THE LIFE AND INSIG

JOSEP CHILTON PEARCE

"*The Life and Insights of Joseph Chilton Pearce,* edited by Michael Mendizza, reveals how Pearce, a modern-day sage, endowed with the courage, strength, and perseverance to challenge conventional worldviews, offered humanity original and penetrating insights into our transcendent nature and vast creativity. Joe's brilliant and original works represent a profound and important contribution toward healing our global dysfunction and ensuring the healthy development of future generations."

BRUCE H. LIPTON, PH.D., STEM CELL BIOLOGIST, EPIGENETIC SCIENCE PIONEER, AND AUTHOR OF *THE BIOLOGY OF BELIEF* AND *THE HONEYMOON EFFECT*

"For many of us, Joseph Chilton Pearce's 1971 book, *The Crack in the Cosmic Egg,* was an early introduction to the mystery and awe of creation. The journey he took through his subsequent books is even more astonishing. This brilliant recap and summary of his work is a must-read for anybody interested in finding the deeper meaning of life and life's experiences."

THOM HARTMANN, AUTHOR OF *THE LAST HOURS OF ANCIENT SUNLIGHT*

"Joe Pearce's rare genius was the way he applied his multidimensional wisdom to a deeper understanding of a child's total development. In my case, he was literally the teacher's teacher. I will never forget him once telling me, 'Teachers teach who they are, not what they know.'"

CHRIS MERCOGLIANO, AUTHOR OF *IN DEFENSE OF CHILDHOOD: PROTECTING KIDS' INNER WILDNESS*

"What a gift to have this distillation of so many of Joe['s]
in one place! Being with him was an experience of 'the m[ ]
imperative' that we all must have. His writings represent a uni[que]
contribution to the deepening challenges we all face today."

"Joe remains a giant. *The Life and Insights of Joseph Chilton Pearce*
is priceless. Joe validated, enriched, and added practical substance
to my lifelong quest to better understand the critical importance
of play. Without Joe's clear descriptions that play is learning, my
explorations would have been less complete. Joe was inspiring, a
role model and mentor."

"Joseph Chilton Pearce's insights into what human beings can
be inspired the founding of Kindred World. Michael Mendizza
guides us through Pearce's decades of synthesized, cross-cultural
fields of science and deeply integrated wisdom toward a welcome
and truer vision of humanity's amazing capacities. This book
describes the new story we all need right now."

"When I first found Pearce's work after training as a psychological
researcher, I was enthralled. As I moved away from a rigid mind-
set, oriented toward material measurement and control, and back
to an interdisciplinary perspective where all truth exists, the seeds
planted by Pearce are now reaching fruition at the Evolved Nest.
I am forever grateful that he had the courage to share his wisdom
and that Michael Mendizza has kept it alive."

THE LIFE AND INSIGHTS OF

JOSEPH CHILTON PEARCE

Astonishing Capacities and Self-Inflicted Limitations

EDITED BY

MICHAEL MENDIZZA

Park Street Press
Rochester, Vermont

Park Street Press
One Park Street
Rochester, Vermont 05767
www.ParkStPress.com

Text stock is SFI certified

Park Street Press is a division of Inner Traditions International

Cataloging-in-Publication Data for this title is available from the Library of Congress

ISBN 978-1-64411-159-8 (print)
ISBN 978-1-64411-160-4 (ebook)

Printed and bound in the United States by Lake Book Manufacturing, Inc. The text stock is SFI certified. The Sustainable Forestry Initiative® program promotes sustainable forest management.

10 9 8 7 6 5 4 3 2 1

Text design and layout by Priscilla Baker
This book was typeset in Garamond Premier Pro with Nexa and Avant Garde used as display typefaces

To send correspondence to the editor of this book, mail a first-class letter to the editor c/o Inner Traditions • Bear & Company, One Park Street, Rochester, VT 05767, and we will forward the communication, or contact the editor directly at **www.TTFuture.org**.

Contents

Editor's Foreword: Joe's Quest for Discovery,
Awakening, and Renewal   vii
by Michael Mendizza

Preface: Saga of Spirit and Psyche   xiii
by Joseph Chilton Pearce

1   *The Crack in the Cosmic Egg* (1971)   1

2   *Magical Child* (1977)   36

3   *The Bond of Power* (1981)   91

4   *Evolution's End* (1992)   133

5   *The Biology of Transcendence* (2002)   176

6   *The Death of Religion and the Rebirth of Spirit* (2007)   230

7   *The Heart-Mind Matrix* (2012)   274

♦ ♦ ♦

Notes   307

Bibliography   313

Index   315

About the Authors   323

Joe's Quest for Discovery, Awakening, and Renewal

One can mechanically copy, imitate, and repeat; but real learning—at any age—the kind of learning that is experienced by the elite athlete, creative artist, or true scientist, is a focused act of discovery about ourselves and our place in the world. Because life is so vast, subtle, complex, and mysterious, the greatest challenge every human faces is to "know thyself." This supreme and forever deepening and expanding act of discovery is a personal and private inner experience. It is a revelation much grander than any idea or concept to be studied. And for the rare, the very few who make this ongoing discovery, their life's passion is revealed and must be shared. And so they do.

Because of their passion, because of their depth of personal experience and synthesis, every once in a while that thing called "greatness" emerges. Not great in comparison to another, but great in the unique story being shared and how that sharing awakens something fresh, new, and powerful in others, something that may never have been discovered without this new story and the unique way it is being told. Joseph Chilton Pearce would turn up his nose at such a pompous accusation of greatness. But he was, and his insights are, potentially life-changing for all who listen, behold, and embody the stories he shared with millions around the world.

There was a single driving quest, something mysterious yet so real and tangible that Joe could not let go. When asked why he explored the unifying mystery in all of his writings, he replied, "To understand our astonishing capacities and self-inflicted limitations."

And what are our self-inflicted limitations? Very simply, we don't understand the nature of our own mind. Therefore, our approaches to parenting, schooling, higher education, organized religions, the corporate and private sector, each of these, in their own way, creates a reality that is in conflict with our true nature, which is nature with its astonishing creative capacities.

Joe's collected works are one coherent, lifelong exploration of these basic questions: *What are we and are we expressing the miracle nature intended, and if not, why?* Each of Joe's books represents a new vista, a unique point of view. Each book is also simultaneously part of a larger whole. Each volume digs deeper, expanding this mystery and creating a new vantage point to launch the next exploration.

As author/businessman Stephen Covey wrote in *Seven Habits of Highly Successful People*, "The first habit is *to begin with the end in mind.*" This anthology of Joe's life and insights offers this *end*—to begin one's journey with Joe into the mystery of what we are and might still become.

Joe complained of being pigeonholed. Indeed, childhood is the experience that sculpts the adult. To understand where we end, we must look carefully at where we began. Approaching Joe's insights is often like the parable of three blind men describing an elephant. One declares, "The elephant is like a snake." "No, it is like a tree," says the next. "No, no," insists the third, "it is like a wall."

Readers of his best-known book, *Magical Child,* will assume that Joe was interested in child development, and he was. Reading *The Crack in the Cosmic Egg,* one assumes he was interested in altered states, ESP, and so-called psychic phenomena. All these assumptions are true but miss the larger meaning that Joe explored and shared.

The Life and Insights of Joseph Chilton Pearce is the first book to the fence separating the subtle and physical. This shift of perspective gave what the anthropologist Mircea Eliade termed "the ability to intervene in the ontological constructs of the universe." This was Eliade's scholarly description of the non-ordinary events brought about by Tibetan yogis, with whom Eliade spent ten years back in the 1930s. (I read his magnificent account *Yoga: Immortality and Freedom* years later.

I found that in any extreme or even ordinary daily event, through a kind of willful, voluntary throwing away of self and self-preservation, the ordinary course of events could be reversed, changed, or modified. This was not one part of my mind playing games of let's pretend with other parts. My whole being moved in total accord with my acceptance of non-being as simultaneously an equal part with my being in that moment. Again, this was not some lofty psychological or spiritual "death" of ego, loss of self, or any such aggrandizement, but rather a peculiar acceptance of death as a foregone conclusive part of that moment. Therefore, there was nothing to lose! And, I found that in that state, that fire—no matter how extreme—did not have to burn me, nor gravity hold me, nor ordinary cause produce its ordinary effect over a wide range of events.

To find that the structure of reality was negotiable when one was free of all internal conflict was a momentous discovery. And I realized that all internal conflict is produced by our fear of possible harm or death. The great irony of this is that there exists for us a state in which harm really can't happen within a particular single event if we bypass our block of fear and open ourselves to this other perspective.

To fully rid one's self of the fear of death or injury is nonsense since the body has a mind of its own, and it never changes its mind. But *one can accept one's death as already an accomplished fact of this instant moment and so can be carried beyond that mind of the body, and beyond the fear of death that lies in a different worldview.*

I was delighted to find the work of neuroscientist Paul MacLean and his half century of research at the National Institutes of Health, on the "triune nature" of our brain, the fact that we have within our heads three radically different brains and behaviors, including that basic "body-brain."

Through MacLean's work I saw how fear of any kind throws us into an ancient survival mentality that literally shuts down all higher modes of evolutionary awareness. And these higher modes of our neural system hold an open-ended possibility through which we can modify, modulate, and change the reality structure of that moment. When Carlos Castaneda* brought out his remarkable books, I saw that he clearly knew that fear of death blocks us from our full spectrum of humanity and potential. (Whether one accepts Castaneda's literary vehicle for presenting this fact or not is beside the point. He certainly knew about and must have experienced this truth—and far more fully than most of us.)

Further, I was to eventually realize that this was the very issue of the cross and my hero-model's willingness to be crucified. Someone had to break through this deadlock on our species' consciousness if our evolution were to unfold and we were to develop the higher neural structures nature had worked out for us. Through this development alone we can be delivered from our murderousness toward ourselves and each other, this violent murderousness of which our fear of death ironically drives us. So our greatest hero and model did what he could for us, there two millennia back, misinterpreted and mythologized as his efforts were.

During this period of my life I had classes all day at the university and worked an eight-hour graveyard shift all night, six nights a week. I was doing poorly at both and walking in my sleep. In general desperation I found that through the same shift of cause-effect brought about by reckless abandon, I could turn over to IT the actual operation of that infernal IBM machine I ran all night, and IT would run the machine for me. This was a high-speed operation wherein error was frequent and costly. But through unconflicted behavior I could turn the machine over to IT, and I could sleep throughout my entire night shift. And sleep I did, quite genuinely, dreams and all, yet with eyes open and body busy, IT handling everything. The difference was that IT then ran that machine and was infallible. IT couldn't err so long as I trusted IT implicitly.

---

*[Carlos Castaneda was a Peruvian-born author (1925–1998) who wrote a series of controversial books on Shamanism. —Ed.]

picnic spot and friends, high above. My friend, knowing of my extreme vertigo (I had refused to go anywhere near the edge up there) jokingly challenged me to climb the cliff with him, even though it was quite rotten indeed and almost vertical. Not to be "chicken," the term for people like me back then, I went along, though terrified. We got no more than ten, maybe fifteen feet up when the whole section began to simply crumble, and down we dumped, covered with sand and shale, white and shaken.

On looking at my friend's pale face, that peculiar quirk leaped inside me, that instant knowing of what can be done if one throws one's self away. "I'm going up," I said without fanfare, and started up again, my friend shouting that I was crazy, he wasn't responsible, he wouldn't carry my body out of there, and so on. I simply started up and kept going, my assuredness absolute. I knew I could not fall or be hurt. Every single handhold, every toehold, collapsed under my weight and almost immediately I could see nothing up ahead of me for the dust and debris that was falling from my handholds. I knew, however, that so long as I didn't stop, even for a second, as though to search for a hand- or foothold, that all was well, and I would continue to go up. I knew that any hesitancy, the most fleeting shadow of doubt, would be the end of me, and this knowing gave a most extraordinary sense of freedom and sheer joy.

I went up very fast, amid a peculiar whistling sound, which formed around me, perhaps from the enormous gulps of dusty air my exertion demanded. I felt that I was embedded in layers of whistles, layers of sound, which both sustained me, and through which I moved. At one point I glanced down through the dirt and dust and spotted my friend on the beach, a tiny ant figure immensely far below. At that sight my exultancy grew to wild dimensions, and within what seemed but a moment my feet and legs were no longer scratching and clawing into the cliff face as they had been. Only my hands were now in contact, while my body was swinging, back and forth, beneath my upstretched arms. I was not moving vertically, but at a backward diagonal, the cliff face arching overhead toward the ocean behind me.

I had come to the overhang of cliff on which we had made our picnic, an overhang formed by the roots of the scrub growth covering the small area. With my body swinging free, looking down and seeing no cliff at all, just space, I experienced the single most exuberant joy I would ever know, increasing my clawing kind of swimming up and out through dirt, debris, and space. What my hands found to grasp is a mystery, but suddenly they grabbed what I knew to be grass, and I was up and over the edge. And there before me was the rest of the picnic group, astonished, to say the least, over this apparition suddenly coming up from thin air.

The great bubbling up of exuberance within me was now so intense that I was completely incoherent. I began to shout, a peculiar screaming kind of animal Tarzan cry of triumph that roared up from my body without any volition or control. I pounded the ground, pounded my chest, and screamed, for, I was told later, some ten minutes or more. By then my friend, seriously upset, had come up from the long, roundabout trail.

The upshot was we all went back to the site the next weekend to settle the arguments of belief or disbelief by checking out that impossible passage. Some doubted their memory and the whole event when we viewed that treacherous overhang from the vantage point of another neighboring overhang. My friend on the beach was subdued and silent, for indeed, he had watched as I traversed the near-sheer cliff face in a veritable landslide of rocks and sand and then some twenty feet of that reverse incline, going out toward the ocean as well as up. My sensation of body swinging freely below my hands had been quite genuine. The logic of the event just didn't add up.

In retrospect I realized that my wild and near hysterical elation was somehow connected with having accepted and taken into myself, so to speak, my death, and then in some manner, gone beyond it.

My next discovery was that an unconflicted person has dominion over a conflicted or divided person. This doesn't have to imply a demonic domination but simply demonstrates the difference between the states of conflicted and unconflicted behavior. I was immune to danger or disaster in any unfolding event so long as I remembered to let

IT do the job and not allow myself to have a knee-jerk reflex and fall into fear. Miraculous or impossible events could unfold once I "abandoned all hope" and turned events over to this peculiar form of will.

Again, however, I found that this was never a negotiable decision; one either accepts this instant opening and falls into it as it opens or not. It is always an instantaneous "offering" made in a split instant or on behalf of an actual event itself, but only in the moment of that event. And one either agrees or not in that very same split instant. No thought is involved in such a decision since there is no time for such, and thought inevitably brings doubt.

Back in the early 1980s mathematician Ralph Straugh, having completed all the levels of the Japanese martial art Aikido and four years of work with Moshe Feldenkrais* in Israel, told me that no person can attack another without a deep, non-ordinary level of agreement between aggressor and victim. I recalled Meister Eckhart† saying, "Listen, when this birth takes place within you, no creature can hinder you." The birth Eckhart referred to was the "birth of God in the soul," but there are undeniable similarities between Straugh and Eckhart's point of view. There are many names *for* and facets *of* the shifts our spirit can bring about. This isn't a religious, theoretical, philosophical, or semantic issue, nor one of logic. This is the alogical "crack in the egg" of reality and the way creator and created give rise to each other.

The automatic dominance of a person in unconflicted behavior over an ordinary conflicted person brought matters to a head for me. I found that by shifting into unconflicted behavior I could sell anything to anybody. I dropped my all-night schizoid battle with IBM's machinery and became a salesman, and of all things—sterling silver (the only opening for a raw recruit who had never sold anything). Selling to poor, innocent, working

---

*[Moshe Feldenkrais (1904–1984) was a Ukranian-Israeli engineer and physicist who founded the Feldenkrais Method, a system of physical exercise that aims to improve human functioning by increasing self-awareness through movement. —*Ed.*]

†[Meister Eckhart (1260–1328) was a German theologian, philosopher, and mystic. —*Ed.*]

to know which was which, nor the character to respond appropriately.

So, not from noble virtue or lofty principle, but from fear and trembling, knowing that I was hopelessly out of my depth, I quit selling then and there and resisted any temptation to monkey around any further with the ontological constructs of my world. Eventually I took another job, held on somehow at the university, and played it straight. And eventually I lost my intimate contact with this opening into another part of myself and reality, though later I fell back on it in a couple of situations of dire extremity.

In my thirty-second year, sitting in my office in silent, wordless contemplation one day, I felt the presence of my hero-model strongly and fell out of my body into a vast ocean of silence that left nothing to report on, once coming back into my ordinary state. Thereafter for some three years I moved in a fluid drive wherein everything worked to perfection, with almost no effort on my part. I knew myself and family to be ultimately cared for, nurtured, intimately loved, and protected by some deep interior place within. This fall into grace was preceded by an intensely exciting period of discovery. I had, among many great writings, read Paul Tillich's* mammoth *Systematics of Theology* in its entirety, a huge trilogy my department head confessed he had despaired of reading but which I found both a challenge and delight. I read every available work of Søren Kierkegaard's, and wondered how his book *Purity of Heart Is to Will One Thing*† could be at once the most soul-shattering, unhinging event and yet an exquisite intellectual-aesthetic-spiritual feast.

And so, I began working on my first book, which was to become, twelve years later, *The Crack in the Cosmic Egg*...

---

*[Paul Tillich (1886–1965) was a Christian existential philosopher and Lutheran theologian. —*Ed.*]
†[Danish philosopher, theologian, and poet, Søren Kierkegaard (1813–1855) wrote *Purity of Heart Is to Will One Thing* in 1847. —*Ed.*]

1

---◆---

The Crack in the Cosmic Egg (1971)

Challenging Constructs of Mind and Reality

THE BACKSTORY FROM JOE
From an Interview with Michael Mendizza

My first book, *The Crack in the Cosmic Egg,* which I wrote and rewrote for twelve years, was a protest against the prevailing academic consensus view, which narrows our perceptions and limits us to grim necessity, as William Blake would say, "to the death of spirit."

In my twenty-third year of life I underwent a series of paranormal events, which challenged the foundations of classical thought. These events took place with abundant objective witnesses. Over time, however, I watched how these witnesses screened out or blurred over their own perceptions, and I realized this was a necessary move to keep intact their established consensus of what was real. This selective tendency of the brain-mind is part of a general maintenance system, which keeps our collective world experience stable, and seems to function below awareness, healing little rifts in the fabric of the known.

Since these paranormal events were my direct experience, not just witnessed, I questioned their meaning, which opened a whole new realm of possibilities, and I wondered how much of our potential this automatic survival-system filters out. Through studying child-development, I saw how our cultural worldview was formed by our social models and how this view is locked into the very neural structures of our brains, not as opinion but as our world-forming, perceptual-conceptual process. When writing *Magical Child,* I started giving workshops and seminars to get feedback on my ideas. By the time I completed the book, this feedback had enlarged my original focus to include our *amazing capacities and self-inflicted limitations.*

Crack was a direct outgrowth of these experiences. By then I had gotten a couple of degrees and was teaching in college, and I kept making the error of occasionally mentioning some of these things that had happened. It didn't suit very well with any of my teaching colleagues.

I was the only one in our humanities department who understood William Blake, and to me, Blake was like a Bible. William Blake was one of the few people I had ever read that I immediately, instantly identified with, as well as him saying, "Where you see white I see black" and so on. Well sure, that's the way it was. And so my teaching colleagues asked me to come in and help them when they were required to introduce William Blake in their humanities courses.

These colleagues were much more advanced academically than I. At that point I had only a bachelor's degree. I remember Bill Williams, the great pragmatist, who had done his doctorate under Walter Kaufman at Princeton. Bill came up to me and in a kind, fatherly way said, "Joe, I hate to tell you this but my colleagues and I have drawn the conclusion that you're hopelessly mad." That was a delightful thing to hear because William Blake had been considered "hopelessly mad." To my way of thinking that was literally confirmation that I was on the right track.

I realized that to be absolutely sane within the run-of-the-mill ordinary concept of things would mean to be pretty bad off. So in defense of myself I began writing the book *The Crack in the Cosmic Egg.* That was in the late fifties. I was writing the book in protest, having been called mad by my colleagues and was simply trying to present my take on things and why I thought the way I did. I tempered it a great deal and took out anything that I thought was too extreme. I could have thrown in a lot of wild things going on, but I wanted to be accepted by my colleagues and, at the same time, to do so without a complete betrayal of myself and how I experienced the world.

EXCERPTS FROM *THE CRACK IN THE COSMIC EGG*
(Begun in 1958. First published in 1971.)

Introduction

An awareness of the creative force of mind is springing up increasingly after a gestation of nearly two millennia. If the dark forces of the Pentagon or the technician mentality do not destroy us in their death throes of naïve realism, the childhood of Man could well draw to a close within our own time. Then it may be that we shall "seize the tiller of the world," as the Jesuit priest and idealist philosopher Teilhard de Chardin (1881–1955) dreamed. This seizure can only take place as a "crack in the egg," whatever shape the egg might have by then. The reality-shaping function operates automatically in spite of us, but this breath of life that structures all things is also the deepest level of our very minds, and available to any of us, even now. The technique for making this function consciously available will be clarified—hopefully in the following pages—for that reader with perseverance and an open mind.

J.C.P.

WILLIAMSTOWN, MASSACHUSETTS, JUNE 1970

Circles and Lines[1]

A change of worldview can change the world viewed.

There is a relationship between what we *think* is out there in the world and what we *experience* as being out there. There is a way in which the energy of thought and the energy of matter modify each other and interrelate. A kind of thought-mirroring takes place between our mind and our reality.

We cannot stand outside this mirroring process and examine it, though, for we *are* the process, to an unknown extent. Any technique we might use to "look objectively" at our reality becomes a part of the event in question. We are an indeterminately large part of the function that shapes the reality from which we do our looking. Our looking enters as one of the determinants in the reality event that we set.

Jerome Bruner, of Harvard's Center for Cognitive Studies, doubts that there is a world available for "direct touch." We are not in a subjective trap of our own making. Rather, we *represent* the world to ourselves and *respond* to our representations. There is, I would add, a subtle and random way in which "the world" responds to our representations too.

We used to believe that our perceptions, our seeing, hearing, feeling, and so on were reactions to active impingements on them by the "world out there." We thought our perceptions then sent these outside messages to the brain where we put together a reasonable facsimile of what *was* out there. We know now that our concepts, our notions, or basic assumptions actively *direct* our percepts. We see, feel, and hear according to what Bruner calls a "selective program of the mind." Our mind *directs* our sensory apparatus every bit as much as our sensory apparatus *informs* the mind.

Holding to this idea today are the "tough-minded," whose boastful posturing of a "realistic, no-nonsense objectivity" cloaks a narrow and pedantic selective blindness, a realism that sees only what has been established as safe to see. Yet there is a way in which physical and mental events merge and influence each other. A change of worldview can change the world viewed. And I am not referring to such parlor games as influencing the roll of dice. The stakes are higher, the relationships more subtle and far-reaching.

Reality is not a fixed entity. It is a contingent interlocking of moving events. And events do not just happen to us. We are an integral part of every event. We enter into the shape of events, even as we long for an absolute in which to rest. It may be just this longing for an absolute in occur, in a clear example of the circularity of expectancy verification—the mirroring by reality of a passionate or basic fear.

There are "mutations" in the metaphoric fabric of our "semantic universe," as Lévi-Strauss* has called our world-built world. The cults seized these novelties previously, and, in their longing for magic, alluded to shadowy cosmic mysteries. Rather, trance states prove to be forms of metanoia, a temporary restructuring of reality orientation. Some fundamental restructuring of mind underlies all disciplines and pursuits. Mathematician and physicist follow the same mirroring of idea and fact, just on a wider scope, from a different set of metaphors, with a different set of expectancies, and from a different aesthetic.

William Blake claimed that "anything capable of being believed is an image of truth."

Our imaginations cannot set out to find the cracks in the cosmic egg until someone lays the egg. New representations for reality, new ideas, new fabrications of fantasy searching for supporting logic must precede the final "discovery" by which verification of the notion is achieved.

It has been claimed that our minds screen out far more than we accept; else we would live in a world of chaos. Our screening process may be essential, but it is also arbitrary and changeable. We pick and choose, ignore or magnify, illuminate or dampen, expand upon or obscure, affirm or deny as our inheritance, adopted discipline, or passionate pursuit dictate. At root is an aesthetic response, and we invest our aesthetic responses with sacred overtones.

Among the potentials of resyntheses of our current reality, one possibility must be selected, heard as a question one might answer, and seen as a goal one might achieve. Every choice involves such a commitment. Once we have made an investment and corresponding sacrifice of other possibilities, our life is at stake.

A mind divided by choices and confused by alternatives is a mind robbed of power. The body reflects this. The ambiguous person is a

---

*[Claude Lévi-Strauss (1908–2009) was an anthropologist who developed the theory of structuralism. —Ed.]

machine out of phase, working against itself and tearing itself up. That person is an engine with sand in its crankcase, broken piston rods, and water in its fuel lines. In spite of great effort and noise, nothing much happens.

Metanoia restructures, to varying degrees and even for varying lengths of time, those basic representations of reality inherited or in the past. On those representations we base our notions or concepts of what is real. In turn, our notions of what is real direct our perceptual apparatus, that network of senses that tells us what we feel, hear, see, and so on. This is not a simple subjective maneuver, but a reality-shaping procedure.

The difference between Einstein's relative universe and the dream-time cosmology of the Australian aborigine is not a matter of truth or falsehood, realism or illusion, progression or regression, intelligence or stupidity, as the naïve realists have claimed. It is a matter of aesthetic choice. Each system produces results unobtainable to the other; each is a closed exclusive.

The American poet Robert Frost (1874–1963) saw civilization as a small clearing in a great forest. We have hewn our space at no small cost, and the dark "out there" seems ever ready to close in again.

Platonists and Stoics have always assumed the forest to be ready planted. Corresponding ideas of what was "out there" were planted also in our minds, leading us by heuristic devices until we finally stumbled our way to various discoveries and conclusions. The gods and fates looked on, rather as we would watch rats in a maze.

Consider, however, that the kind of trees we succeed in felling at the clearing's edge need not have always *been*. Indeed, there may be no trees at all in the depths of that dark. Rather, the forest may shape, the trees may grow, according to the kind of light our reason throws.

The nature "discovered" is determined, to an indeterminable degree, by the mind that sets out to discover. We can never know the full extent we play in this reality formation. It will never be computable or reducible to formula. An ultimately serious commitment of mind, however, can be the determinate in any issue, overriding randomness and change.

A mind finds its definition of itself not by confrontation with *things* so much as other minds. We are shaped by each other. We adjust not to the reality of a *world* but to the reality of other thinkers. When we have finally persuaded and/or badgered our children into "looking objectively" at their situation we can then relax since they are being *realistic.* What we mean is that they have finally begun to mirror our commitments, verify our life investments, and strengthen and preserve the cosmic egg of our culture.

It is our ideation that shapes our children. We provide an enriched environment, visual, aural, tactile stimuli to furnish the best supply of raw materials, but our own background determines what we decide makes up a "rich environment." And then, quite naturally, we expect our children to shape this material into a pattern verifying our commitments. We look for agreement.

The child's mind is autistic, a rich texture of free synthesis, hallucinatory and unlimited. His mind can skip over syllogisms with ease in a non-logical, dream-sequence kind of "knight's-move" continuum. He nevertheless shows a strong desire to participate in a world of others. Eventually his willingness for self-modification, necessary to win rapport with his world, is stronger than his desire for autonomy. Were it not, civilization would not be possible.

Maturity, or the becoming of adjusted reality, restricts and diminishes this "knight's-move" thinking and tends to make pawns of us in the process. The kind of adult logic that results is dependent on the kinds of demands made on the young mind by parents and society. If we believe our social view sacred and made in heaven, we tend to shut off a deep potential in which many of the terrors and shortcomings of our logic and reason might be averted. Exclusion of possibility is necessary to narrow and hold the mind. The price of excluded possibility buys a prism that opens on specialized worlds. We lose and gain. But the autistic mode of mind offers a way around severe loss.

The emerging mind will have mirrored *whatever* model it had during that formative period. The pattern formed in this plastic stage becomes firm. It hardens into the functional system of representation-response we call a worldview. Once done, there is no undoing of the system except by metanoia resyntheses.

Even this mutation is dependent on the materials available for mutation—conversion is a creative process, but not magical.

This pattern formed by the mirroring of child mind and social pressure is not only the means then available for *coping* with a world and other people; it largely determines what shall be coped *with*. This worldview is then the screen allowing only related data in, as well as the synthetic process determining the final cognitive shape of that admitted material. The pattern shapes the kind of world to respond to and the world response that must then be made.

The infant's dreamlike association of ideas is slowly won over to an agreement of *what* should constitute reality. By the time our reasoning has developed enough to reflect on the process by which our reasoning has formed, we are part and parcel of the whole process, caught up in and sustaining it. By the time the young rebel reaches the age of rebellion he is inevitably that against which he would rebel, his linear thrust ending as a pale reflection of the circle from which he would break.

Anthropologist and cross-cultural researcher Edward Hall (1914–2009) writes that it is impossible for us to divest ourselves of culture, for it has penetrated to the roots of our nervous system and determines how we perceive the world. We cannot act or interact except through the medium of culture.

There is no magic, there is only *The Creation*. There is no supernatural, but there is an infinite number of possible natures.

We used to think of the nervous system as a simple telephone switchboard, bringing in messages from outside. We know now that the system is every bit as much an "editorial hierarchy"—a policy-making device determining what is perceived.

The open end of human potential is built into the blueprint of mind, and is contained in that mode I have called *autistic*. This is blocked, however, by blindness of *viewpoint*, and yet the autistic can be structured and realized only by assuming viewpoints. The openness nevertheless happens to us in peripheral and unsuspected ways. One of the most intriguing of these ways is in the procedure of ultimately asked and passionately adhered to *questions*.

Mirror-to-Mirror[4]

Man's mind is a mirror of a universe that mirrors man's mind.
What a thing is is to an unknowable extent determined by
or influenced by what we think it is, though the
mirroring is subtle, random, and unfathomable.

The seventeenth and eighteenth centuries displayed a mania for labeling and cataloging every commonplace item on the globe.

British mathematician and philosopher Alfred North Whitehead (1861–1947) felt that several centuries of contemplation of this basic stuff was needed. What grew from all this was a method of *agreement*—agreement on the kinds of phenomena that could be "objectively" considered, and the way by which such speculation could be verified. The method of agreement was strengthened by its own careful restriction to those events to the same "common objectivity." This kept intact the particular fabric of belief in process of being woven. Thus the growing frame of reference centered on a desire for an *order of nature* that would reflect the medieval faith in the rational order of God.

Eventually these self-verifying successes built a system of hypotheses that became self-sustaining. Science became a *reality-shaping* structure, creating its own unique ecology.

The scientist detaches himself from the commonplace assumptions of his discipline; commits himself to a new construct; his passion gives him his selective blindness to ignore the contradictions and negatives, and, by his superior degree of attention, he sees what he needs to see; his decorum assures the love of form, the etiquette toward the object of desire that keeps him in the brotherhood. Having placed his intellectual and professional life on the line (losing his life that he may find it), he has the freedom and willingness to be dominated by the object until the work of creation takes over. Then his life both serves the new work and is justified by it.

Jerome Bruner* wrote of how science postulates empty categories on purely logical grounds, and then, when appropriate measures have been found, "discovers" the content needed to fill the category. When the neutron was disintegrated, its products—the electron and proton— did not behave according to the law of the conservation of momentum. Something had to yield; surely it was not going to be the law, on which too much else depended, so the Italian physicist Enrico Fermi postulated a third particle of zero charge and zero mass, which he called the "neutrino" or little neutron. The mysterious third particle, without mass, charge, or much of anything, was finally considered to have a spiral orbit; several years after its hypothetical beginnings, evidence for it took on more and more reality aspects until finally it was "discovered."

William Blake considered our capacity for imagination to be our "divine genius." Jesus was Blake's most truly imaginative man since he could bridge the logical gaps. In his marginalia to Joshua Reynolds,† Blake claimed that our truest self was in our innate ideas with which we are born. He did not mean this in the Platonic sense, but as the capacity for creative and original thinking, independent of mechanical information from a world. Biological and economic necessities as formative devices were denied by Blake. "The eternal body of man is the Imagination, that is, God himself. . . . It manifests itself in his work of art (in Eternity all is Vision). Man is all Imagination: God is Man and exists in us and we in Him."

What Blake's vision releases on earth is released in heaven. If an imaginative seed, the gist of an idea, can be planted, even though contrary to existent evidence, the seed can still grow and sooner or later produce confirmation. Data can be found to bolster the conviction.

---

*[Jerome Bruner (1915–2016) was an American cognitive psychologist. —*Ed.*]
†[Sir Joshua Reynolds (1723–1792) was an English portrait artist who promoted the "Grand Style" in painting, which depended on the idealization of imperfection. William Blake stated that "Reynolds had been hired to repress art." —*Ed.*]

others. What takes place is a reproduction of the natural development processes of early experience.

The ability to relinquish reality and enter trance states must wait until a fairly firm reality picture is itself built up. Trance abilities are lost unless retained by the associations mentioned, somewhere in early adolescence. Somewhere between twelve and fourteen logical development, which means a final adjustment to the world-of-others, becomes the complete criterion of concept—the ruling hierarchy of mind. This hardening of worldview generally represses the autistic modes with their free synthesis into fully unconscious, lost potentials.

The small percentage under discussion retains the autistic mode as a freely possible subset. Trance entrance bypasses the ordinary criteria for data selection and draws on the ordinary world as needed by the novel suggestions induced.

The most important aspect of autistic thinking is that it has no value judgment. It has no criteria for what shall or shall not be synthesized. This same qualification and limitation holds in all trance states a point of major importance and one overlooked by cults. The person in the trance, though he or she has an enormously rich background to draw on for synthesis, remains a blank slate—at least when the entrance is through a hypnotist. The person can draw on background not from his or her *own* value system, since that has been suspended to *create* the trance state, but draws on one's background perceptually in response to the concepts of the hypnotist. The "over-all ego" retains its ordinary relationship with both hypnotist and world. It is the partially regressed subsystem that is surrendered to the hypnotist's control. And it is this subsystem that is receptive to novel thought formations, novel restructuring of the perceptual world.

An interesting account of a self-induced anesthesia appeared in a medical journal (1963), when the well-known doctor Ainslie Meares underwent a tooth extraction. The dental surgeon performing the operating described the details. First an incision had to be made in the gums, laying bare the bone over the third molar. This bone was then removed with a chisel, exposing the roots of the tooth near the apices, after which the tooth was removed by forceps. No anesthetic was used. The dental surgeon asked Dr. Meares to write out his own subjective reactions.

Dr. Meares, the patient, had published widely on therapy and had served as president of the International Society for Clinical and Experimental Hypnosis. Thus the integrity of the two doctors seems beyond question. Meares was capable of self-induced trance. Though normally sensitive to pain, he was well aware of the anesthetic possibilities of trance. He explained to the surgeon that he would signal "ready" when in the proper state of mind, and that he would also signal should it be necessary to halt the proceedings.

The idea of halting the operation never occurred to Meares. When he heard the chiseling of the bone he knew an instant's irrational anger that the surgeon might have injected anesthetic without his knowledge since he felt no pain. The doubt quickly vanished, however, since he realized that he felt every detail of the work being done, just without the pain of it. There was, further, almost no sign of blood during the operation, or any trace afterward. Dr. Meares suffered no after-effects, felt perfectly normal, and took his family out to dinner that night.

Here then is the technique of the hook swinger, the fire walker, the cultist, adapted to specific beneficial needs by an intelligent medical man. He carried into a trance state his own ego awareness. He had predetermined the idea around which his subset would orient. He had filtered out those elements of his ordinary world that he did not want and had set up his expectancies for those he needed to retain.

The trance part of his experience was a voluntary releasing of his ordinary logic, while logically controlling the autistic results. That portion of logic that cannot escape ambiguity, which cannot avoid the excluded possibilities, was bypassed. The secret involved is thus an inner agreement with one's self.

There is, then, this capacity of the adult to bypass the world selectively, while drawing on that world for a particular synthesis.

That is the way it works, and no system or method, including religion and science, has yet gotten around it because there is no place to get to—the function is the only thing there is.

It might be wondered why the Aborigine boy had to undergo a terrible initiation in order to enter dreamtime and its totem world.

The reason is that the adult world of dreamtime was an abstract, intellectual construct. It was not just raw material from an informational "out there." Its logical complexity could only be grasped by a mind that had developed to the logical level, which, as Piaget points out, is in early adolescence. Then the worldview developed to that point was disintegrated as a rational structure, while its acquired information was retained. The totem and dream state then acted as screens channeling percepts and determining the autistic synthesis. The system produced according to its premises as any cohesive, logical structure should.

Trance states repeat the basic process by which worldviews originally form in the mind by first bypassing that worldview and opening the autistic or unconscious to restructuring. The triggers for the new syntheses are given either by a conscious directive or by assumed cultural expectancies. These serve as concepts for the directing of percepts in new ways. Trance is a dramatic, if temporary and limited, kind of metanoia.

The "crack between the worlds" is neither a "real world" nor an opening into such—for there is no such thing as a "real world" other than that one from which one makes such a statement. The crack is only a capacity, an ontological function, a possibility for processing an infinite number of worlds—none of which is absolute. To leave one you can only structure another one or face dissolution.

So now my book leads, as did my search, to its final goal—another kind of path, strangely similar to don Juan's, as unique, as difficult in vastly different ways, with an even more daring goal. I believe it is a path with a heart—though I must recognize that it is only one of an infinite number of possible paths, and that no heavenly hierarchy sanctions it or gives it a final edge. This pack hinges on analyzing the process by which paths function, and, as don Juan would say, by exercising the self-confidence to claim knowledge as power, seizing the tiller by which realities are made.

Don Juan and Jesus[7]

We are finally confronting the mirror of our true selves—
we are that fate. We are in our own hands.

Don Juan and Jesus consider the world to be an arbitrary construct, not an illusion as in the East or a fated absolute as in the West. Since the world is an arbitrary construct, the means of construction, not a particular construct, or the products of a construct, are the focal point of attention.

Don Juan and Jesus believe the materials of the world to be subject to dramatic alteration and reorganization by an activity of the mind. Both systems work to lower the threshold between reality-adjusted thinking and autistic thinking without loss of identity. Both systems have analyzed the way that reality events shape and then dissolve the structure of a common domain that the selective world agreed upon in ordinary social thinking. Such dissolution would ordinarily threaten the ego-personality, which has been centered and formed by the common domain—this is a risk assumed.

Both don Juan and Jesus have as a goal the seizure of the ontological function itself and both attempts hinge on a complete surrender *to* the function. Through a sacrifice of self and absolute obedience to the *way* of the system, union with the process of reality is achieved.

Don Juan seized the ontological process to construct paths of "breathless wonder." Jesus seizes the process to bridge the modes of mind. Don Juan is in love with eternity. He is a kind of hedonist of the psyche. Jesus is in love with time. He is a pragmatic Hebrew, concerned over his fellow man. The aesthetic differences of goals, of techniques and disciplines, give dramatically different results. But the process of attainment is similar.

Don Juan and Jesus see the world as a matrix for continual resynthesis. Both recognize the world as an agreed-upon and practiced construct in a continuum of possible constructs. Both recognize this as true with any and all possible worlds.

Don Juan created private but equally real worlds for personal adventure, and accepted as a natural part of his path the isolation within his created point of view. Carlos experienced this as "the aloneness of a single person on a journey." Jesus recognized that no communicable, shared reality is possible except by agreement between the participants of that world. So his system was to carry don Juan's open synthesis *into* the ordinary world. Jesus will break with the world of common agreement, but only under special circumstances and for special goals.

The crack in the egg is sought by Jesus to restructure some specific problem area in ordinary reality. His system works only in relationships between people. His non-ordinary states are created as *shared* states by the constant focus on the needs of the other. No isolation is engendered. Two or three can gather together and reach a non-ordinary consensus, a point of agreement different from that of the ordinary world. Group agreement gives a mutual feedback of verification sustaining the non-ordinary even in the ordinary. Carlos might call feeding the five thousand a special consensus of non-ordinary reality, or healing the man with a withered arm a special consensus about ordinary reality. In all cases, filling some need is Jesus's motivation and this proves to be the only way his particular crack is sustained.

Earlier I mentioned the psychology professor walking the fire by holding the fakir's hand (see page 19). [x-ref] Without the fakir as trigger, without seeing him actually walk, it is difficult to see how the professor could have been so seized. But the fakir was neither the reason for the phenomenon nor the bearer of magic. The restructuring ability was innately within the professor all along, a part of the very mechanism of his being.

Those with ears to hear would understand. Jesus spoke to his "Kingdom" as like a leavening, the kind the baker puts in the flour to give life to the inert ingredients. Only a tiny bit of leavening is needed to work and raise large quantities of flour. Beware, though, Jesus warned, of the leavening of the Pharisee, the world of legalistic split-thinking and rationale; and beware the leavening of Herod, the world of power battening on the brother's blood, the final demonic, the forces of death. Beware because *all* leavenings work, all raise the flour, and equally well.

Leavening is ontological, neutral, impersonal, natural. Jesus said that his "'Father' judges not." God is the function of leavening, not the capacity for choosing types of leavening. Judgment is given to the "Son." Man chooses. God responds automatically. That is the way the process works. Don Juan said there was an infinite number of paths and that we should choose our paths with care.

Reality-adjusted thinking was Jesus's point of departure. He did not break with logic or "law," the reasoning functions of mind. He spoke of perfecting logic in order to go beyond it. His child-metaphors have meaning only against an adult background. The first demand he makes is that the ego-centered, reality-thinking personality must be surrendered. Unless you hate your life you cannot follow where he goes—not just because ambiguity would result from trying to hold two orientations at once—unless you are willing to give up your worldview structured from infancy, those concepts directing your percepts cannot be restricted.

An indeterminately wide capacity for resynthesis is incorporated in the structure of our minds. This capacity is blocked, though, by the very system of logic which *must* be developed to structure the mind to the point where resynthesis is then possible. No resynthesis is possible to us until an initial synthesis gives a ground on which to stand.

It is not just fortuitous that somewhere around age twelve logical development begins to firm up, and that *this* is the age of the archaic transformation rites. Neither is it fortuitous that this is the age when our educational system breaks down most seriously (try teaching in a junior high school) or that mythological overlay gave this as the setting for Jesus's first manifestations of seizure, and so on.

The world is the matrix from which all things must operate. To be realized, made real, is to be born into the world. In order to be in the world, one's worldview must shape according to the shape of that world. The logical process of structuring the mind into a modified relation with the world of man maybe arbitrary but it brings about the only reality available. Any restructuring is then equally arbitrary—a matter of choice and commitment—but it is a restructuring.

When the ordinary mechanics break or lead to destructive results, disease, and so on, the crack is needed to restructure events. Since the ordinary mechanics are infinitely contingent, accident is inevitable. But the crack opens to that mode of thinking itself infinitely contingent and capable of infinite synthesis. The way down and out is an instantaneous restricting of some isolated, specific point of relation, a carrying of the non-ordinary to the ordinary, and an equally instantaneous establishment of the ordinary mechanics.

Cracks in the egg cannot be built into a cosmic egg. They can only come about when the embryonic form expands and needs room beyond its genesis. The crack is found by the time-tested technique found in all systems of necessity: a repeating of the initial process of worldview formation. A surrender is made as a "child" to a father-figure who gives sureness and confidence that one *can* give over his life, his conceptual framework, to the image and receive it back enlarged.

In all education, metanoia, or change of concept, there is some form of duplication of this worldview structuring. Those children who had initial experiences of entry into fantasy and return to reality with their parents may have an edge here. Perhaps we can see why education fails so sadly; why there are at best mostly technicians and too few physicists; why "hardness of heart" may be built in from infancy.

When Jesus said "no man comes to the Father but through me" he was simply stating this very case. His "Father" is a very specialized and carefully delineated symbol of transference designed to give that "loosing on earth" that we want "loosed in heaven."

In our day we tend to dismiss suggestions of "unconscious" cultural forces, since we deny properties of mind other than those of an electro-chemical, biological nature. This notion makes it difficult for us to understand culture in general.

As Bruner stated, "Life creates myth and finally imitates it." Jesus, seized by the catalytic synthesis of the long quest, translated the answer in flesh and blood, giving a concrete symbol of the new cultural synthesis. He set up the expectancies for new possibility and gave the pattern for the best representation we could make of life for the best mirroring response. He used dramatic restructurings of ordinary reality as examples of the possibilities—whenever he could find a person willing to suspend an ordinary worldview and enter into a subset with him.

He used these restructurings as don Juan did with Carlos, to try to show the arbitrary character of ordinary reality and the equality of other possibilities.

Long centuries of sacrifice by hook-swinging took place in India before broken by that believer who was seized by the notion that he really *was* the temporary incarnation of the god, as the priests had represented for centuries. Once that notion had been realized, dramatically concretized, and made real, no bodily harm ever came again to the "victim." The mythos leads the logos.

Recognizing that "what we loose on earth is loosed in heaven," Jesus tried to give the *kind* of loosing we should do, the kind of representation we *should* make of God, or life, if we want the non-judging mirroring process of reality to work to our best advantage. It was a purely practical, pragmatic venture. He set up a pattern of representation, an image of transference, a pivot for restructuring, by which we can, "becoming as little children," achieve a new hierarchy of mind, a way down and out to freedom from fate.

The large category of the unknown rains on just and unjust alike. This function "judges not." Any question asked with ultimate seriousness merges into this unjudging ultimacy and tends to express itself. Any sowing enters this contingency and tends to set up its own reaping. Any worldview organizes a world-to-view. Any representation of God produces accordingly. Understanding and accepting responsibility for this function can make us free.

To move against the certainties and energies of "the world" calls for an equally sure conviction and a concentration on balance of mind. To center all the forces on the restructuring of an ordinary event in a nonordinary way called for exceptional organization of self.

Jesus promised his followers: "Whatever you ask in my name will be given you."

What do you want?" is the only question eternity can ask of time, and it is our divine gift to answer by asking our own question. Desire, passion, curiosity, longing, novelty, daring, creativity, productivity, lust for life, ecstasy, joy, adventure, all these are the highest thrusts of life, the most divine of attributes, the most sacred of possessions. And all these have been the attributes *mistrusted* and *condemned* by that dark priesthood probing for control, domination, and battening on the brother's blood. Without these seeds from time, however, without these vital gametes from the larger body of man, the womb of eternity is barren.

The "Will of God" shaped as the new metaphor for the old Greek Fate. The "Son of God" was no longer rational man; the "Father" no longer the logos-shaping mythos, the symbol of transference; the "Spirit" no longer the threshold of mind; "God" no longer that divine-demonic, non-judging, amoral, raining on just and unjust alike, the hard taskmaster reaping where he sows not, doubling the talents, any talents, mirroring any desire, and crying "More! More!" Less than all will never satisfy." By the Greek perversion these became Olympian figures rather than psychological symbols of ontology. They were abstracted from all reality. Jesus's Way, the greatest of human Eureka! ventures, became a fairy tale, a mundane, ridiculous, pious fraud.

Christendom has largely ignored Jesus's insistence that acts greater than his would be a product of his system. Based on Greek logic as it is, rather than on the non-structured and open Way, theology never understood or really believed in those happenings. Since miracles represented cracks in the egg beyond all probability, the self-styled guardians of the egg, determined to protect man *from* himself, projected those cracks into the nethermost regions of inaccessibility.

The "interventions in the ontological construct" attributed to Jesus and promised for his followers are as logical within *his* premise and system as are different reality states in don Juan's fire walking in the Hindu's, or atom bombs in the scientist's.

Man is the imaginative tool or technique by which life "thinks" in a rational, value-giving and limited way, selecting that which might be real. We have received only a mirroring of our own limitations, and have thus seen ourselves fated, by the Classical view. Calling God "Nature" has not changed the resulting fate. A change of metaphor will not make a bad idea good. To attribute human qualities to God is to have mirrored back *just this quality* of limitation, trapping us in our own logic.

There is no magician up there pulling strings if his whim and fancy can just be tickled by the right words. There is no Moral Governor of the Universe, no oriental tyrant able to grant amnesty if we can but find flattering enough incantation. There is no divine mind with beautiful blueprints. There is no super-computer behind the scenes able to out-figure the statistics if we could but hit on the right combination to trigger the mechanism.

The formative process of life is non-ambiguous since it is equally all possibilities. Any non-ambiguous idea becomes an organizing point for realization in this process. Ordinary logical thinking is ambiguous and enters only indirectly as one of an infinite number of random contingencies that may or may not be decisive. Non-ambiguous impressions and notions are generally "below the limen of feeling," and so appear to happen as fate when becoming points for formative realization. Fear, for instance, takes on an ultimate, non-ambiguous nature and tends to create that which is feared. Hatred is the same, trapping the hater in his own hell. A conscious, passionate, single-minded intensity tends to dampen out ambiguity and achieve a realization. Ultimate ideas in that "secret place of mind," the rock-bottom of real belief, shape one's ground of being.

We *must* become aware of the force of mind and develop a balance between the modes of thinking. The materials for achieving this wholeness have been in the common domain for two millennia now, though continuously evaded by our failure of nerve. The current dilemma allows no further evasion. Langer's "boldness of hypothesis" is not just desirable but crucial for survival.

We are finally confronting the mirror of our true selves—we are that fate. We are in our own hands.

Our next step will hinge on opening to the total process of mind and that means that shadowy area encompassing the whole development of psyche.

Do you not see how logical thinking, in order to even function, must limit to a specific, and that this specific is then the only apparent reality—and how this fragmented form of thinking then orients quite naturally around the notion of *scarcity,* the idea that in order to *have* we must take from and deprive others, since only a limited amount can be seen? Do you not see that fragmented thinking turns all others into potential enemies, until we live, as Northrop Frye* said, "As armed crustaceans, damned to a perpetual alarm and crisis, where life itself is a threat to life?"

The new direction outlined here in my book can be seen as harbingers of a new and larger season in our own cycle, and we will manage, I do believe, to hold through this winter of confused discontent.

As for myself, however, today is the day, and I dare not wait for some slow cultural drift finally to pave the way that I might easily float into some nebulous social salvation. I cannot depend on "them" "out there" to order into coherency this small sphere of my only present now.

Vision and Reflection[8]

"Perfection," Northrop Frye claims, "is the full development of one's imagination. The timid reflective thinker sees perfection as a quality abstracted from a real thing, and thus the sole property of an abstracted and unreal god. Perfection is the utilizing of all the modes of mind, finding that the Trees of Life and Knowledge are twins from the same taproot. Perfection is daring to embrace the universe itself as our true dimension, daring to steal the fire of the gods, to walk on water or fire

---

*[Northrop Frye (1912–1991) was a Canadian literary critic and theorist who gained international fame with his first book, *Fearful Symmetry,* which led to the reinterpretation of the poetry of William Blake. —*Ed.*]

unafraid, to heal, to claim plenty in time of death, to behold boldly that desired, and become what we have need to be."⁹

Vision is creative imagination using the eyes as windows to see *with* actively and not *through* passively.

Vision sees life as an "eternal existence in one divine man." Reflection sees life as a series of cycles in nature. We vacillate our life away between the two notions, never fully conscious of either. Reflection is Blake's *Diabolos,* the nihilistic impulse of self-doubt reminding us of our helpless frailty and increasing our dependence on the current priesthoods. If the fire walker listened to this side of his nature, he would never walk on fire. As Blake said, "If the sun and moon should doubt, they would immediately go out."

We need an image, a mythos, representing a way upward and outward where creative longing can be released and not denied. But reflective thinking seizes the insight given by vision and turns it into a dogma that makes for reliably ineffective, lifeless supporters of the world.

There is no absolute "out there" of logic, reason, love, goodness, or perfection. Nature is amoral, indifferent, operating by profusion. Needing these things we can only become them by boldly holding them as our rightful due. Lie creates myth and then strives to fill it by imitation.

The American philosopher Susanne Langer (1895–1985) warned that our losses to science should not be taken lightly. And what we have lost is our psyche, our very soul. Mass psychosis and sickness of soul are the price we are paying for letting a product become our absolute, letting a tool become master. The young rebel lashes out blindly at this living death to which he is condemned and which he must support, for which he must fight. The tragedy is that by the time he senses a deadly trap he has become—by the very process of reality formation—that against which he instinctively rebels. As don Juan said, "When you find that the path you are on has no heart and you try to leave that path, it is ready to kill you." Very few men, he observed, can stop deliberately at that point, and leave the path.

Reality is what we *do* know, that the world, as it is for us, is one we represent to ourselves for our own response. So it is with nature, God, "ultimate matter," and so on.

In a peculiarly prophetic vision a century and a half ago, Walt Whitman asked, looking up at the vast universe of stars: "When we have encompassed all those orbs, and know the joys and pleasures in them, we will be satisfied then?" "No," he realized, "we but level that lift to rise and go beyond."

It is time to see man in his true perspective, as Whitman did when he wrote: "In the faces of men and women I see God, and in my own face in the glass, I find letters from God dropped in the street, and everyone is sign'd by God's name."

Whitman writes, "I am ever shutting sunrise out of me lest sunrise kill me." This is the given premise on which the function rests, that which we can shape into a level to lift, that toward which we can rise to go beyond—a light of which I cannot speak except to those who would know already of what might then be said—beyond our words, where speech itself is superfluous, a knowing beyond the clouds of all unknowing, an answer beyond all questioning.

For here is the catalyst that shapes Eurekas! and gives syntheses beyond our mind's wild reach. Here is the catalyst that acts when it has something to catalyze, and always remains unchanged in so doing. Here is the unattainable, that I cannot will or think into my being, falling into my life even as itself, fleetingly, unbelievably, outside all structured thoughts, strivings, systems, and games. Here all paths are opened and synthesized, our freedoms underwritten and assured within.

2

$\blacklozenge$

Magical Child (1977)

Rediscovering Nature's Plan
for Our Children

THE BACKSTORY FROM JOE

I've known two things: One is an extraordinarily beautiful and ideal childhood up until about age seven. Then all hell broke loose; and the contrast of those two things I've never forgotten. There were tremendous experiences at age four and up on Dorchester Hill, playing all by myself under the great oak tree, at one with nature. You were the great mother's child at that age. I think of my friend Dave, a remarkable guy, who said, "We must rediscover living in constant astonishment." That is the experience of that whole period. We're in constant astonishment over something so wonderful, this life that we get to live. It is being one with nature, and you have conversations with every little flower and talk to the trees. No joke. This is who we are.

Then came the nightmare of my first day of school. We had no kindergarten. My family lived a block from the school, and my mother simply said, "Today you've got to go to school. Go down to the second building and open the door and knock on that first door on your right and that's Ms. Carpenter's room, and she's your teacher." She was also my Sunday school teacher and my godmother. So everyone figured we would get along beautifully. I quickly became Ms. Carpenter's pet, just obnoxiously so. I could do no wrong in Ms. Carpenter's room. Unfortunately, no one could do anything right in her room, except me, and it made quite a contrast.

We had eight months of schooling because the community couldn't pay their teachers for more than that. This was in 1931–1932. I went into the room, and the first thing Ms. Carpenter did was divide all the children between the bright eyes and the busy bees. The bright eyes were all those who were dressed fairly well. The busy bees were all the poor boys wearing their older brother's huge coveralls. They came out of the mines from the south side. It was strictly a social thing. The bright eyes were given all the attention; the busy bees were just shoved away. I was aware of that the very first day. My golly, what about the rest of them, I thought? I had this huge thing that rolled up here in my chest. What about the busy bees?

I'll never forget little Joiner Tribute. He wore these huge big coveralls from one of his older brothers, and he was always dirty. We had to sit at these desks and do nothing. Joiner didn't know what else to do so he pulled the little girl's hair in front of him, and Ms. Carpenter thundered back at him. She tied Joiner's hands behind his back to teach him not to pull the little girl's hair. And poor Joiner, not knowing what else to do, began to whistle. Well, what does a boy do with himself? He's stuck there sitting in his chair, and his hands are tied behind his back. What does he do? So he began to whistle, and Ms. Carpenter, to teach him a lesson, to teach us all a lesson, tied a gag on his mouth at which point little Joiner Tribute started to cry. Ms. Carpenter took him and put him in the kneehole of her desk and didn't let him out until school was over. And we could hear him crying away in his kneehole.

To me all this was horrible. It sounds like I'm trying to dramatize all this, but at that point *I was Joiner.* This was happening to me, and I suffered the contrast with those who were favored. And I was the most favored of all the favorites. To me this was a nightmare. I was plunged into a nightmare world called school, and I went home and declared, "I would never again go back to school."

My older brothers and sisters were there. They all laughed and laughed. They said, "You have to go back to school." I said, "No, I own myself. They don't own me." And they said, "Oh yes they do. You'll have to go back to school or they'll put you in jail." So, the nightmare was really growing. Going to jail was another nightmare piled on top of poor little Joiner—a nightmare of a nightmare. "What do they mean they will put me in jail?" And I began to just shout out in this terrible defiance, "They can't do this! I own myself!" Then my oldest brother, who was very sophisticated, being in his later teens, said, "If you don't do what they tell you, they'll put Mamma in jail." And to me that was the final ultimate horror. I went completely, I mean seriously completely, berserk. I ended up screaming in hysteria, "But I own myself, I own myself," over and over and over until finally my mother held me, trying to calm me down.

So this story of my life was that I did not own myself, and I objected to that violently. I played hooky from that point on. It was very difficult to get me there. I would do anything to keep from going to school. In the third grade little Joiner Tribute died of pneumonia. I was convinced he died because of his treatment the first day of school. It was the silliest thing in the world, but I lived with that the rest of my life. Little Joiner died because of what happened to him the very first day of school.

EXCERPTS FROM *MAGICAL CHILD*

The Second Bonding: Yin and Yang[1]

> *We have no notion of what intelligence is or what it is*
> *designed to do. Above all, we do not know what the mysterious*
> *difference between male and female intelligence is all about.*

At issue is the unbonded male child or the insufficiently bonded male. His need of bonding is biologically crucial, and the biological structure resulting from insufficient bonding is a warped, non-natural biological organism. . . . The unbonded female might become neurotic and be unable to bond to her child properly, but the unbonded male goes very subtly mad. Unless rooted to that mother matrix, his other matrices cannot form, and his machinery loses its balancing mechanism, its governor. He runs amok. What the unbonded male does is spend his life turning back on that matrix, trying to force from it that which is lacking. And what is lacking is his source of personal power, his possibility, and his safe space. Lacking these, he turns and uses his strength to rape. He rapes either crudely or with sophistication, that is, bodily, or intellectually, raping the earth matrix with technology. And he then has the chutzpah to set up an entire cultural criteria system for judging intelligence according to how successful one is in this rape of matrix.

The difference between the drive for the rape of the physical body of a particular woman and of the physical body of the living earth is only a difference of degree (perhaps a college degree). The same imbalance is at root. The non-bonded male has no safe space and turns to force this from the matrix. To dominate her becomes his passion, to violate her if need be to win from her that elusive magical nutrient every female seems to have but which the unbonded male cannot get or beat out of her. . . . The rapist himself does not understand the real hunger that drives him.

The Monstrous Misunderstanding[2]

Our problems are largely man-made, caused by ignoring nature's plan. Nature herself worked out all problems eons ago.

The material in this book has led me to a position so at odds with current opinion about the child mind and human intelligence that I have been at some loss to bridge the gap. At issue is a biological plan for the growth of intelligence, a genetic encoding within us that we ignore, damage, and even destroy. The mind-brain is designed for astonishing capacities, but its development is based on the infant and child constructing a knowledge of the world as it actually is. Children are unable to construct this foundation because we unknowingly inflict on them an anxiety-conditioned view of the world (as it was unknowingly inflicted on us). Childhood is a battleground between the biological plan's *intent,* which drives the child from within, and our anxious *intentions,* pressing the child from without.

Nature has provided that the human child be more dependent on a caretaker for a longer period of time than any other species. If parents and society honored nature's purpose behind this long dependency and slow maturation, the child would discover and respond to the world without concern for the utility or value of his/her discovery. If the child were allowed to develop this natural worldview, logical maturation would develop a utility, value, and ability almost beyond our imagination. Children throughout other parts of the world do, in fact, continually display abilities far beyond our accepted norms, though not for long.

What is going wrong in all technological countries today that infantile autism and brain damage are increasing at an epidemic rate, that childhood suicides are increasing yearly, that growing numbers of parents are beating infants and tiny children to death, that schooling is becoming increasingly unproductive, traumatic, even hazardous and improbable to maintain, and so on? I found that none of these problems, isolated to themselves is solvable. And I found that we make a serious error if we think children are only reflecting the tensions of the adult world. Rather, it may be the reverse. The issue is the nature of the child mind, human intelligence, and our biological connections with the earth system on which the development of the mind-brain depends. Until this issue is clarified and corrected, our problems can only multiply.

At one point, I felt that the book was impossible for me to write, that the implications were too vast and too sad to articulate. I underwent some depression when I began to see the potential of the child and the monumental tragedy that befalls us anew with each generation. I knew guilt over my own experience as a father and nostalgia over the loss of potential I had once felt so keenly. Only by delving as completely into the material as was possible did I finally see why I was *not* guilty, why none of us are, and why blame is largely fruitless. Once I had achieved this insight the material showed me the extraordinary and profound potential and hope that an understanding of the child's (and our own) mind-brain holds.

As a biologist, Jean Piaget felt that psychology had erred by starting with the grown human and working backward to the child, carrying into research the biases and viewpoints of a mature logic. The end product of a biological organism, he said, is not the best place to start if you want to understand that organism.

Piaget found that the child goes through clear developmental stages in this growth of intelligence—stages that parallel physical growth. He found that the child's brain system and structure of knowledge undergo specific transitions on a kind of timed maturational basis. At each of these shifts, the brain then processes its information in new ways and develops new ways for interacting with a larger experience. These shifts of logic, according to Piaget, are genetically determined and occur in all children in the same sequence at about the same age—much as physical growth does, I might add.

Herman Epstein, a Brandeis University biophysicist, has found evidence of periodic brain-growth spurts in all children at about the same stages in their development. At these periods the brain actually grows new biological materials for learning. These spurts occur roughly every four years, all but one coinciding with Piaget's periods of logical transition. Brain-growth spurts seem genetically predetermined in the same way that Piaget's developmental stages do, and I take it as obvious that these are all part of an integral genetic coding for the growth of intelligence.

Magical thinking implies that some connection exists between thought and reality; that thinking enters into and can influence the actual world. Child thought is based on this attitude for the first seven or eight years. The central question of psychologies and educational research has been given. How can the child be made to attend to reality? Or how can we make the child abandon magical thinking?

Each generation uses its children to its own ends, Otto Rank* once claimed, and magical thinking has been one of the stumbling blocks to using our children as we would like to in service to our technology. Has

*[Otto Rank (1884–1939) was an Austrian psychoanalyst, writer, and teacher, who for twenty years was a close colleague of Sigmund Freud. —Ed.]

nature, then, made a monumental error in creating a child who compulsively spends most of his or her time in the apparently nonproductive and even anti-survival activities or fantasy, magical thinking, and play? The implicit, almost axiomatic answer of our whole modern treatment of children has been *Yes!* Nature has apparently erred, in spite of the fact that this seems to go against the entire thrust and fabric of evolutionary adaptation and selection. But the child's world has recently been collapsing almost as fast as our adult one. Is it not possible that our ideas of the child and nature are in error instead?

My task has been to sketch the picture of the child's mind and nature's plan for intelligence. This is a large terrain, and discrepancies are probably inevitable. But I stand by my sketch of human intelligence and intend this book to be an aid in the correction of a monstrous misunderstanding.

Promise Given: A Magnificent Heritage[3]

The human mind-brain system is designed for functions radically different from and broader than its current uses. An astonishing capacity for creative power is built into our genes, ready to unfold. Our innate capacities of mind are nothing less than miraculous, and we are born with a driving intent to express this capacity.

This book discusses a corresponding, beautifully coordinated biological plan for the development of intelligence. Indeed, we find that body growth, so self-evident, follows the needs of the mind-brain's development in perfect synchrony. To allow full development of intelligence, we must acknowledge and cooperate with this biological plan. In so doing, we will find that most of our current problems with infants and children will never materialize. For our problems are largely man-made, caused by ignoring nature's plan. As stated earlier, nature herself worked out all problems eons ago.

Back in 1938, for instance, Harold Skeels (1901–1970), of the University of Iowa, was nearly drummed out of the American Psychological Association for his studies suggesting that I.Q. (the intelligence quotient of a person) was directly related to environmental conditions, particularly the nurturing of home and family. For everyone knew that intelligence was innate, a fixed genetic factor. Everyone was tragically wrong, of course, and eventually Skeels was recognized. Intelligence, like the body, can be injured or nurtured, stimulated, or starved.

To say that every child is a potential genius may sound ridiculous and even cruel, but to take current statistical norms as the standard or natural for the child is far more ridiculous and surely more cruel.

Intelligence is not assigned only to the brain and nervous system. Every cell of our bodies is an intelligence of staggering complexity, and every cell acts intelligently. The mind-brain-body is a wonderful array of intelligences ranging from the simpler life forms of the cell and old brain to the most complex (neo-cortex). Each human being contains the patterns of all thinking forms developed over the millennia.

In moving from simpler to more complex thinking organs, life's growth has been toward a more open intelligence and a more flexible logic. The more open the intelligence, the greater totality of the earth that hologram can express. Furthermore, an open intelligence is one that can structure a knowledge of an increasing amount of experience and compute the widening range of information gained by that experience. By flexible logic, I mean a brain system that can differentiate between its experiences, combine them, and synthesize new ways to interact with more complex kinds of experience. Open intelligence and flexible logic combine so that the more we learn through personal experience, the more we *can* learn, the more phenomena and events with which we interact, the greater our ability for more complex interactions.

Development is the interaction of the intent within and the content without. Intent moves the child toward interaction with the content out there. The intent within must always be given its content from without. The more extensive and complete the child's interaction with the content of the world out there, the more extensive the resulting structure of knowledge within.

Intelligence is the ability to interact, and this ability can grow only by interacting with new phenomena; that is, by moving from that which is known into that which is not known.

From birth, the growth of intelligence is a progression from the concrete toward the abstract. By concrete, I mean the physical substance of this living earth (its rocks, trees, people, winds, things) and its principles (such as "fall down, go boom" and "fire means burn"). By abstract, I mean the products of the mind-brain's own creativity (thoughts and ideas) rather than the actual material substance of the earth.

All thinking arises out of concreteness, which means out of the brain patterns resulting from actual body movements of interacting with actual things. But thinking then moves toward autonomy, that is, moves toward independence of those concrete patterns or physical principles. This progression toward pure thought is itself genetically programmed and unfolds in neat, sequential stages. To nurture intelligence in the young is to honor this progression from concreteness toward abstraction. This means that intelligence must first be educated in an accurate and full interaction with the earth as it is in order that the mind-brain might structure a knowledge of this earth. This *is* physical knowledge or basic body-knowing. Only out of this kind of knowing can abstract thought develop, such as an understanding of the law of gravity rather than "fall down, go boom" or the laws of thermodynamics rather than "hot, don't touch."

Our children have been signaling to us for years that things are critically wrong for them. In our anxiety-ridden concern to "equip them fully for life," we have been deaf and blind to their distress calls. And now our training techniques, our teaching systems, our behavior modifications and motivations are turning into chaos, both for our children and for ourselves. Perhaps at this critical point for the survival of the species, we can do more than make another futile gesture toward patching up the holes in our exhausted system of ideas. Perhaps we can seize this cubic centimeter of chance that history is giving us and move, not just to correct some of the more blatant and tragic errors we have made with children, not just to curb the battered-child syndrome, but actually to turn again to that three-blllion-year development lying within us, that uncanny wisdom of the body clearly programmed into the child as unbending intent. In learning to learn again, we can learn of this wisdom and allow our children (and so ourselves) to become the free, whole individuals this good earth has prepared us to be.

Matrix Shifts; Known to Unknown[4]

Matrix is the Latin word for "womb." From that word, we get the words *matter, material, mater, mother,* and so on. These refer to the basic stuff, the physical substance, out of which life is derived.

The womb offers three things to a newly forming life: a source of possibility, a source of energy to explore that possibility, and a safe place within which that exploration can take place. Whenever these three needs are met, we have a matrix. And the growth of intelligence takes place by utilizing the energy given to explore the possibilities given while standing in the safe space given by the matrix.

The biological plan for the development of intelligence is based on a series of matrix formations and shifts; that is, human beings are designed to grow in intelligence by learning about and gaining ability to interact with one source after another of energy, possibility, and security. The sequence is from early concrete matrices to ever more abstract ones, that is, from the matrix of our given life substance to the matrix of pure creative thought. Each matrix shift propels us into another set of unknown, unpredictable experiences, which is the way intelligence grows. Each matrix shift is both a kind of birth because we move into greater possibilities and a kind of death because the old matrix must be given up in order to move into the new.

These matrix shifts follow a set cycle. First, the mind-brain must structure its knowledge of its matrix.

Second, the mind-brain develops bonds (forms of communication and rapport) with both its present matrix and the new matrix into which the child must eventually shift as genetic maturation unfolds.

This bonding process provides a bridge between matrices so that the unknown of the new matrix will have sufficient points of similarity with the known of the old matrix. Then, the mind-brain can accommodate or learn about and adapt to the new. Nature would never (of her own choice) propel the child into a new matrix without sufficient preparation, because the child would be unable to adapt or survive in the new. And remember that nature programs entirely for success.

Third, when we have structured a knowledge of the matrix we can move successfully within it. When we have established bondings with the new matrix we shift functionally from dependence on the known matrix and move into the next stage of development—the next matrix. We move into the new matrix only by standing on the old matrix.

Fourth, having shifted matrices, we then have the possibility of a wider, more creative relationship with the former matrix. We find (*only* after leaving a matrix) that we do not lose that matrix but are able to interact with it in far more flexible and creative ways.

To relate creatively and to explore all possibilities, independence from the matrix must be achieved. To relate fully with the mother, the infant must leave the womb and, eventually, the dependency relation with the mother. . . . This means that every stage of development is complete and perfect within itself. The three-year-old is not an incomplete five-year-old; the child is not an incomplete adult. Never are we simply on our way; always, we have arrived.

Everything is only preparatory to something else that is in formation, as day must fade to night and night to day. But all this is part of an infinitely contingent natural system that simply lies beyond our conscious grasp and is, in effect, none of our business. The intricacies of the three-billion-year system are not necessarily available to, or needed by, our short-term understanding. . . . The cycle unfolds according to a genetic timetable that is roughly the same in all cultures.

What the biological plan does not, and apparently cannot, take into consideration is the failure of development within any particular stage. That next stage unfolds, regardless. . . . For instance, if the mother's body is producing massive amounts of adrenal steroids during pregnancy, as a result of chronic anxiety, maltreatment, or fear, the infant in the womb automatically shares in these stress hormones; they pass right through the placenta. That infant is locked into a free-floating anxiety, a kind of permanent body stress. If you have ever undergone a fright that startles your entire body, you know the body feeling of this stress state. Consider, then, having just such a flooding of fear without any conceivable reason for it; that is what a free-floating anxiety is. Locked into this tension, the infant in utero cannot develop intellectually or establish the bonding with the mother in preparation for birth. However, nature cannot program for this variable and wait for the damaging effects of chronic stress to be removed. Growth (at least physical growth) goes right ahead while intellectual growth struggles along as best it can in its crippled state, slipping farther and farther behind. If the infant does not spontaneously abort, it will be born deficient in intelligence if not in body, highly prone to early infantile autism or childhood schizophrenia, or dysfunctional in a wide variety of ways. At best, the child will have to use its intelligence to try to compensate for its deficiencies. The timed unfolding goes right ahead, and the child's deficiencies accumulate. The greater the deficiencies, the more stringently the system must compensate. But meanwhile, the wheels roll on; the intelligence meant to be fully absorbed in the present and adapting to it is back somewhere trying to get the machine working. If the first matrix formation is incomplete or insufficient, the next matrix formation will be doubly difficult.

The overall design is open-ended and is limited only by the individual's capacity for interaction, never by the possibilities for interaction. By its very structure, the brain's capacity for concept structuring and synthesizing can never be exhausted, and our independence and capacity of mind, designed to grow from that brain capacity, can only add to and go beyond this flexibility and freedom.

Physical interaction with the mother (or permanent caretaker) furnishes the infant with his/her basic set of brain patterns through which sensory information can be organized into perceptions. The mother *is* the infant's world, hologram, the content for his/her intent; she is the infant's power, possibility, and safe space.

The biological plan provides that the infant be given exactly the kinds of sensory motor tools (physical capacities) needed to do one thing in the first eight to ten months of life: structure a knowledge of that mother as the matrix. Once this critical task is accomplished, nature provides that the infant be given the physical and mental tools necessary to move slowly out from that mother and explore the living world around him/her. The infant can do this fully and successfully only to the extent the mother is the absolutely unquestioned safe place to which the baby can always instantly return and be nurtured. Only when the infant knows that the mother matrix will not abandon him/her can that infant move into childhood with confidence and power.

The biological plan provides that the child remains squarely rooted to the mother while exploring and structuring a knowledge of the earth matrix. This worldview structuring takes some seven years to perfect. When knowledge of the earth matrix is completed, at around age seven, nature provides that the child functionally separate (through a division of labor in the mind-brain system) from direct dependence on the mother as the base of exploration and shift to the earth itself as the safe place to stand.

From the years seven to eleven (roughly), the child structures a knowledge of this personal power in the world. This knowledge of the self (one's mind-brain-body organism) as matrix grows through the child's physical interactions with the physical body of the earth, much as the early infant structured a knowledge of the mother through sensory interactions with her. Dramatic and profound new modes of interaction unfold for development during this late-childhood period. Autonomy—becoming physically independent of parental help and learning to physically survive the principles of the physical world—is the goal of the period. Development of this personal power prepares for a shift of matrix from earth to self.

By adolescence, the biological plan is that we become our own matrix, consisting of mind-brain and body. In the logic of differentiation, mind-brain activity slowly distinguishes from body activity or body-knowing, that concrete knowledge structured throughout childhood. The biological plan then drives us toward the fifth matrix shift, when mind-brain should functionally (through distinctions of brain processing) separate from body.

Standing on the matrix of the concretely oriented physical body, mind-brain interactions (pure abstract thinking) should begin matrix formation; that is, the mind-brain should eventually become its own matrix, its own source of power, possibility, and safe place to stand.

At some point after maturity, mind should begin a functional separation or logical differentiation from brain processes. This is the final matrix shift about which we can have any direct knowledge. At that point, mind is capable of operating on the structures within its own brain and restructuring its experienced reality accordingly. At that point, personal awareness is no longer contingent upon or dependent upon any concreteness. Thus, the progression from concreteness toward abstraction would be complete.

The entire progression can be seen as the growth or development of autonomy, both as a physical organism in the physical world and as a personality in the realm of thought. We have, in effect, only two matrices: the physical matrix, progressing from womb, mother, earth, and physical body, and the abstract matrix of thought, progressing from relationships, the ability for interaction.

The biological plan is wrecked when the intent of nature is met, not with appropriate content, but with the *intentions* of an anxiety-driven parent and culture. Interaction can only take place when content matches intent. Inappropriate content brings about reaction, not intellectual growth. Anxiety results when the child is forced into mismatched relating of intent and content. Interchange with the matrix and growth of personal power then break down, but the sequential unfolding of maturation goes right ahead. The child's ability to interact falls more and more behind and more and more energy must go into compensation. The young person's intelligence is still back there trying to make the first matrix functional. Finally, there is a breakdown in the mind-brain balance, which was designed to be smoothly synchronous.

When the capacity for abstract creativity and pure thought does not develop properly, the solution is not to try to force earlier and earlier abstract thinking, as we now try to do. Rather, we must provide for full-dimensional interaction with the living earth, without allowing abstract ideas to intercede or obscure, so that a sufficient concrete structure may be built from which abstractions *can* arise.

Understanding follows knowing, and knowing results from actions, and proper actions can follow only some deep, intuitive hunch that bypasses ordinary thinking. Our first step is to consider that it just might be possible that nature knew what she was doing when she devised this three-billion-year developmental plan.

Intelligence as Interaction[5]

Through interaction, intelligence grows in its ability to interact. We are designed to grow and be strengthened by every event, no matter how mundane or awesome. The flow of nature and seasons, people, extreme contrasts, apparent catastrophes, pleasantries—all are experiences of interaction to be enjoyed and opportunities for learning, leading to greater ability to interact.

With what is human intelligence designed to interact? With anything and everything possible. If there is anything intelligence cannot interact with, that intelligence is crippled. A fully developed intelligence is one designed to exchange energies with anything existing, without ever being overwhelmed. A mature intelligence should be able to interact on three levels that correspond to and arise from the three stages of biological growth. These levels are first, the ability to interact with the living earth according to the principles and natural laws of this earth; second, the ability to interact with the earth according to the principles of creative logic developed in the mind-brain system; and third, the ability to interact with the processes and products of the mind-brain system itself, which means the thoughts and creations of our own mind, the minds of others, and the whole thought system underlying our reality. Any definition of intelligence that does not encompass these three categories of interaction is incomplete. Any development of intelligence that does not move through these three modalities falls short of the biological plan for intelligence and betrays nature's three-billion-year investment and trust.

Intelligence can only grow by moving from that which is known into that which is not yet known—from the predictable into the unpredictable. Moving into the unknown is possible only when there is a secure matrix to which the child can make an immediate return, and the younger the child, the more immediate and constant this return must be.

The only criterion we have for what the infant, child, young adult, or adult is learning or has learned is interaction. Can the child or person interact, or is his/her life one long chain of reactions to or acts of aggression against? When people express reaction-aggression, they are expressing not just a crippled intelligence but what they have actually learned.

Growth of the infant-child's ability to interact means increased rhythmic patterning in the brain and corresponding muscular responses. This growth can be slowed almost to a standstill by subjecting the growing child to demands inappropriate to his/her stage of development; that is, by trying to force the child to learn or deal with information or experience suitable to a later stage of development or by keeping them locked into an earlier stage. Then the child learns that learning itself is difficult and frustrating or non-rewarding. Even when the child manages to comply with demands suitable to a later stage, premature involvement can cripple intelligence, although the damage may not show for years.

For instance, abstract knowledge, such as adult idea systems and opinions, is designed for the later years of development. Forcing the early child to deal prematurely with adult abstract thought can cripple the child's ability to think abstractly later on.

The first ten years or so are designed for acquiring a full-dimensional knowledge of the world as it is and learning how to interact with it physically and mentally. This growth of knowledge and ability should lead to the ability to survive physically in the world. With the security of a full knowledge of survival, the young person could then move freely into abstract thought. His/her intelligence could then attend the true maturation of the mind-brain. Not incidentally, the concrete knowledge from which survival grows is also the concrete structure of knowledge out of which abstract thought arises.

Direct physical contact with the world—taste, touch, even smell—are often either discouraged or actually forbidden in the parent's anxiety over the hazards of germs and imagined threats. Without a full-dimensional worldview structured in the formative years, no earth matrix can form, no knowledge of physical survival can develop, and no basis for abstraction and creativity can arise. A permanent anxiety and obsessive-compulsive attachment to material objects will result. And anxiety always cripples intelligence; it blocks the development of muscular-mindedness, the ability to interact with the unknown and unpredictable. Anxiety is the source of the fall of the child somewhere around age nine. Its roots are deep, it branches prolific, its fruit abundant, and its effects devastating.

Stress and Learning[6]

Our senses bring us a ceaseless stream of reports concerning our world, but these grow humdrum and tedious. A surprising amount of life is repetitious, and after a time, any repetition tends to be screened out of awareness. We shift the editing of repetitive sensory reports to automatic brain processes in order to free our awareness for internal processes of thinking such as daydreaming. We spend a large part of our adult lives establishing routines that allow us to function with a minimum of sensory sampling.

The unknown is a set of circumstance whose outcome we cannot be sure of. The unknown-unpredictable imposes sensory data that do not fit the brain's established editorial policies well enough to be handled automatically by various subordinates. Then the editor in chief, I, the decision-making self, must be summoned to the scene. All body processes must be alerted.

When this happens, the pituitary gland releases hormones that activate the adrenal steroids. These hormones stimulate and activate the body-brain system in whatever amount the situation seems to call for.

This organizing of the body and brain to deal with the immediacy of an event and respond accordingly is *stress*. Such an activating and coordinating of the body's muscular system with the sensory system and awareness shuts out imagination and gives a direct sensory involvement, the immediacy that we call *excitement.* The infant is born into the world in a state of general excitement or stress.

Stress is the way intelligence grows. At moments of extreme stress, the pituitary gland produces a hormone called *adrenocorticotrophic hormone* (ACTH), which, in turn, activates the adrenal steroids, tightening up the body's defense systems. Scientists have injected rats with ACTH and found that the rats immediately produce large quantities of new proteins in the liver and brain. Proteins of this sort seem instrumental in both learning and memory. And on being injected with ACTH, the rat's brain immediately grows massive numbers of new connecting links between the neurons.

Such stimulated rats prove to be far more intelligent and adaptable than non-stimulated rats. They can learn faster than ordinary rats, solve problems more easily, adapt more quickly, and survive much better. Before converting your high chair to an electric chair, however, bear in mind that although the stressed mind-brain grows in ability and the unstressed one lags behind, the overstressed one collapses into physiological shock and shuts out everything. Stressing the system is only *half* of the natural cycle of learning.

The rhythm of intellectual growth is movement into the unknown-unpredictable, or stress, and assimilating or digesting it back into the known-predictable, or relaxation. Each such assimilation and adaptation to the unknown increases the scope of the known, the relaxed state. Correspondingly, each such adaptation increases the ability to move into more unknowns, presenting even greater stress or unpredictability, because of the broader base of predictability through which we can assimilate the unknown and make a proper accommodation to it.

Failure to assimilate and accommodate to new information breeds the confusion and anxiety of unresolved stress . . . The weight lifter builds his power through stressing and relaxing his muscles. Muscular-mindedness is built through successful practices of stress-relaxation. This gives personal power and is the source of joy. However, the cycle can take place only from a firm matrix or known base of power, and our job as parents is to make sure that this construction is successful in the infant-child.

The mother is the infant's first matrix and the source of his/ her possibility. She is the place of power of which the child builds muscular-mindedness and develops autonomy, the self-sufficient strength to separate from her and become independent. If this matrix does not become fully structured, if such a security and strength are not given from birth, intelligence will have no ground on which to grow. The growing intelligence (and, God knows, the so-called mature one) that has no firm matrix has no choice but to devote its energy and attention to trying to secure that matrix. Without that safe place to stand, no energy can be utilized to explore possibility, intent cannot move into content and know fulfillment, and the stress of the unknown-unpredictable becomes a chronic threat. We then spend our lives trying to avoid this threat.

An intelligence whose matrix as mother has not formed sufficiently at birth cannot explore and structure a knowledge of the earth on a full-dimensional level. For this child, the earth as matrix cannot become functional, as designed, when the child is about seven years of age. Rather than the whole world becoming the source of possibility, energy, and the safe place to stand, it becomes the enemy, the adversary, the danger. The person denied the first matrix remains grounded in that earliest stage, trying to establish some arbitrary and artificial safe place of his/her own making. It is a compensation that never works.

The New Demonology: Exorcising Nature[7]

Why should—indeed, how *did*—stress become the enemy within? Obviously the life-giving balance of stress and relaxation has been seriously upset. We are locked into a cultural stress-stress atmosphere in which relaxation becomes almost impossible unless it is chemically induced. It is stress-stress that truly proves to be the enemy, an alliance with death; but so is relaxation-relaxation because if such a state completely takes over, we must put that body six feet under.

To trace the root causes of this notion of stress as the enemy within us would take volumes because it would lead to the unraveling of the whole fabric of current life. I shall focus on only the most significant assumption that underlies this notion and show how it is the real issue before us. This assumption, which really cripples us, is so axiomatic, so much a part of our whole web of beliefs, that to question it seems ridiculous. The assumption runs like this: In this three-billion years of experimenting, life has evolved our huge and brilliant mind-brain system in order that we might have the intelligence to outwit and so survive this life system that has evolved us; that is, we really believe that we have a superior brain in order that we might outwit nature, and we believe we *must* outwit nature in order to survive her. Outwitting means acting against, dominating, overcoming, and removing the causes of stress.

Would a three-billion-year experiment in genetic coding really have produced as it finest production a brain whose only purpose is to outwit itself? Yet, we believe, apparently with a tenacious passion, that the purpose of human intelligence is to predict and dominate the infinitely contingent and interacting balances of a universal system. We call our supposed successes in this venture *progress* and believe that the purpose of our lives is to contribute to this progress. Finally, we gauge all our interpretations of intelligence according to this belief, at which point we surely fall—long and hard.

Interaction between the mind-brain and its source of information has been rigorously and religiously denied by Western logic, if not *most* cultural logic. Interaction with the living earth would imply that the earth responded in kind, interacting with us. And the one cardinal rule of all classical Western academic belief, which is very much in power over our minds today, is that the mind has absolutely no relation to the world other than to be informed of that world through the senses and to make some sort of intelligent reaction to that information. This belief has automatically robbed us of personal power. Having no personal power to draw on, we are reduced to only one source of power: tool usage.

Our body of knowledge and tool development has never given, is not presently giving, and almost surely will never give us either physical security or well-being. The more vast and awesome our tool production has become, the greater our anxiety, hostility, fear, resentment, and aggression. But the direct correlation between our anxiety and tool production is almost beyond our grasp because our intelligence is itself the result of our conditioning by and within that very body of knowledge. Our intelligence is trained to believe that any imperfections in the reality resulting from our activities, such as personal anguish, misery, and fear, simply indicates the need for improvements in the body of knowledge and/or improvements in tool production, distribution, and application. Even as our body of knowledge splits us off from our lives and creates anxiety and unhappiness, it conditions us to believe religiously that escape from our misery lies in perfecting that body of knowledge. (Therein lies the current generation's sincere belief in schooling as the way out of our dark ages.)

European and American researchers have long observed that infants do not smile until some two and a half months after birth (on the average). Nor does the early infant display sensorimotor learning or general adaptations during this time. Because such a prolonged period of incapacity, with no signs of intelligence being manifested, is quite unique in this world, many learned papers have been written about the smiling syndrome and post-birth lack of intellectual response in infants. Freud, in early neurological studies of infants, wrote about this strange vegetative condition, and theories have grown out of his theory in typical academic style. Our body of knowledge finally included as a matter of fact that babies do not (indeed perhaps should not) smile during this ten- to twelve-week period after birth because intelligence is nonexistent during this time.

In 1932, Professor Katherine Bridges* noted that the newborn seems to come into the world in a state of "general excitement" but that this excitement quickly changes to distress. Pleasure or smiling, she observed, appears some two and a half to three months later. Psychoanalyst René Spitz (1887–1974) wrote about the smiling syndrome and its late appearance signaling the beginnings of some crude intelligence. The infant has only two states in this period, he observed, "quiescence," which meant

---

*[Author of *Social and Emotional Development of the Pre-School Child,* published in 1931. —*Ed.*]

unconsciousness or sleep, and "unpleasure," which meant being awake. Spitz noted that for the first two and a half to three months, the infant either cries or sleeps and little else. Spitz based his position on "Freud's concept of the neonate as a psychologically undifferentiated organism. "This organism still lacks consciousness, perception, sensation, and all other psychological functions." At another point, Spitz writes, "I follow Freud's opinion that at birth there is no consciousness, accordingly, there can be no awareness or conscious experiences. . . . Thus it is rare to find the smiling response before the third month of life."[8]

Burton White, of Harvard's center for child development, found research futile for about the first two months of life because the infant only sleeps, cries, or feeds during this time. Until smiling begins, he maintained, there is no intelligence.

The question arose: Why is intelligence so slow in forming? No other species has anything comparable to this long delay in at least some form of intelligent adaptation. In answer, theories arose, of course, giving rise to other theories, concerning this period of stupor, total helplessness, semi-consciousness, massive sleeping, excessive crying, and a generally precarious hold on life. Spitz, in fact, assumed that the entire first year of life was devoted solely to physical survival.

Naturally, an acceptable answer emerged: The human infant is born *prematurely*. We are rather like marsupials without pouches. And naturally another question arose. Why is the human born prematurely? Again, an answer dutifully emerged, one in keeping with the whole fallacy. We are born prematurely because of our big brains. Notice that the head of the infant at birth is much larger than the body. Problems arose when humankind got up on its hind legs and started walking upright because this posture closed in the pelvic area and narrowed the birth canal considerably. With this huge head, full of all those brains, if the infant were to grow to full term in utero, his head would be too large to pass through the now-narrowed canal, so the human infant must be born prematurely to get out at all.

No less a person than Jerome Bruner of Harvard's Center for

Cognitive Studies, surely one of our more brilliant researchers, developed this idea. The assumption is terribly wrong, but the academic rationale growing around it began to include more contradictions blithely ignored because once an idea is accepted into the body of knowledge, everyone "knows" and no one questions it. Everyone "knew" that no smiling occurs for some ten to twelve weeks because infants are born prematurely and have no intelligence during that time. If a mother reported some smiling before that acceptable date, the cryptic diagnosis was "gas pains."

Meanwhile, in 1956, Marcelle Geber, under a research grant from the United Nations Children's Fund, traveled to Africa to study the effects of malnutrition on infant and child intelligence. She concentrated on Kenya and Uganda and made a momentous discovery. She found the most precocious, brilliant, and advanced infants and children ever observed anywhere. These infants had smiled, continuously and rapturously, from at the latest, their fourth day of life. Blood analyses showed that all the adrenal steroids connected with birth stress were totally absent by that fourth day after birth. Sensorimotor learning and general development were phenomenal, indeed miraculous. These Ugandan infants were months ahead of American or European children. A superior intellectual development held for the first four years of life.

These infants were born in the home, generally delivered by the mother herself. The child was never separated from the mother, who massaged, caressed, sang to, and fondled her infant continually. The mother carried her unswaddled infant in a sling, next to her bare breasts, continually. She slept with her infant. The infant fed continuously, according to its own schedule. These infants were awake a surprising amount of the time—alert, watchful, happy, calm. They virtually never cried. Their mothers were bonded to them and sensed their every need before that need had to be expressed by crying. The mother responded to the infant's every gesture and assisted the child in any and every move that was undertaken so that every move initiated by the child ended in immediate success. At two days of age (forty-eight hours) these infants sat bolt upright, held only by the forearms, with a beautifully straight back and perfect head balance, their finely focused eyes staring intently, intelligently at their mothers. And they smiled and smiled.

New European-type hospitals were being erected in Uganda at the time of Geber's studies. Only the upper-class Ugandan families could afford such luxury, of course, and the women of this class naturally followed the fashion of having their children in hospitals. These hospital-delivered infants, it turned out, followed the same civilized schedule American and European infants do. Geber found that they did not smile until some two and a half months after birth. Nor were they precocious in any sense. They showed no signs of sensorimotor learning, displayed no uncanny intelligence for some two and a half months, at which point some signs of intelligence were apparent. Blood analyses showed that high levels of adrenal steroids connected with the birth stress were still prevalent at two and a half months. These infants slept massively, cried when awake, were irritable and colicky, frail and helpless. So the issue was not in some racial predisposition toward early intellectual growth. The issue lay solely with what happens to the newborn infant in hospitals.

What happens is quite simple. The infant is exposed to an intelligence determined to outwit nature, an intelligence distrustful of anything natural, an intelligence with a vast array of tools at its disposal with which to outwit and, in fact, supplant nature entirely. And in that outwitting and supplanting, damage is done that is incalculable. Future historians will shudder in loathing and horror at the hospital treatment of newborns and mothers in this very dark age of the medicine man and the surgeon and their uses of chemicals and cuttings. The chemicals dull and stupefy both mother and infant, making birth hazardous, prolonged, difficult, and extreme, so tools are used for grappling, clawing, sucking the infant out when the natural processes have been made impossible.

The Ugandan mother works around her house until some five minutes before delivery. In about an hour, she is out on the streets again, showing her new infant to her neighbors and relatives.

Frederick LeBoyer (1918–2017) was a conventional French obstetrician who delivered 9,000 babies by standard methods. He noticed that

France, a nation of 50 million persons, had over 1 million dysfunctional children. He began to question general birth practices and realized that hospital deliveries were damaging the infants. He quit his practice, retired to India for three years where he carefully studied native procedures for child delivery in very remote, so-called primitive areas. He combined what he saw with his own scientific background and came up with a synthesis. He returned to France and began a new form of delivering infants into the world. And the babies he delivered *smile,* beautifully, continuously, rapturously, from some twelve hours after birth.[9]

I personally know of several infants, delivered in the home by their own parents, who have smiled continuously from the first hour of life. And why not? They have been met with love, care, concern, and above all, gentleness and quiet.

Time Bomb in the Delivery Room[10]

All the anxiety-ridden fallacies of our day seem to congregate in the hospital delivery room where they bring about a disaster that remains largely undetected because it works like a time bomb. None of the parties to the crime ever has to pay, for the explosion takes place in slow fusion over the years and creates such widespread and diverse havoc that few bother to tract it back to see who lit the fuse.

The fallacies are personified in the figure of the medicine man, who, donning his bizarre and frightful masks and cloaks and surrounded by an astonishing array of mechanical wizardry, sets about to outwit nature. Aided by an equally impressive array of chemicals he sets about to help the victim-patient-mother avoid the stress inherent within the strange unfolding nightmare. Lost to sight—almost incidental and peripheral to the play of ego, money, and power involved— is the infant, the new life trying to unfold. As everyone "knows," this psychologically undifferentiated organism lacks consciousness, perception, sensation, and all other psychological functions. Accordingly, there can be no awareness. So the attitude is: get the infant out of the way quickly so that we adults can enjoy our self-drama.

When the proper gestation period is over, and the infant is ready to leave his/her first matrix and embark on the great venture into the world, it is *his/her* body that releases the hormones triggering the entire birth-delivery system. The mother's body picks up the hormones released by the infant, which, in turn, trigger her hormones into action. These hormones are passed back to the infant, and back and forth it goes. The two systems, mother's and child's, are designed to work together for a quick, efficient delivery. The birth canal is, after all, very short.

The resistance of the medical people to natural childbirth is understandable. Resistance is displayed to anything natural. The natural does not pay and does not need the professional, who robs you of what is naturally yours and sells it back to you at a dear price. Childbirth as a natural, euphoric, and ecstatic experience—as reported by primitives, hippies who birth in their own dirty homes, or other uncivilized specimens—obviously will not do. Childbirth is, and will damned well be *kept,* dangerous, difficult, painful, complicated, obscure, mysterious, and vastly beyond the grasp of a simple *layperson* (someone who does not even know Latin anatomical terminology). How could women be kept frightened enough to jump through those medical hoops, assume that unnatural position, submit to the series of insults and violations of person and child, and keep those husbands shucking out all those bucks if such a notion as natural childbirth were to take hold?

A number of years ago, a doctor by the name of William F. Windle became concerned over childbirth practices. He made a careful analysis of hospital deliveries throughout the United States and noted, with some alarm, two questionable procedures: the widespread, automatic use of premedication and anesthetics and the usual practice of cutting the umbilical cord as soon as the baby's body was clear.

Windle then made the simplest of tests. He took pregnant monkeys and treated them to all the benefits of our modern medical practices. At the time of labor and delivery, he administered anesthetics in a body-weight ratio equivalent of that given the average laboring human mother in the hospital. At the birth of the infant, he cut the umbilical cord at the average time he had found practiced in hospitals. In every case, Windle's newborn monkeys could not get their breath and had to be resuscitated; that is, artificial means had to be used to help them get their breath going. (Our hospitals now have various machines to aid in this process.)

In the natural world, of course, this never takes place. Unless an animal infant is stillborn, it breathes the instant that its head clears the cervix. Little monkeys have enormous capability soon after birth. Almost immediately, they can cling to their mother, who resumes her ordinary life quickly, toting her infant with her, giving him a bit of assistance in those first few hours as he clings to her. In a short time, the infant is physically autonomous, on his feet, jumping about, leaping away from his mother and back to her.

Windle's infant monkeys, whose nature had been outwitted by clever human devices, showed no such agility or ability. Indeed, they were totally helpless. Not only could they not cling to the mother, they could not get their limbs under them at all. The mothers, dazed by the drugs and the greatly lengthened labor (which anesthetics automatically cause), could do little to assist. Windle had to step in to keep the little creatures alive. And how long was it before these medically delivered infants achieved some normality, got their limbs under them, and began some preliminary sensorimotor learning? Some two to three weeks.

Newell Kephart, director of the Achievement Center for Children at Purdue University, finds learning and behavior problems resulting from minor undetected brain injury in 15 to 20 percent of all children examined. Goldberg and Schiffman estimate that 20 to 40 percent of our school population is handicapped by learning problems that may be related to "neurological impairments at birth."

Windle closed his report, published in *Scientific American* in 1969, with this comment:

> "[Our experiments] have taught us that birth asphyxia lasting long enough to make resuscitation necessary always damages the brain. . . . A great many human infants have to be resuscitated at birth. We

assume that their brains, too, have been damaged. There is reason to believe that the number of human beings in the U.S. with minimal brain damage due to asphyxia at birth is much larger than has been thought. Perhaps it is time to re-examine current practices of childbirth with a view to avoiding conditions that give rise to asphyxia."[11]

Breaking the Bond: Our End Is in Our Beginning; Our Beginning Is Our End[12]

Author Jean Mackellar told me of her years in Uganda, where her husband practiced medicine. Local mothers brought their infants to see the doctor, often standing patiently in line for hours. The women carried the tiny infants in a sling, next to their bare breasts. Older infants were carried on the back, papoose style. The infants were never swaddled, nor were diapers used. Yet none of them were soiled when finally examined by the doctor. Puzzled by this, Jean finally asked some of the women how they managed to keep their babies so clean without diapers and such. "Oh," the women answered, "we just go to the bushes." Well, Jean countered, how did they know when the infant needed to go to the bushes? The women were astonished at her question. "How do *you* know when *you* have to go?" they exclaimed.

Dr. Melvin Konner, in his studies of the Zhun/Twasi, an African hunting-gathering culture, found that the mothers always knew when the infant was going to urinate or defecate and removed the child to the bushes ahead of time. The mother sensed the general state of the infant and anticipated the infant's every need.

These mothers and infants have *bonded*. Bonding is a nonverbal form of psychological communication, an intuitive rapport that operates outside of or beyond ordinary rational, linear ways of thinking and perceiving. Bonding involves what I call *primary processing,* a biological function of enormous practical value, yet largely lost to technological man.

Marshall Klaus of Case Western Reserve's University Hospital in Cleveland, Ohio, has made the most articulate, thorough, and brilliant study of bonding to date. He has shown how bonding is a carefully programmed instinctual response built into us genetically. The mother is genetically programmed to bond to the infant at his/her birth, and the infant is programmed to expect her response. Indeed, without it, the infant is in grave trouble. Bonding may even involve specific hormones, and *breast-feeding may prove one of the most critical factors in establishing the bond.*

Carl Jung once said that the child lives in the unconscious of the parent. I am distrustful of the word *unconscious,* but surely Jung was correct about the function involved. The truth is the fully conscious parent encompasses the psychological state of the child. They participate in shared functions that need no articulation, that simply call for spontaneous response, a mutual meeting of needs, and a mutual fulfillment on emotional-intuitive levels.

Crying seems to be a distress signal employed when other signals fail. If this final form of communication consistently fails to bring response from the caretaker, the infant then learns that it has no power over its world at all and sinks into apathy.

Klaus, however, makes the astonishing claim that if properly bonded with the mother, the child should *never* cry. Crying, he states, is an unnatural, abnormal, uncommunicative expression, an emergency distress mechanism only. And in those societies where bonding is practiced, crying is, indeed, quite rare. Other forms of communication are used, and the infants and children develop the sense of personal power such responsiveness gives.

Bonding is stage-specific. Nature has designed the bonds to be established in the hours immediately following birth.

The issue is not sweet sentiment. The issue is intelligence, the brain's ability to process sensory information, organize muscular responses, and interact with the environment. In order to be assimilated and accommodated by the mind-brain, the unknown experience must have a sufficient number of points of similarity to the known. This is the cycle of stress-relaxation involved in all learning. If there is no way of relating the new to the old, the brain cannot process that information. Confusion and—anxiety must then result, and the learning must prove negative.

I will return to this bonded child later, for this child still has more to teach us. For now, however, I need to return to the hospital-delivered infant (my five and yours, I dare say). The infant has been prepared for the greatest single act of learning or growth of intelligence ever to take place. What does the infant learn? What happens to this highly absorbent mind?

First, as childbirth activist and author, Suzanne Arms, has detailed so well, the entire procedure of delivery gets seriously delayed and complicated out of all bounds in hospital delivery. Drugs, particularly anesthetics, specifically slow up the synchronous movements by which the infant is expelled from the womb, and delivery gets extended to tortuous lengths. Fear and anxiety build in the mother, and pain follows swift and sure. The pain calls for more medication, as does the anxiety. And what of the infant? Its little body has begun a massive outpouring of adrenal steroids preparatory to the great push and adaptation, but the movement does not come. The baby's body continues it outpouring of hormones. Stress piles on stress; the expected natural cycle of stress-relaxation is not forthcoming. After hours of this, both mother and infant are exhausted.

Then there are all the medical interferences, the carelessness, and the callousness. Coupled with the conditioned reflex of fear are the operating amphitheater atmosphere, that deadly table, and being forced to lie down (or even be strapped down), which completely eliminates any last hope of muscular coordination. This is followed by drugs that incapacitate both mother and infant. (The average anesthetic passes through the placenta to the infant in forty-five seconds.) Long before delivery (deliverance), mother and infant have been kept at a climatic point of tension, able to achieve no resolution.

What happens? Because the natural expulsion process is by now thoroughly fouled up, instrumentation is used to "assist" the mother in expelling the baby. In addition to the now commonplace practice of episiotomy (severely cutting the mother in a manner that would be considered major surgery at any other time and often causing permanent damage), forceps and suction machines are casually used to claw or suck the infant out of the mother's body, by grabbing that fantastically fragile, all too sensitive, and utterly precious head. The vast majority of such instrumentation is not necessary; and only in a rare emergency could an episiotomy be justified, even with all the complications caused by the medicine man's bag of tricks. The simple truth is that he likes to use his tricks; he likes the drama and importance of his image, wielding all his mechanical toys, showing the incompetence of nature, and establishing his own superiority.

The semi-drugged, overstressed, and exhausted infant is, of course, generally unable to take a breath, even if given ample time to do so. The many new, unused coordinates of muscles are confused and malfunctioning. Its body is reacting only; all synchronous interactions have long since been destroyed. In addition to the prolonged body fear of oxygen deprivation, when the baby is finally sucked or clawed out of the mother, his/her entry is into a noisy, brilliantly lit arena of masked creatures and humming machines. (The hum of fluorescent lighting alone is an overload, much less fluorescence itself, which, as the world's greatest authority on lighting, John Ott, makes perfectly clear, is disastrous to infants.) Suction devices are rammed into the mouth and nose, the eyelids peeled back to that blinding, painful light and far more painful chemicals dropped into the open eyes. The baby is held by the heels and beaten on the back or subjected to a mechanical respirator; at this critical, oxygen-short period, the umbilical cord has been cut. The child is cleaned up a bit from the blood of the episiotomy (which will knock mother out of the picture for quite some time); placed on cold hard scales to be weighed like any other piece of meat in a factory; wrapped up (of all things, to protect him/her from those demon drafts), bundled off to a nursery crib, screaming in pain and terror, or rushed semiconscious and half dead to any incubator, a far worse fate than a crib.

This rush is necessary because attention is focused on the cut, bleeding, injured, drugged, and depressed mother. Her comfort is the issue. Her postpartum blues will be discussed in some psychological journal, which will ask whether there really is such a syndrome. She herself, somewhere in her daze, feels that it was all so wrong. Something magnificent, earthshaking, universal, godly, numinous, near mystical was supposed to happen and did not. She wants her baby, and all she gets are sharp commands and reprimands. Nature has done everything possible to make the newborn's venture into the unknown a success and a great learning by guaranteeing a return to the known. What the infant actually learns at birth is what the process of learning is like. The baby has moved from a soft, warm, dark, quiet, and totally nourishing place into a harsh sensory overload. The little one is physically abused, violated in a wide variety of ways, subjected to specific physical pain and insult, all of which could still be overcome, *but the infant is then isolated from the mother.*

It is impossible to overstate the monstrousness of this final violation of a new life. No book can ever express the full ramifications of this crime against nature. This isolation neatly cancels every possible chance for bonding, for relaxation of the birth stress, for the activation of the sensory system for its extra-uterine function, and for the completion of the reticular formation for full mental-physical coordinates and learning.

The failure to return to the known matrix sets into process a chain reaction from which that organism never fully recovers. All future learning is affected. The infant body goes into shock. The absorbent mind shuts down.

During this period of shock, sensory closure, and retrenchment, there is virtually no development. How could there be? And all the other preprogrammed stage-specific developments are systematically missed, throwing the system farther behind.

Consider now the male child, whose hold on life is automatically more precarious than the female child's. In nearly all cases, the doctors circumcise the male infant on the second or third day of life. They cut off the foreskin of his penis, nearly always without anesthetic. After all, the infant—suffering excessive stress, in a state of shock, and all too often with a crippled reticular formation—seems to be a vegetable, so why not treat him as one?

Does it hurt? Of course it does. How could it help but hurt? And this is just one more of those massively negative learnings etching into that new brain-body system.

I can only dare parents, if they are going to allow this criminal act, to demand they be allowed to *watch* the performance. Just go watch, remembering that the infant registers pain just as you do. If the infant is not already in a complete state of shock before the operation, he certainly will be afterward, as parents would be if they were to observe and comprehend what is happening. Remember that the practice is a recent addition to our century's atrocities committed on children; bear in mind the growing incidence of sexual inadequacies and dysfunctions; remember that 80 percent of all silent crib deaths are male infants. Ask your doctor, though, and he will scathingly dismiss criticisms, reassure you that it's perfectly all right, and make you feel rather stupid for even asking.

Dr. Marcelle Geber spent one year (1957) doing long-term studies of 300 of these home-delivered infants in Uganda. She used the famous Gesell tests for early intelligence, developed at Yale University's child development center. The pictures of the forty-eight-hour-old child—supported only by the forearms, bolt upright, perfect head balance and eye focus, and a marvelous intelligence shining in the face—are no more astonishing than those of the six-week-old child. At six to seven weeks, all 300 of these children crawled skillfully, could sit up by themselves, and would sit spellbound before a mirror looking at their own images for long periods. This particular ability was not to be expected in the American-European child before twenty-four weeks (six *months*) according to the Gesell tests. Between six and seven months, the Ugandan children performed the toy-box retrieval test. Geber showed the infant a toy, walked across the room, put the toy in a tall toy box; the child leaped up, ran across the room, and retrieved the toy. Besides the sensorimotor skills of walking and retrieval, the test shows that object constancy has taken place, the first great shift of logical processing in the brain, at which point an object out of sight is no longer out of mind (the characteristic of infancy and early childhood). This test, successfully completed by the Ugandan children between six and seven months of age, was not to be expected until somewhere between the fifteenth and eighteenth months in the American and European child.

Throughout these extremely critical transition periods, during which the infant's brain is prepared for massive new learnings, every encounter with people is a stressful situation with no forms of nurturing or stress-relaxation at all. At the height of this stress, the infant is isolated, which very plainly means abandoned. There, in proximity to only material things (the baby blanket), the child must manage again to achieve some stress reduction in order to survive; the need of physical skin stimulus to facilitate this reduction finds only that baby blanket, a *nonhuman* source of stress reduction. What is the great learning? What is being built into the very fibers of that mind-brain-body system as the initial experiences of life? *Encounters with people are causes of severe, unbroken, unrelenting stress, and that stress finds its only reduction through contact with material objects.*

The net result of this has been a collapsing social order, on the one hand, and a generation with an increased passion for consumer goods, on the other; and this generation can only breed more of the same. That is, the long-range effects of the materially bonded child are a breakdown of interpersonal relations and an obsessive-compulsive attachment to material objectives.

Obsessive-compulsive attached to objects, Linus with his security blanket, in the comic strip *Peanuts,* is the tragicomic symbol of the effects. This occurs simply because the organism learned, in its primary learnings, which take precedence over all others, that although stress comes from human encounters, relaxation or escape from stress comes from encounters with physical objects. So we have a nation—and more nations all the times as our disease spreads—in which a breakdown of interpersonal relating is coupled with obsessive-compulsive attachment to material things.

Bonding is a psychological-biological state, a vital physical link that coordinates and unifies the entire biological system. Bonding seals a primary knowing that is the basis for rational thought. We are never conscious of being bonded; we are conscious only of our acute *disease* when we are not bonded or when we are bonded to compulsion and material things. The unbounded person (and bonding to objects is to be very much unbounded in a functional sense) will spend his or her life in search of what bonding was designed to give: the matrix. The intelligence can never unfold as designed because it never gets beyond this primal need. All intellectual activity, no matter how developed, will be used in search of that matrix, which will take on such guises as authenticity, making it in this world, getting somewhere.

I need to clear up an issue concerning the Ugandan child. If these children are so smart, why aren't they all rich, as the old saying goes? Why aren't they all Einsteins? How come they live in those grass shacks and often starve?

In Uganda, according to the strict, unbreakable custom or taboo of that culture, the mother specifically, carefully, completely, and without any forewarning, totally abandons her child when it is about four years old. She suddenly refuses even to acknowledge the child's existence. The child becomes invisible to her, as it were. The child is then sent to a distant village to be raised by relatives or is given to neighbors to raise. The psychological shock of abandonment is overwhelming to the child. Severe depression develops, and many children do not survive the shock at all.

At this critical point of total vulnerability, the child is prepared for what can only be termed "bonding to the culture." The child learns the taboo system and locks into it with depression. What is then learned is that to break the taboo, to act against the rules of the society, will mean banishment from that society. That would mean another abandonment; and the dread of this final and complete form of abandonment drives the child to accept without question the strictures and qualifications the taboo system imposes. And at that point, growth of intelligence largely stops.

Establishing the Matrix[13]

This mother is responsible, able to respond. She responds to the needs of her body with the same respect and care she will show for her infant in and out of the womb. She responds by making her own preparations for delivery, birth, and bonding. During the last months of pregnancy, she works specifically for bonding with her unborn child. She may have a simple tune she hums to her infant over and over. She will sing or hum this same tune during delivery and birth as one of her many bonding cues. She talks aloud to him/her continually because she knows that the infant hears and responds physically with synchronous body movements.

She keeps communion with the child, thinking positive and creative thoughts. They are already friends. She attends to her child, becomes aware of different movements and responses. She is, from the first signs within her, learning about her child, learning to take her cues from it and respond accordingly.

Knowing anxiety to be the great crippler of intelligence, she works purposely for a calm response. She begins each day in quiet meditation, establishing her union with the flow of life and with her child. She closes each day in the same way and makes her time in between a living meditation, a communion and rapport, a quieting of the mind to tune in on the inner signals. She reduces all the fragmenting intentions of life to the single intent of her act of creation.

She does not indulge in doubt. She chooses what she will entertain in her mind, and she chooses confidence, which means moving with faith. She knows the contents of her mind are matters of her own choice—that anxiety contents stir adrenal steroids that are passed on to her child.

She knows what to do by heeding the three-billion-year biological coding built into her genes. Her knowing is not articulated, thought-out, coherent, or verbal. She is just a coordinate of smooth actions. Her thought is her body action, and in this she is like a child. She is gripped by that same intensity found in deep play (skiing a dangerous slope, scaling a cliff face, fast tennis): the total attentiveness and single-mindedness of confrontation, an ultimate encounter. Every move, act, signal heeded is an unbroken flow of controlled abandon. By being responsible, she is in her power, a joyful response to a body-knowing that "breathes" in her.

Safely on her belly, the just-born baby begins to relax. The infant has picked up the mother's familiar heartbeat and hears her familiar hum. Points of similarity are beginning to emerge. The child breathes more regularly, each breath is easier. Within a few minutes, breathing is steady and regular, as the mucus in the tubes clears. Contact with the mother's nipples triggers the afterbirth into play; the contractions of the discharge of the placenta aid in sending the final reserves of blood and oxygen to the infant.

At this point, any others in the room leave. This first hour after birth is the most critical time in human life. For now the bond is established in strange, mysterious, and unfathomable ways. Anyone else around literally gets caught in the magnetic fields of attraction weaving back and forth. A great love affair is being born, a love affair that is sensuous, sexual, spiritual, mental, quietly ecstatic. As Marshall Klaus puts it, "they must learn to make love with each other."[14] The self has divided and reunites with the self. The hologram part starts immediately moving into and reflecting the whole. Only in the great second bonding, many years hence, will life again enter into this same ecstasy.

Far more important than the problem of nourishment or even ease of body stress, fear of abandonment is based on fear of a thread of a collapse into chaos, a loss of the means for concept structuring. The mother is the conceptual channel for interacting and responding to the world as intent prompts him/her to do. The mother represents the building block, the cornerstone of meaning, the pattern around which the child's mind-brain structures its whole body of knowledge. The infant-child must have a constant reinforcement of this basic structure if new experience is to be continually accommodated.

By never separating in these critical early days, the mother is surprisingly free of the child in comparison with the average anxiety-ridden parents during those first ten to twelve weeks of adjustment.

World as It Is[15]

Nature programs the child to do two things from ages one to seven: structure a knowledge of the world exactly as it is, on the one hand,

and play with that world in ways that it is not, on the other.

Structuring a knowledge of the world takes at least six years because the world is filled with many things, and its processes and principles are strict. The child is programmed to interact with the actual world: a place of rocks, trees, grass, bugs, sun, moon, wind, clouds, rain, snow, and a million things; a world that runs on principles, where cause and effect balance, where "fall down, go boom" means skinned knees, where fire burns, and hot means don't touch.

New patterns for sensory organization and bodily action form in the child's brain only as interaction with the world through the body. Throughout childhood, a full-dimensional and accurate concept is an internalization of an external act.

Around age seven, a dramatic shift of brain growth and logic will occur. The child's matrix will (or should) shift from the mother to the earth and will then have the living earth as the place of power, the safe space, and the source of possibility. The child will be bonded to that earth. These bondings will grow until the ability to interact opens to breathtaking dimensions.

Nature has designed it so that mother is matrix. Father is vital as the bridge from mother to the world somewhere in that second year of life and to the larger world of society around age seven. Father draws the child out from a symbiotic kind of relation with the matrix into ever larger matrices. But each matrix shift encompasses the former. Alienation or isolation from a matrix is destructive.

This drawing out is like the sun's drawing of moisture from the earth in order to send that moisture back in a life-giving rain. Father and mother are rather the stress-relaxation poles for the child. The father is the pull into the unknown; the mother is the known, the touchstone. In balance and harmony they provide the perfect ground for growth.

The child, roughing-in a world knowledge, wanders without rhyme or reason, and plays. He or she has no goals other than the moment, and no other time exists. To the child the time is always now, the place is always here, the center is always "me." For this is the way a world knowledge is structured. At the same time, the parents institute an underlying strata of order.

If correctives are needed, they are concrete. The parent picks the child up firmly and removes him or her form the bounds of transgression. They let the child know without apology that boundaries are to be observed. The single word *no* suffices if the parents are absolutely consistent in their own minds, free of ambiguity about their actions, confident, decisive, and expecting full compliance.

Firm boundaries give strength to the bond and clarity to those areas open for exploration. The child clearly registers the parents' power of decision and their confidence in their decisions. The child feels bonded to strength and accepts the boundaries and restrictions without frustration or hesitancy because he or she is geared to take cues from them, and the decisions are in keeping with his or her intent.

Primary Perceptions Bonding with the Earth[16]

"I see white light coming out of your head and fingers," reports little Jessie. "There are bright colors around your face and body." Larry, aged seven, sees white light moving in and out of people's bodies. He sees red light around trees and orange light around dogs. Bryan, seven, sometimes sees specks of color float around her bedside. So go the reports from children studied by James Peterson, author of *The Secret Life of Kids.* Over the past two years, child psychiatrist Gerald Jampolsky has studied some 150 children, who, between ages three and four, have also reported extrasensory perceptions. Jampolsky's cases fell largely into classical extrasensory categories: clairvoyance, in which events taking place beyond the range of vision or hearing are reported by the child; telepathy, in which information or messages come from specific people at a distance; precognition, in which an event is perceived before it has actually taken place.

Considerable literature exists on ESP and psychic phenomena among children. Eloise Shields presents evidence that telepathic ability peaks at age four, at which time their parents may begin to be aware of such activity. An English acquaintance of mine, who considers herself psychic and who can certainly pick other people's brains remarkably well, told me that her two daughters displayed astonishing psychic abilities at age four. These abilities proved to be in the ESP categories, with telepathy between mother and children being the strongest. Sadly, the abilities faded by age eight, a source of chagrin to the mother.

Why age four? Why do such abilities so often fade at seven or eight? Do all children possess such abilities? If not, why not? Can these abilities be encouraged? Are they worth encouraging? Of what use could such capacities be?

These talents are biological, part of nature's built-in system for communication and rapport with the earth, part of our bonds with that matrix, part of the emerging system for survival, related to the division of labor, almost surely stage-specific in their unfolding, and no more fragile or rare than general intelligence.

ESP is simple reception from the primary process, designed to enhance well-being and security and to give information over a wide range.

When a child reports some phenomenon that the parent has no grasp of, as many of Jampolsky's and Peterson's children did, the parent is usually disturbed. This negativity is immediately apparent to the child and weighs against his/her repeating the experience. Sooner or later, the child's concern for bonding, and later his/her concern for social consensus, will lead to selective inattention, screening out that kind of experience.

To consider ESP a rare gift is to miss the significance of our whole heritage and take the easy way out. There are no errors programmed into our biological plan. Primary perceptions are bondings to the earth and no more rare than the infant-mother communions observed in Uganda. Such communions are not found in our country simply because we treat our infants differently and so we get a different product.

Primary perceptions are designed to establish links between self and world, and they utilize sound biological procedures in the brain. Primary perceptions furnish a way of drawing on nature's body of knowledge and of being informed by this general field of awareness as needed for well-being.

We observe all sorts of marvelous qualities unfolding that then disappear, and we assume that they were simply passing aberrations and so *should* disappear. Some people respond that my examples are not typical and so not valid. From where are they taking their models? From the lowest common denominator after the damage has been done, just as Spitz and the rest assume over and over for generations, that the newborn should be a vegetable because Freud said so.

Transforming the Given: Dancing through the Crack— Operational Thinking[17]

Ernest Hilgard of Stanford University found that children become highly susceptible to suggestion at age seven. This suggestibility peaks around age eight to eleven and fades around age fourteen. At seven, the child undergoes a brain-growth spurt and a dramatic shift of logical processing. Because individuality is just becoming functional at seven, the purpose of the new logic and the new learning capacity is to gain self-sufficiency or autonomy, independence, and the ability to survive in the world.

At seven, the brain can construct concepts out of imaginative ideas or possibilities that apply to the immediate reality, and such a pattern then functions as any other concept does: as a pattern by which the brain puts together sensory information. An abstract concept based on an idea about something can put together the situation information coming from that thing. *The abstract patterns act on that stimulus according to the idea about its source rather than its actual structure.* And that, roughly, is how operational thinking works on its incoming sensory information.

The Balinese child, by imitating her superiors, operates on her incoming sensory information and changes it. She knows, without thinking about it, that the fire will not burn her because she sees the other dancers and knows that they do not get burned. She knows that by imitating their body gestures, she, too, will have their powers over the world and go unharmed. This is what she has unconsciously practiced in imitative play for years. The difference now is that, with her new logic and new brain growth, her imitative movements bring about a corresponding concept of action patterns in her brain, as always and just as non-consciously. Thus, she bends some aspect of the world to her desire, not by some intellectual knowing of how to manipulate information, but by the same kind of automatic work within her brain that makes all conceptual growth and change possible. Her system operates on the incoming information through a combination of patterns: those from the world of cause and effect and those from the idea system of her models.

The child's sensory information must bring in reports of the fire, the flesh, and the effects of the two; that is what her primary world concepts and body-knowing are designed to do. However, this information is contrary to her well-being, and concrete operational thinking, having been given (through suggestion) a model for another possibility, follows suit and operates on the information, changing it into something more compatible. Her thinking bends the world out there to the inner desire not to be injured. All that is needed is for the child to furnish the function; her mind-brain furnishes the structure. The only way the function can be furnished is the actual physical interaction. The assimilation-accommodation cycle, which was missing in fantasy play, is filled in by the new logical capacities. The play on the surface and the conceptual work beneath it merge as needed or as opportunity arises.

The pianist plays on the piano; a piano tuner operates on it and changes its structure, keeping it in top form and harmony. The child's conscious self plays on the world; logic and intellect operate on and keep the instrument, the child's body, properly tuned and in harmony with the world. The wonder is, both performers—world structure and child structure (mind-brain)—perform on the same instrument at the same time and in keeping with the needs of each.

The findings of biology and physics no longer allow the assumption that world and mind are separate elements. A world without thinking would have no life. It is thinking that creates a planet different from, say, the dead moon (assuming it is dead). There is no way to distinguish the planet from its planetary life any more than to distinguish a live body from the life of its cells. Remove the life from its cells, and you have a different body. Earth without life would be a corpse. To assume that a relationship does not exist between the cells of life produced by the larger body of life is ridiculous. To assume that individual life can exist without accommodation and provision by the host body earth is ridiculous.

In the examples of the Eskimo and animals, their relationship with their environment includes a range of communion beyond their long-range senses of sight and sound. In the same way, the child has relations with his world beyond sensory range, and these concern his well-being in the same way as those of the animals do. But no matter how clearly nature might signal, as with the fox on the riverbank, the child must have the necessary receptors developed to receive and comprehend those signals. The only way these receptors can be developed is to be recognized and encouraged by parental nurturing.

The concrete concepts about the world can, of themselves, offer only the concrete world experience. Fire can, of itself, only burn. The world offers no abstractions out of itself. It has created the human mind-brain to do that.

A man came to a magical child seminar as a result of an experience that had unnerved him and threatened his academic and rational world-view. His eight-year-old son was whittling with a knife, slipped, and severed the arteries in his left wrist. Following an instant's panic at the sight of the spurting blood, the father, as if in a dream, seized his screaming son's face, looked into his eyes, and commanded, "Son, let's stop that blood." The screaming stopped, the boy beamed back, said "okay," and together they stared at the gushing blood and shouted, "Blood, you stop that." And the blood stopped. In a short time, the wound healed—and the father's world almost stopped as well. He knew disorientation and confusion. He could not account for his own actions or the words he had heard himself speak, and he surely could not account for the results. He did not understand that the child is biologically geared to take reality cues from the parent; he did not know of the high suggestibility of the eight-year-old, of concrete operational thinking, or that at his age his son was peculiarly susceptible to ideas about physical survival. But some part of him *did* know and broke through in the moment of emergency. All the son needed, of course, was the suggestion and the support.

The creative logic unfolding during this late-childhood period can be summed up as *reversibility thinking,* an ability that Piaget calls the highest act of human intelligence but, sadly, the rarest. Full reversibility thinking does not unfold until adolescence, but its early concrete form is what the examples I have cited have displayed. Reversibility thinking is, to use Piaget's description, "the ability of the mind to entertain any state in a continuum of possible stages as equally valid, and return to the point from which the operation of mind begins." A simpler statement would be: reversibility thinking is the ability to consider any possibility within a continuum of possibilities as true, knowing that you can come back to where you started from.

At age seven, children have as passionate a longing for creative interactions and learning as they earlier had for explorations of the world. The mind-brain-body system *wants* to learn; that is what the brain-growth spurt is for. The longing this brings about is a drive, just as the longing genital sexuality brings about is a drive. Learning is a non-conscious biological process and will take place automatically when the models given are appropriate to the needs. In cultures where children are allowed to interact with adults, these children immediately imitate adult survival practices during the years from seven to ten or eleven. This is their play, and they develop great skill at it. The peculiar thing about culture has been that it takes the accidental forms of creative logic or reversibility thinking that occurs and ritualizes them, then turns them into religious acts instead of correlating them into a fabric of action. Such ritualizing happened on Bali, and among many Eastern cultures.

At this point, our Western logic breaks down before an irresolvable paradox. To us, you cannot have it both ways. You cannot dance on the coals without even a blister while beneath those coals pigs and pineapple or whatever are roasting. Frozen in our no-man's-land of confusion between world and reality, having lost the best of both worlds, the organization and the extent of our logic is either-or. Between the *either* and the *or* lies a rigorously excluded middle that we Westerners feel we must maintain, or else our whole semantic universe will collapse into chaos (as, in fact, it might). And through that excluded middle, ignorant of our logical niceties, the little Balinese child blithely dances.

There are different ways by which the brain can operate on its data and change those data. The Balinese child simply imitates, and any reversing of ordinary cause and effect takes place peripherally and in true play. The father and son stopping the blood and healing the wound did not reverse a process so much as directly operate on concrete material. Left to his own devices, the child would have bled to death. What they did was through verbal suggestion, the temporary power of the father, and their combined interaction. On their own, the severed artery must bleed, the heart must pump, the fire must burn. They are the world's principles, subject to law, understandable by analysis, standardized and predictable. They constitute the reality of the world or, we might say, physical reality. But add *idea* or abstraction, and you add mind-brain. Add mind-brain to the world and you have not reality as it is in the world but reality as a construction, a created reality. Human-reality experience and the world as it is are not synonymous phenomena, although they partake of the same substance. This is why the laws of one operation cannot possibly fit the other, why ordinary scientific testing, which is designed to discover the world's principles, is not appropriate for a study of earth *plus* mind.

Mind is the catalyst that changes the earth into created reality experience, precisely what the earth has moved toward in its 3 billion years of genetic experimentation. Separating mind from world is a massive denial that splits our conscious awareness from our primary process. From this split state, the scientist (and fellow victims) rightly concludes that any two-way exchange between earth and human cannot exist.

All the earth can do with fire is burn, as it is supposed to do. There is no chemical change in the fire or in the child when she walks on that fire. There are no molecular shifts, no mind over matter, no mystical mumbo jumbo, no deep esoteric secrets of cosmic space, no hidden pyramid numbers of astrological trickery, no superpowers of flying saucer super-minds. The relationship between concept sets and functions in the mind-brain changes, and the relations between mind and its matrix, between microcosmic and macrocosmic hologram, change accordingly. The functional changes do not take place in awareness; they furnish awareness.

Through the function of play the work takes place and creativity unfolds. The missing link of earlier child play is added to the abilities within that child at seven; she walks the fire in play, still responding only to intent, as she did in her first hour. But what accommodates to what? The fire or the flesh? Ah—that is admittedly mystery, thank God, mystery that keeps play and work neatly divided, although they must merge for creation. This is the paradox and the reason that play is the only way the highest intelligence of humankind can unfold.

The Two-Way Flow: Assimilation-Accommodation[18]

Uri Geller, for those readers who did not follow this minor-major comedy, was an Israeli entertainer who could apparently bend metal without touching it, make broken or stopped watches run for short periods, and occasionally make an object disappear, and who displayed undeniable extrasensory perception. Interested researchers tested Geller's abilities at the Stanford Research Institute in California. The tests were conducted by only one of the dozens of nearly autonomous departments making up this complex (3,000 employees), but those connected with the investigation, which went on for months, were convinced that the *Geller effect* was genuine. Papers stating this opinion were published, and a storm of protest broke out, for academic dogma and was brought into question. . . . So Geller's discrediting was undertaken. Soon we Americans found out—to the disappointment of some and to the relief of others—that Geller was a fraud, a charlatan, a cheat.

Then a funny thing happened. Geller went to England in late 1973 to perform his fork-bending stunts on television for the British Broadcasting Company. Geller had observed that people in his audiences occasionally had keys bend in their pockets, rings twist and break on their fingers, and so on while he was doing similar things on the stage. The notion grew that perhaps Geller could operate through people and maybe even at long distance. Or perhaps other people might possess the same odd ability he did. On the English television show, Geller invited all those people out there in television land to join him, to participate in his metal bending by holding forks or spoons themselves to see if the phenomenon might be repeated. Some 1,500 reports flooded the BBC, claiming that forks, spoons, anything handy had indeed bent, broken, moved about—there, in the homes of Britain. . . . Surely such hysterical claims are often noted, and no validity can be granted such business at all. The funny thing was that the vast majority of the claimants were between the ages of seven and fourteen, the period of suggestibility and concrete operational thinking.

During the same period, and operating within his own circuit, Mathew Manning, an English teenager, had been doing Geller-type acts since experiencing a poltergeist seizure at eleven years of age. Dr. Brian Josephson, of the prestigious Cavendish Laboratories at Cambridge University (where DNA's double helix was born), winner of the 1973 Nobel Prize in physics, and a principal in the investigation of young Manning, said: "A redefinition of Reality and Non-Reality is needed now. . . ." We are on the verge of discoveries, which may be extremely important for physics. We are dealing here with a new kind of energy. This force must be subject to laws. I believe ordinary methods of scientific investigation will tell us much more about psychic phenomena. They are mysterious, but they are no more mysterious than a lot of things in physics already. In times past, "respectable" scientists would have nothing to do with psychical phenomena; many of them still won't. I think that the "respectable" scientists may find they have missed the boat.

Whether or not Geller was a fraud, then, is beside the point. We have stumbled on a potential that eclipses the investments and institutions of our culture. The full extent of the power of suggestion has just barely been touched upon. Creative logic has been glimpsed. A new aspect of concrete operational thinking has opened. The key to the logic of survival has opened into plain view.

No one involved in Geller effects has the slightest idea how the phenomena occur, no more than the Ceylonese understand how they walk on fire. Geller effects take place without a person's doing anything and often without a person's even "willing" anything to happen. Concrete operational forms of reversibility thinking are not necessarily conscious or controllable. We can function that way, but we cannot analyze the structure by which such reality experience takes place.

From age seven to about age fourteen or fifteen is the period the biological plan prepares for this learning and development. Uri Geller reports his first phenomena of this sort occurred when he was seven. The phenomena broke into Mathew Manning's life at age eleven.

Yet, precisely at this point of the reversibility of the ordinary flow of assimilation-accommodation, the academic stronghold rises to reject the phenomena. The entire history of Western man rests on the unquestioned assumption that the mind-brain is a *one-way* receptor of information from its world, designed only to interpret and react in adaptive ways to this information. And the only adaptive ways academically recognized and allowed are those using mechanical devices or ineffectual muscular defense stances. This institutionalized belief that the mind has absolutely no influence over or relation to its world except through dominating tools has now created a nuclear terror reducing everyone to total impotence and fate. We deny our true nature at our peril because such denial always creates a demonic counter-energy of destruction. The crux of our social stance is entirely and squarely this issue of our relation of our mind and our reality, our world and our created experience.

Dr. Joel Whitton of Toronto found in his work with Mathew Manning that the old brain (cerebellum and brainstem) seemed to be involved in the actual psycho-kinesis displayed by Manning. Whitton writes that "psychic functions are not a higher or different degree of concentration . . . but an unknown or outside force that creates it." Because of the involvement of older-brain parts, Whitton suggests that psychic functions are not random gifts or space-age abilities, but "an innate function and ability in homo sapiens that probably goes back to the earliest history of man."

Perhaps our myths are correct, and our problem is one, not of evolving a higher mentality, but of reclaiming our lost state. Whitton's comment is of interest to me because I have suggested, in my earlier book *The Crack in the Cosmic Egg*, that non-ordinary phenomena and primary perceptions would be found to center in older-brain functions.

Pause with me, then, to consider these 3 billion years of genetic experimenting leading to the human being: moving from concreteness toward abstraction, through thousands of experimental species, to achieve a logic that can conceptualize with unlimited flexibility, an intelligence that can move through infinite realms of content (the more it knows the more it can know), and a means of survival beyond species survival, a personal survival needed by the kind of individual resulting from the development of such an intelligence.

Have these eons of effort, passing all notions of time as we use the word, have as the goal of this greatest expression magical parlor tricks? Bending spoons? Every movement, every random effect in development has purpose and design. What, then, is the purpose of altering the principles and/or parts of the world itself? These capacities are the logical extension of play, and play is in the service of survival.

Survival play is not developed, of course, and a phenomenon occurs in the children of all cultures somewhere between eight and ten years of age, right in the middle of this concrete stage, a phenomenon that shatters the young life yet receives scant attention. Quietly forming below awareness is a conceptual structure that surfaces as an exquisitely silent anguish, hidden beyond discussion or clarification: the awareness that one must die. The concept of death as one's personal destiny, with no possibility of evasion, unfolds as a function somewhere around age nine. Concepts structure information into meaning regardless of the nature of the concept, and this concept changes everything. Once filtered through this particular abstraction, experience is never again the same. Play disappears and becomes intentional and competitive. The self tries to take over the conceptual work beneath, and childhood dies.

The Cycle of Creative Competence[19]

Through creative modeling, model-parent furnishes the youngster with the principles of mind needed for moving beyond the principles of the world.

Just as the Balinese child could, at such a point, walk the fire and not be burned, so this child's brain immediately assimilates the father's instructions, and his body accommodates to the operations of mind. The blood loss stops, and the wound begins to heal. (Again, this is not hypothetical. I am simply reporting. I could add examples from personal experience.)

What are the possibilities of suggestion to the concrete operational child? The implications stagger the imagination. We draw back and dismiss the potential; our deeply ingrained pessimism over the human condition forces our surrender to professionalism.

Professionalism and the institution grow out of our fear over reality criteria. In the case of the injured child, for instance, the average parent would have little capacity for responding to the needs of the situation. She or he would, instead, react. Conditional to surrender personal power and ability to the professional, the parent would have to rush the child to a hospital or doctor. Even if the parent knew of the personal possibilities for power in such a situation, fear of social condemnation (if the parent failed) would prove incapacitating and would force him or her to react rather than respond.

The child whose parent panics and rushes him/her to the professional (that person who stands between self and personal power) undergoes a deep and abiding learning. The child learns that the parents do not have the personal powers that she or he believed them to have. The child learns that the parents cannot act on his or her behalf and that the matrix is not the safe space, the place of power and possibility that these must be bought from the professionals. Muscular-mindedness grows by finding that when one gestures to the matrix, the matrix gestures back with a mirroring and enhancing of power and possibility. The parent who panics and shifts responsibility thus dispels the child's own sense of personal power and ability. The child learns that she or he is as impotent as the parents. The stage is then set for the child's own surrender of responsibility to the professional. Later, as a parent, this child, too, will have no choice but to react in panic and throw him-/herself on the mercy of the professional (at their astonishing prices). The child's growth and education will, in turn, also be in the lack of the power to act. . . . Then the professional is the only hope left, and, of course, will capitalize on our incompetence and will work to keep us incompetent (lest the professional should have no return business). . . . So the parents of the magical child educate their youngster in body signals and corresponding responses.

The parents capitalize on the magical child's belief in their omnipotence. They encourage his/her innate idea that they have power in their world and that through them the child can share in this power and develop his/her own. Should the child become ill for some reason (although for the bonded child, such unwholeness is rare), the parents assure him/her that they have the personal power to heal. They then devote their full attention to that healing because far more than a temporary body misalignment is involved. Learning is involved; the development of the ability to interact is at stake. Through a continual suggestion, reassurance, and reaffirming of their power and their ability to lend him/her that power, the child's suggestibility receives the idea of healing, and the inner work responds. The child learns that mind has dominion over the world.

Throughout this period, the parents have continued to encourage, enhance, and respond to the child's primary perceptions. They practice telepathy by using the hypnagogic and anagogic periods right before sleep and on first waking. During these brief periods, they exercise this capacity with their child just as assiduously as a parent might exercise toilet training. They practice remote viewing, encouraging the child to sense particular target areas chosen for the day and to report his/her sensing to them. Through such play, these primary perceptions grow enormously during the stage of suggestibility because the parents are suggesting and entering into specific experiences with the child.

Little by little, the child's play on the surface and his/her conceptual work beneath the surface move closer to synergy, which will finally unfold during adolescence in fully reversibility thinking. This synergy takes place as the child learns to be selective about what she or he selects from the continuum of possibilities to be given fantasy-play reality. The use of imagination and fantasy have been free-ranging, as they should have been. Now, with the growing rewards and successes from concrete operations, the child's capacity for imagination becomes more devoted to the needs of physical survival and well-being in this world, and in this way outer and inner increasingly mesh.

Thinking about Thinking: Formal Operations[20]

Somewhere around age eleven, the brain undergoes another growth spurt. At the same time, another logical shift takes place, giving new ways of processing information. Susceptibility to suggestion hits its peak, from which it will slowly phase out as one of the characteristics of the mind-brain by about age fifteen. Formal operational thinking, the ability of the mind to operate on and change information, its own brain unfolds for development. As usual, it is only an intent within and must receive its initial impetus from outside sources, but this dependency on modeling will fade as the new ability develops. The thrust of the biological plan during this period is for the mind-brain to become its own source of possibility.

Through formal operations, the mind can experience information and perceptions from its own creative thought alone. Out of its vast pool of knowledge the brain can then create its own stimuli and experience perceptions from its own abstract conceptions. Thus, suggestibility will eventually be phased out as a needed tool. The magical child's perceptual experience will then have a wide source of possibility: relating to the earth as it is, a matrix of stable background that is experienced every day; creatively relating with that earth through concrete operations of mind, giving possibilities beyond the earth's own principles of cause and effect; relating with the possibilities of pure thinking, imagination, abstract conceptual constructions, and the resulting perceptual experience (not found in any concreteness or operation on concreteness), which means a reality created entirely within, and mixtures of these three ways of processing and/or creating information. To this last category must be added the possibilities of one person creating abstract perceptual experience and sharing it with another person or persons and the interactions between them in creating consensus realities.

At age eleven, the young mind still needs examples and guidance in order to build a sufficient body of pure abstractions. Suggestibility is at its peak at this period. At age seven, the child's suggestions for possibility needed to be given in concrete form, directly in front of him/her, or by specific concrete instruction and suggestion. His/her capacity for imitative play then moved his/her body accordingly, and the new abstract concepts were formed out of this concrete action. At eleven, suggestions can be given without direct modeling or concrete referent. The eleven-year-old Japanese, Juni, simply heard a newscast about children repeating Geller's exploits. Juni immediately knew he could do so and did. John Taylor found that older children and teenagers could imitate after only hearing of some possibility; they had a sufficient ability to create abstractions not based on concreteness.

The meshing of play and conceptual work is the whole thrust and meaning of development and the way by which we move from concreteness to abstraction. Earlier, we saw how the early child's play remained distinct from the conceptual construction of his/her worldview. At age seven, when individuation begins to function, play can, if trained or guided, begin to mesh with concepts, as we noted in the Geller children. This capacity may be directly tied with individuation and fading egocentricity. . . . An art form is a medium of expression, and the medium determines the art.

All our creativity, then, has so far been a combination of formal and concrete thinking, and this is surely one of the great combinational forms available to us. But with due respect, awe, and wonder for this kind of creation, I would point out that it is limited, nevertheless, to the concreteness of its medium. The mature intelligence should be able to interact with the possibilities of the living earth, that living earth plus the creativity of the mind, and the processes and products of the mind-brain itself. So far, we have used this third category of possibility only in relation to the second category; that is, the mind-brain has not become its own matrix, as planned genetically for the period of late adolescence and maturity. . . . What, then, would be a truly mature form of creativity?

Renewing the Promise[21]

At the end of the magical child seminar, I have frequently been asked: "Okay, what do we adults do now about our child and our own split selves?"

Bonding is the issue, regardless of age. The parent who can start off with a new infant is lucky because by bonding to that infant they are bonding to the undifferentiated primary process. Learning to take our cues from the child and make a corresponding response means learning to heed and respond to the primary process within ourselves as well. Children can teach us an incredible amount if we are willing to learn, and because they are biologically geared to take their cues from us, they learn as we do.

Some specific steps are certainly apparent. Holding, with body bonding—eye contact, smiling, and soothing sounds—is something all of us can use. Anything that blocks bonding should be avoided. Hospitals for delivery, bottles for feeding, cribs for sleeping, playpens and strollers for isolation, daycare centers for not caring, nursery schools for not nurturing, pre-schools—all create abandonment and weaken the bond. Surely, a parent would do everything possible to protect the child from premature literacy and be warned about television. To nurture the magical child is a full-time responsibility.

Surely the same holds for us adults who would reclaim our lives from anxiety's grip. Our lives, too, are filled with cues concerning real needs. The biological plan might go underground in this strange semantic reality of ours, but it is impossible for it to be extinguished.

The father who was suddenly moved to join his son in stopping the flow of blood had somehow broken through the noise level of his ordinary anxiety and followed the subtle signals of his body. A certain risk seems inherent in this kind of action, though, because it leads into unpredictable territory. Indeed, we have historically referred to this kind of non-ordinary response as *left-handed thinking* because the right hemisphere [of the brain], which runs the left hand, seems the repository for this kind of effect. Cultures have always represented this left hand as the sinister, dark, and evil largely because of its unpredictability. Had that father followed the predictable path of reaction, an entire chain of predictable forces would have been enacted: perhaps the sympathetic rescue squad and dramatic sirens wailing, sympathetic police and dramatic hospital emergency room, sympathetic doctors and nurses and maybe even the drama of the local news media and a human-interest story. Surely vast machinery would lie idle if left-handed thinking were to be employed habitually.

Our anxiety conditioning leads us to believe this left-hand process is tantamount to death itself, and our conditioning sets up buffers between this dark unknown and our ordinary awareness, which is sustained by verbal feedback and that which is right. Attuned to this noise, we lose our communication with the subtle power of the rest of our being. To become quiet and respond according to these subtle signals seems to be the equivalent of giving up our last defense. Yet, the moment we can drop such defenses, even for a brief time, and respond to our left hand, we shift matrix from anxiety to the primary process within.

God works, and man plays—or that is the way the scheme is set up and meant to be. I like it that way. As soon as I try to do all the work, I have tried to be God, and I mess everything up. The harder I play, the harder God works. Sometimes we get caught up in a spinning around of this work-play. Sometimes everything catches fire in this work-play spiral, a spiral of fire such as the author Blaise Pascal experienced and scrawled about on that piece of paper one marvelous night: "Fire! Fire!" he wrote, "not the god of philosophy, but the God of Abraham, of Isaac, and of Jacob." He had fallen into play, was never the same again, and carried his scrawled response in the lining of his coat, next to his heart, all his life. . . . Perhaps this is not a very detailed prescription, but it will meet the needs of any child entrusted to us—the offspring we begot or will beget, conceived or will conceive eternally begotten in ourselves.

3

◆

The Bond of Power (1981)

Meditation and Wholeness

(Reissued in 2003 as Spiritual Initiation and the Breakthrough of Consciousness)

THE BACKSTORY FROM JOE

The *Bond of Power* explores my bond with Muktananda and Siddha Yoga, which represented the classic Eastern tradition or worldview, and David Bohm, Einstein's protégé, one of the most influential physicists of the twentieth century, representing the Western worldview. I wrote the book in Muktananda's ashram in India, where I spent time for twelve years. Meanwhile, back in 1958, I came across David Bohm's writing titled *Causality & Chance in Modern Physics,* and it blew me out of orbit. It was Bohm's first great work. Bohm was heading toward a Nobel Prize in Physics had he not gotten in trouble with the McCarthy business. He refused to sign the Loyalty Oath that was sweeping the country. No, he said, this is an affront, not only to me and physics but also to the whole academic world. They took away his citizenship and forced him out of the country. It was an unbelievable, terrible injustice. He landed in Brazil and later in London at Berkbeck College, where he and I met several times.

Of our limitless innate capacities only those given a model environment will open and develop. Bonding is the issue, regardless of age.

I considered Muktananda and Bohm each a different matrix or model, representing completely different worldviews. As a child is empowered by bonding with his or her parent, we are empowered through our bonds or relationships with individuals who have developed in themselves powerful ways of perceiving and being in the world. Both Bohm and Muktananda were expressing different worldviews of life, relationship, and creation and used very different metaphors to describe these forces, one Eastern and the other Western. *The Bond of Power* explores this.

In fact, the things that went on in India are just what you read about and they were all true. They all happened to me or for me. I felt it a great grace and privilege to be able to experience those things. But the event, which led to Muktananda, was as wild as any. I was in that little place of mine up there in the Blue Ridge, two miles from the nearest paved road and completely cut off from the world.

The woman who was helping me run the Magical Child workshops came in one day and said, "You've got to go to Oakland," and I asked, "What for?" She said, "To meet this incredible guy that I met. This tremendous thing happened in his brain. He's a guru from India." A friend of mine and I had formed the Guru of the Month's Club in utter disgust over the parade of gurus coming to this country. I had utter contempt for them. I got furious at her, the idea that we'd drive to Oakland to meet one of those guys; that she had actually gotten sucked in by one of the shysters disgusted me, and I refused to do it. And yet another person who had read my book found out and he sent through my publisher a copy of Muktananda's book, *Play of Consciousness,* and I opened it up to look at it and here was, I thought, a picture of a doped-out rock star on the front cover. He had, wow, a crazy look to him and on the cover it said *Play of Consciousness,* and I thought, my God, I don't have time to read that now. I'll look at that tonight. That night I turned on my little Aladdin kerosene lamp and sat down to read. I said, well I'll just have to see what this shyster is saying before I throw the book away. And I opened it and read about two sentences of the first page and here it came, this huge weight pressing me down. I was gone.

I fell through this great blackness in this incredible space, and when I came to I saw what I thought was blinding white light in my eyes. We were two miles to the nearest road. How could anybody be shining a bright light through that window of ours? I looked again and the bright light was coming from this white marble alabaster bust statue of Jesus. Here was this white alabaster image of Jesus right in front of me and all this light was pouring from that, brilliant light. I looked more closely and the eyes of the statue were brilliantly alive and locked onto my eyes. Then the statue leaned over and blew up my nostrils and I went out again, except this time, into a far more rapturous and ecstatic out-of-body experience.

Finally, I came back. Here I was, sitting on my couch in my cottage up in the mountains with the lantern going and this book on my lap and I had the biggest life-changing experience. So I put the book aside and I said to my wife, Karen, "Wherever this guy is, I'm going." I started reading further the next day, and I found that one of the ways Muktananda gives Shaktipat (the passage of power from the one who has received to the initiate) is through breathing up their nostrils. And that cemented it. I mean, what more do you need? Shaktipat or Śaktipāta (Sanskrit, from *shakti* "psychic energy," and *pāta,* "to fall") refers in Hinduism to the transmission (or conferring) of spiritual energy upon one person by another.

I met Muktananda. They ushered me in. I sat down, and his interpreter started talking to me, and the first thing I did, looking straight at Babba, and I got embarrassed by it but I went ahead and I blurted it out, and said, "Babba, I think you're Jesus." And he laughed and laughed and slapped his knee and just roared. And then he stopped and looked me straight in the eye and pointed and he said, "But of course, and so are you." So we got off to a good start. He then spent the next couple of hours telling me about every facet of the heart. He said, "At the center of a heart is the point from which the whole universe arises, comes out in a great swirl of an energy we call Shakti, the creative energy of the world, and Shakti dances around the center of the heart, the center, which we call Shiva, the primal God in the heart, and Shakti is his counterpart that dances the world around him, creating the universe for him to witness.

And therein you have the whole picture of creation, where it comes from, out of the heart," and he went on. It took him about two hours. That led to the writing of the book *Bond of Power* and then my next book, *Evolution's End*. And from that point everything in my life has centered on what I began to describe as *the intelligence of the heart*.

EXCERPTS FROM *THE BOND OF POWER*

Introduction[1]

In some off-guard moment, a thought that illuminates new territory can explode in our heads and change the shape of our thinking and our lives. This "postulate, which arrives full-blown in the brain," is a function of mind, which holds the key to our nature, development, and fulfillment.

This phenomenon is rare. It comes as creative inspiration, scientific discovery, the Eureka!, the mystical revelation, the conversion experience. Its source has been a matter of debate. Trace the function *to* its source, though, and the mystery of our brain, mind, creation, and creator unfolds. The postulate is like a thread, which, pulled from the wool and warp of our reality, unweaves that fabric and leaves us the threads from which reality itself is woven.

The problem with tracing the roots of creative insight is that thought, no matter its strength or brilliance is not sufficient for the task. The postulate-revelation doesn't arrive in the brain *as* thought, but as the materials *for* thought. Thought is but a tool of the function and seems only peripherally (though vitally) involved.

Revelation is as valid a term as *postulate,* since new information seems revealed to our mind, rather than thought by it. The postulate seems to arise from some deep recess of mind, not brain. I will use the term *insight* hereafter, since it is a "seeing" from within, even when projected without.

Insight seems extra-cerebral, an intrusion into our awareness. It flashes into us always in some moment out of mind, never when we are busy thinking about the subject involved. . . . Insight seems a *grace,* that which is given freely rather than made by our effort. Einstein spoke of his insights arriving like flashes of lightning which, though they lit up the landscape of his mind for only an instant, forever after changed its shape. The only thing that can change the nature of our thought is an energy more powerful than that thought. So there are different modes of mental experience, and the difference lies in the levels of energy involved. Nothing that we can do will insure the arrival of insight, yet insight comes to us only when we are passionately involved in the subject matter concerned, and have thoroughly prepared for its coming.

Ordinary thinking, our everyday "roof-brain chatter," is a weak-energy emergent of our brain, while insight is surely more powerful. That is why the insight function isn't reversible, to be repeated by formula. Our ordinary thinking can (must) prepare for insight, respond to it, but can't manufacture it. A weak thought can't produce a stronger one, but it can attract it.

In his mature years, Mozart's mechanical excellence was so perfected that his genius could speak as direct insight. He would receive a commission for a new symphony and the work was quite likely to fall into his head as a gestalt, arrive full-blown in his brain, twenty minutes of music in an instant out of time. He then had the arduous task of translating that moment out of mind into the myriad of notes, which could, in turn, be translated by others to make the symphony sound in the actual world.

The task of translating insight often proves as great as the work necessary to bring it about. Hamilton spent fifteen years on the quaternions *after* his insight. The famous Belgian chemist August Kekulé's translation bridging the symbolism of a ring of snakes to the hard data of organic chemistry was not simple (see p. 299), nor was Einstein's final neat equation spelled out in that original lightning bolt.

Back in 1958, I had a minor insight, which followed, in my own minor way, the classical pattern of all insight. My insight was, in effect, a glimpse into the mechanics of insight itself. Being of a slow mind (and with four children to raise), it took me some twelve years to finish a "translation." The end result was my book *The Crack in the Cosmic Egg*. In that book I outlined a fourfold procedure found in any creative venture—discovery, or transformation experience resulting in insight. Since that "formula of creativity" is a way to trace insight to its roots. I will summarize it here.

First, to entice insight into our lives, we must be caught up in some passionate quest. (No dilettantes here.) A certain intensity of purpose must be generated, which finally swamps our switchboard, absorbs all our attention, rules out our lesser goals and passions. Then we must work for that mechanical excellence that alone can serve as the vehicle of our genius. We must gather the materials related to, and develop the abilities needed by, our quest. If an artist, we must perfect the mechanics of our art; as a scientist we must thoroughly search the area of our interest; as philosophers we must gather all possible pertinent knowledge; as spiritual seekers we must immerse ourselves completely in our chosen path. The halfhearted endeavor will leave us with only our weak thought and vain imaginings.

Our passionate pursuit, which may take months or years, must feed a massive amount of material into the hopper of our mind/brain. The materials must then at some point "take over," take on a life of their own, dictate their own ends, overrule even the person gathering them. We must feel subservient to our own pursuit, used by it, incidental to it. This ushers in the "gestation period," when the mass of accumulated data and/or ability achieves its critical size and power. Then, within that mysterious realm of insight, the revelation will form. Maybe.

In order to unfold as revelation in the brain, insight must get thought out of the way, at least for the brief instant needed. So the insight arrives in some moment of suspended thought, or simply pushes thought briefly aside.

In my book *Magical Child,* I discussed some of the critical problems facing technological countries today. These conditions are apparently brought about by imbalances of thought connected with technology itself. . . . Technology is sweeping our earth, and our social-mental breakdown seems an outgrowth of that sweep, indicating a mode of thinking out of balance and out of control. As usual in imbalance, our attempts at redress lead only to extremes equally unbalanced. Technology seems here to stay and the issue isn't how to get rid of it (which we don't want to do even though we sometimes hate it) but how to achieve balance with it.

Our personal power seems to be draining right out of us into our machinery and tools. Human survival, development, our autonomy as persons, our long-range genetic goals, all center on development of ability, which means personal power. Ages of genetic expectancy are built into us, cued to expect development of personal power. When this vast expectancy begins to sharply erode, anxiety is the only possible result.

The threat of technology is no more from bombs or pollution as this growing loss of personal power and our ensuing collapse into anxiety. Anxiety is singularly intolerable to the brain system, truly swamps the switchboard and stops all processes, as everything in an anxiety-ridden brain bends toward trying to *remove* that anxiety.

Anxiety is peculiarly contagious. It operates below the limen of awareness—it isn't made of thought, but shapes or influences thought. It creates on contact an uneasiness, a dis-ease, a vague wrongness, even guilt. This contagion affects a child immediately, and in the same way infects even a people largely free of anxiety historically. Anxiety is like the Midas touch. Everything the anxiety-ridden mind touches, in its ceaseless push for release from that anxiety, turns into that from which release is sought.

Carl Jung, on his return from a visit to India in 1937, observed that the Hindu didn't seem to think his thoughts as we do in the West, but "perceives this thought" as though thoughts were ready-made outside the brain and simply viewed like any sensory act. Indeed, Jung's notion agrees with Hindu and yogic theory that thoughts are not originated in the brain but are perceived from a stream of impressions impinging on the brain. . . . At issue here is not the merit of Western and Eastern logics, but a larger definition of mental experience.

The West has its true scientific genius, such as the physicist David Bohm, and the East has its true genius such as the Siddha meditation teacher, Muktananda. . . . Amid the nonsense of a world of folly, the great syntheses are made by genius syntheses, which sooner or later, with luck, filter down to the level of the common domain. The following pages attempt to outline the mechanics of our disappearing personal power, as modeled within the most complete theory of reality the West has produced, David Bohm's *holonomic movement,* and in the most complete person I have known, that exemplar of personal and bonding power, Muktananda. The issues they present are threefold: insight, ordinary thinking, and the bonding power that underlies these rather polar modes.

There definitely exists in this world a bonding power that can arc the gap and bring us to wholeness. This bonding power, like insight, is directly within each of us, a part of our mind/brain/world function, inherent in our very genetic development and the subject of this book.

For the sake of brevity few details are given of the persons involved here. I have used David Bohm's magnificent theory (in my own way) but have left Bohm as a person alone. Einstein considered David Bohm his "spiritual son." Bohm's book on quantum mechanics is standard text the world over; he is probably one of our century's great creative thinkers and has been a personal hero of mine since his publication, in 1957, of *Causality and Chance in Modern Physics,* surely a milestone of Western thought. For the past decade or so he has been closely associated with Krishnamurti—that most Western of Eastern thinkers.

My own life has undergone serious shifts of orientation as a result of my personal experience with Siddha meditation and its teacher, Muktananda. My shift of orientation marks the point of departure for all that follows in this book, yet I have devoted all of three very brief paragraphs to Muktananda.

My wish, then, is that what happened for me bringing about this book, might happen for some of those chancing to read this little work. Then this skirmish between my typewriter and myself will not have been in vain.

Playful Insight[2]

Once a culture or a person collapses into anxiety, no self-effort is effective against that negative power. Only insight has the power to override that negativity and bring the system into balance. Operation bootstrap always fails. Wholeness of mind can't come from any action or thought from a split person, but only through a kind of grace, the power of insight arriving full-blown in the brain.

Whether Kekulé's ring of snakes (see p. 299), Einstein's lightning, or what have you, the function of insight works according to its pattern. Put a sufficient amount of passionate pursuit and collection of materials in, give over personal dominion to those materials, stand back before the insight when it comes, and serve it in its translation you then are empowered to make.

Central to my inquiry was spiritual longing, which included religious rejection and rebellion against the idea of God. The focus of these decades finally centered on my work in child development, resulting in my book *Magical Child,* which I completed in 1976. Tangled into this work were strong personal anxiety and a feeling of failure; disturbed recollections on bringing up my four children, the disaster of our fifth child, a cerebral-palsy victim; emotional residues of the children's mother; her passionate investment in them, and early death.

The central issue of the book and the seminars hinged on child play. . . . I knew Piaget was right in his imitation-model theory of play but I knew that, too, was incomplete. The problem was, I didn't know what play *was* all about. I struggled with the issue for months, read all the research available, and became seriously preoccupied with the problem, which seemed a pivot around which all my years of search gravitated.

In the midst of this activity I received a letter from a reader of my previous books. She insisted that I go immediately and meet an Indian "swami," Baba Muktananda. She sent me a picture of the man, as though I couldn't wait. . . . Muktananda's picture leered up at me like some reckless rock singer, with the most insolent eyes I had ever seen. Most of the would-be holy men at least try to look pious and saintly; this character seemed smug, irreverent, and mocking. I felt a distinct flush of irritation, doubled the mess up and threw it in the wastebasket, without answer.

In the weeks following my receipt of it, while I worked on my book, read research, or did daily tasks, those insolent eyes would occasionally flash to mind, kicking up the same flush of irritation over tricksters rushing over here to bilk the misguided.

A few weeks later, I sat alone at home one evening, reading a new research paper on play. Suddenly the solution seemed to loom up, right under *my* nose if my brain would just pull together and clarify matters. But I hadn't the strength of mind. Hours later, drained and defeated by play again, I leaned back, head in hands, and groaned aloud, "Oh God, what *is* the role of play in our life?"

Nothing in my fifty-year history had prepared me for what then happened. Instantly, without warning or transitional change of awareness, shock waves of ecstasy rushed up through my body. Without disturbing my sense of unity, I became aware of each cell in my body as my individual self. There were billons of me in a wild, exuberant dance of joy. Then I felt myself lifted up and hurled, physically it seemed, like a ping-pong ball, from one end of the universe to the other. My body of billions-of-me passed through galaxies of stars, each star also me, pulsing in rhapsodic interaction. Ecstatic wave succeeded wave, each a crescendo of exuberance surpassing the other, and I shouted over and over: "God is playing with me!"

I knew then what the role of play was, though, not just in child development, but in all of our life. I was weeks articulating that knowing, into words, and rewrote my book on children from that new point. . . . I knew that even the greatest magician can't pull a rabbit out of the hat unless there is first a rabbit in that hat. As Blake said: "A cup can't contain beyond its own capaciousness." What I had perceived was somehow within me and part of me, and so threw my notion of myself into an open spectrum. Something was up. I felt I was waiting for the other shoe to drop.

A series of astonishing and rich meditation experiences took place over those three years. My knowing and understanding were enlarged; my mind was thoroughly plowed, harrowed, and readied for replanting. Early in 1979, the same persistent follower of Muktananda, the one who had sent me his picture, wrote yet again. She had just read my third book, *Magical Child,* and urged me again to go and meet her swami,

Muktananda. He was, she told me, in this country for his third world tour. To help bridge the gap this time, she sent me some of his books including *Play of Consciousness,* on the cover of which was that once-irritating picture. The circle was closing. This time I was open, more able to receive. After a slow and casual start, those books engrossed me, every line spoke to me, everything began to make sense.

One evening I was reading Muktananda's little book, *Siddha Meditations.* A powerful visionary insight unfolded before me, ecstatic surges of power carried me beyond myself, but this time *to* my Self, a part of me I had never so directly encountered before. This lightning bolt proved a point of no return. Blake said: "If a fool persists in his folly he will become wise." As a sufficiently persistent fool, I had at least the wisdom to suspend my folly long enough to go check out this man. If he could, apparently, wreak such happy havoc on my nervous system from a distance, what might direct contact hold in store?

The Genesis of Genius[3]

Muktananda seemed at one moment icy, hard, and remote; the next unbelievably warm and loving. Magnetism and charisma, the stock-in-trade of the public figure, are not applicable to him. There was, though, a breaking inside me, some snap of a high-tension defensive wire, and sense of impending recognition on approaching him. I am familiar enough with projection to realize my own needs were looking for a target, but an obvious power radiated from him in turn.

Muktananda's words seemed conventional enough in some ways, radical and improbable in others. He reiterates, in dozens of ways, that "God dwells within you as *You*. Worship your Self, honor your Self." Equally, he balances this with: "See God in each other. Welcome each other with love." This inner-outer command summarized his position and one is likely to ask: So what's new? Actually, "worshiping your Self" sounds strenuously heretical to Western ears, even as that capitalized Self begins to take on definition.

There are many kinds of genius, and genius is the issue here. There

are people in the world who are simply plugged into a different circuitry, one at a radical remove from the ordinary. . . . That there can be
spiritual genius, a mind-set at a radical discontinuity with the average,
is not so farfetched.

We sense that the genius has powers of mind and character that
we don't have, and his very presence behooves us to move beyond our
ordinary self. This is why the genius is so often stoned by the populace.
This is also why, without genius, we sink into lethargy and inertia.

Just as a mathematical genius breaks into a realm where he inter-
prets his reality mathematically and sees things in a unique way, so the
spiritual genius breaks into a realm that encompasses the total capacity
of mind/brain and creation. He can then range the whole continuum
of experience. This is called "self-realization" because that continuum is
found within the human mind/brain and (reportedly) is recognized as
one's own, actual being, or Self. (The Australian Aborigine's dreamtime
incorporated some aspects of this capacity, which is obviously as old as
mankind itself.)

Surely few terms are as sullied as *guru.* The word is Sanskrit for "dark-
light." It stands for a function of development within us for moving, or
maturing, from ignorance to knowledge, or from "darkness to light. . . ."
The power is called *Shakti,* the process of awakening is called *Shaktipat,*
and the awakening is almost useless—in fact, it can dissipate, unless
there is then an ongoing guidance, or Yoga, to develop the power.

Meditation is the term used for this Yoga, although chanting outweighs actual sitting-still meditation in practice. And Shakti is the
power always at stake. Since Shakti is a personal-universal energy,
Muktananda's Siddha Yoga is more a *tantra,* a generative force, than
a yoga in its classical sense. Muktananda continually links everything
he does with ancient Scripture out of his background and lineage, but
what is actually unfolding around him may be quite unique in history.

I recall as a youngster hearing, with awe, that a single lump of coal
contained enough energy to run a steamship for a year were atomic

energy to be tapped. In 1956, David Bohm proposed that if we compute the "zero quantum energy in a single cubic centimeter of empty space" (which is about next to nothing at all), we would come up with 10^{38} ergs, the explosive power of roughly ten billion *tons* of uranium fission. Bohm spoke of that vast energy in a speck of nothing as "currently unavailable," but, in his youthful optimism, assumed that eventually we would tap into it. . . . Shakti is the energy of creation itself. Allowed to develop within, this energy always moves for unity, it can order into coherence our mind/ brain split asunder by the force of madness about us, and bring us into balance with this awesome universe we carry within our skulls.

The Order of Things[4]

David Bohm's paradigm for physics offers a splendid model for explaining personal power and Shaktipat. . . . Anything manifested in the explicate order is *enfolded* in the implicate order. By "enfolded" Bohm means that anything in the physical universe exists within the energy of the implicate order in a potential state, rather as a tendency toward expression.

Mozart's initial perception of a symphony as an instant's gestalt was the transition, between the implicate order's possibility and the explicate order's pages of musical manuscript, which could be interpreted by others and turned into music.

The difficult part of Bohm's theory for us Westerners, and its direct correspondence with Eastern thought, is that the implicate order is *consciousness*. The energy out of which anything and everything is made is conscious energy, which, of course, calls for a redefinition of consciousness.

The power of consciousness, or the implicate order, is far greater than the power of the explicate order, far greater than *any* explicit manifestation made out of that great energy.

The entire physical world, with its time and space, results from impulses, which manifest by complex mathematical relations of frequencies, within the implicate order. The explicate expression can be thought of as an order arising out of chaos through relating frequencies of energy.

The explicate order, the whole physical universe, is only a "ripple" on the surface of consciousness, and beyond the implicate order itself, according to Bohm, lie vaster fields of even more powerful energies. At the core of it all is what Bohm calls the realm of insight-intelligence, which I take to be the source of creativity where the postulate comes from.

The implicate and insight realms are states, not places. Location can be drawn from them, but they have no location. Time and space can't be applied to them but can be expressed out of them. No energy has time, space, or location, though time, space, and location can be effects of energy. . . . Bohm uses the word *holomovement* for this creative system of insight, implicate and explicate orders of energy. The holomovement is a single unit, a gestalt, an impulse or state, which cannot be divided in any way, but which can be represented in an infinite number of ways.

According to Bohm's theory our mental reservoir is such that the physical universe is but the "merest ripple" on our actual surface, which is the holomovement. The holomovement's mode of being is through the energy of consciousness and all this is, of logical necessity, inherent within the domain of our brain.

The word *brain,* by itself, is where an insufficiency lies, however, for the brain is an explicate-order arrangement, which, by definition, is too weak an energy system for anything beyond explicate-order energy interaction. So we can't say, or imply, that the brain encompasses, as though it owns the holomovement.

The brain, however, is the physical manifestation of the holomovement, and so, like its own hologram, the universe, the brain is but the merest ripple on the surface of consciousness, or the implicate order. The term *mind/brain* allows us to think of the brain realistically. The brain must be seen as an instrument of mind, just as the body is an instrument of the brain. The mind, then, is the holomovement as implied within the brain, but not manifest. Which is to say, the mind is not part of or in physical reality. The *brain* is the way the mind *is* in physical reality. The mind is not "real" in the same sense the brain is real, when reality is considered that which is physical or in the explicate order. To be in physical reality requires an explicate mode of being, and that mode for the mind is the brain.

Insight, as discussed earlier is creative thought which arrives full-blown in, rather than being thought by, the brain. Insight is expressed through the power of consciousness (which in this sense is itself but an instrument of insight). Insight, since of a vastly greater energy, can influence thought, shape it, and keep it coherent. In order to be intelligent and express insight, thought must be open to the power of consciousness and be capable of being *used* as an instrument of insight. No thought is possible except through the power of consciousness, but a certain amount of this energy is inherent within brain construction and the whole explicate order. And, sadly, this energy can be employed in isolation from insight-intelligence.

The biological plan built into our genes is for development of thought as that instrument of insight. This development is, genetically, an orderly, logical, and thorough design. In actuality, in practice, it fails miserably. Thought doesn't develop as the instrument of insight-intelligence, and so never has the full and enormous power of consciousness available.

Our problem is that thought takes over, as Bohm puts it, and becomes self-generative. By self-generative is meant a kind of closed-circuit, tape-looped effect of the brain, wherein the brain feeds on its own output, so to speak, rather than on insight-intelligence. Through enculturation and its resulting anxiety, thought relates exclusively to the brain, the body, and the outer world, and loses its connection with consciousness and insight.

Bohm distinguishes, then, two kinds of thought. The one we generate with our own brain and the one generated by a "deeper mind" and given to us; that is, insight-intelligence.

Self-generative thought, the semantic fabrications of the isolated social-ego, is *autistic* in the original sense of that term: thought that relates only to itself largely because it is unable to relate on a wider frequency. Autistic thinking in this sense is an inner, tape-looped circuitry verifying and feeding back on its own circuit while ignoring (because unable to compute) what is taking place outside the tight confines of its own definition.

This isolated thought develops a passion for prediction and control, trying, within the confines of its own weak and narrow limits, to fathom and "out think" what always amounts to nothing less than the holonomic order itself. A semantic world of chaos and confusion is the only possible result.

Only insight-intelligence and the "high energy" of consciousness can order the limited and disorderly field of our thought into coherence and rapport with the holonomic order, according to Bohm. Insight can act by a direct wave-interference on the brain at the manifest level. This interference can change that brain and make it orderly.

Insight, according to Bohm, is the agent of change, an . . . active intelligence that doesn't pay any attention to thought . . . (which) bypasses thought as of little importance. Insight removes all the blocks and confusions in thought; rearranges the very structural matter of the brain which underlies thought. Bohm says insight can remove that message, which is causing confusion, leave the necessary information there, and leave that brain open to perceive reality in a different way.

What needs exploration here is the relation of thought, consciousness, and insight. Surely, as Bohm claims, thought trying to go beyond its place blocks what is beyond—but what *is* thought's place? What is its role? Often philosophies and theories, particularly Eastern ones, begin to look on thinking as the universal culprit, as a vast error of nature, perhaps. But nothing in our natural endowment is error, and to miss the role of thought is to miss the nature of human development.

Generated mostly by the brain, equated with the isolated, fragmented, and anxiety-ridden ego, dissociated from the coherency and energy of the whole, our thought is nevertheless the vehicle of creative imagination. Surely, thought in its undeveloped and undisciplined state, given to gibberish and foolishness as it is, and locked into compulsive roof-brain chatter, blocks that which is beyond. But this has nothing to do with its potential or what nature intended for it.

Thought, consciousness, and insight form a trinity, one which can't, in the final analysis, be divided. Thought is *man;* insight is *God;* consciousness is the bonding-power, the connecting force, the Holy Spirit, that Shakti or energy which underlies all reality. The issue is what brings about insight, or what is our relation with God?

A great answer is no answer to a person who has not asked that question. . . . Were insight to break into an unprepared or weak mind/brain, no reordering would take place and no translation into the common domain would be given. Outside the phenomenon of Shaktipat, there are no cases of insight-revelation of any stature taking place without proper preparation simply because the law of development precludes such a possibility.

An exception to the preparatory period of thinking seems to be found in *grace*—insight or beneficial events that seem freely given, not of our making and not clearly deserved. Even here connecting links can be found. A split system is always seeking wholeness, just as a newborn infant is automatically expecting and primed for appropriate responses.

So the answer for our anxiety-ridden and crippled thought is not to escape the world or try to shut it out, but to see it for what it really is, invest in our seeing, and be what we are designed to be. The only way to be as designed is to get into and remain in alignment with the function of creativity, the instant-by-instant creation of our universe. Then our thought, personality, and life have the power of the universe behind them.

Instruments of Mind[5]

The words *mind* and *brain* are often used interchangeably and the results are confusing. Body is an instrument of brain; brain is an instrument of mind; mind can be considered an instrument of consciousness, which, in this sense, can be considered an instrument of insight-intelligence. Certainly body and brain are a unit; brain isn't much good without body, but if we are going to use the word *brain* we clearly don't mean the pancreas or liver. The same distinction must be held for mind and brain.

The late Wilder Penfield, one of our century's great brain surgeons and research persons, offered a distinction between mind and brain (an offering rather rigorously turned down by our current biologists and brain researchers). In his long career, Penfield removed the top of the skulls and probed the brains of some fifteen hundred people. Since the brain has no feeling, only a local anesthetic is needed to open the skull. The patient is then conscious and responsive.

Penfield's operations often lasted for hours, as he took advantage of this open-skulled opportunity to explore. He found certain tiny areas of the brain, which, when electrically stimulated, gave the patient a full, five-sensory replay of some event in the patient's past (say, for instance, falling off a haystack in grandfather's barn at age seven). So long as the spot was stimulated, the event would run its course and stop.

The patient would report the replayed event to Penfield as it took place. Yet the patient was open-eyed, looking at Penfield as he did so. Two distinctly different reality-events were taking place at the same time for him and the patient reported the two as equal, though his logic ruled that he had to be "just remembering" the barn incident. "But," Penfield would ask, "where are *you* that you witness two separate but equal events?" The patient would reply: "Just watching both."

From many such cases Penfield concluded that mind and brain are separate entities; that mind perceives the brain's perceptual functions but is not the result of those functions; that mind has no memory or content that brain furnishes those on demand or as needed; that mind "runs," and in turn draws its sustenance from, the brain. Penfield mused that if we could ever prove that mind could under any circumstance receive its energy from any source other than the brain, we would know that "immortality" was functionally possible.

Consciousness is not an emergent of the brain, but that force that powers the brain. Even bodily awareness and ordinary verbal thought are "emergents" of the brain only because they are consciousness as processed through its instrument *of* brain.

One of the most significant but ignored facts from brain research is that researchers can't find where in the brain perception occurs. The whole fallacy of mind as an emergent of brain breaks down in light of this fact, so the fact is simply ignored.

David Bohm spoke of the physical world, the implicate order supporting it, "vaster energies" beyond, and a final core of insight-intelligence. For untold centuries Siddha psychologists, the "realized beings" or geniuses of the East, have spoken of the holonomic movement in terms of "bodies."

The one unanimous agreement is that consciousness and the universe are of the same substance; all is mental experience. Yogic psychology speaks of four bodies: first, the *physical* body, its brain and its world-out-there. This is the explicate order, of course. Next comes the *subtle* body, which is the same as, or partakes of, Bohm's implicate order. Next is the *causal* body, which is the realm of potential without even "implications" of any manifestation in it; and finally comes the *supercausal* body, which is the witness of all states, the final core of awareness, the final "receiver" of perceptions. The causal body or state is what Bohm referred to as "vaster energies beyond the implicate," and the supercausal is the realm of insight-intelligence, from which the postulate-revelation and all creation springs. This last state is without attributes or impingement on it from anything of which it is aware and is the goal of the practice of *choiceless awareness,* of which Krishnamurti speaks, and is, of course, the *self* in Siddha Yoga terms.

Yogic psychology states that perceptions register in the subtle body. The reason research can't determine exactly where perception takes place in the brain is because it *doesn't*. The ghost in the machine is not detectable by the machinery. People in great pain report occasionally that they have left their bodies and looked down at them. When they leave their bodies, body pain no longer has anything to register on.

Yet the subtle body *can* register perceptions independently of the physical body. Ordinarily the two are intricately connected; the subtle permeates the physical and interacts with it point for point; receives its perceptual information; is its twin, powers the body, and yet can detach from it and leave the body on "automatic pilot." When the subtle detaches from the physical, the receptors of the physical senses are no longer in the body, and consciousness is withdrawn from the brain. (Some yogic adepts can withdraw the subtle receptors from specific areas of the body, at which point those parts of the body are anesthetized.)

Development of ability is the whole thrust of our biological plan of life, since ability is the vehicle by which we can move *beyond* the physical.

In childhood, most anxiety generates out of a general fear of abandonment, brought on by failure to bond with the parents. Our later failure to bond with the earth, society, and so on, both confirms and perpetuates that anxiety.

By the very nature and mechanics of our brain's worldview construction in infancy and childhood, we have no choice but to identify with the construction we make, which we must make. Since we must pattern ourselves and our worldview after our culture and parents, when that is a disordered system for our modeling, we are ourselves disordered in precisely the same way.

The force, which alone can straighten us out, is the power of insight-intelligence operating through consciousness. And this must, of genetic inevitability, be interpreted by our survival mechanism as anti-survival. Our disorder can't help but drive continually to maintain its own disorder. We strive continually to use the forces of order for maintenance of our own disorder, in spite of ourselves.

The result is that our whole genetic drive, once warped, can't reorder itself. And change, as yogic theory states, real conceptual change in a human, becomes the rarest single event in the world. Instead of change we get an infinite rationalization, as our drive for autonomy maintains itself.

Bohm speaks of a "deeper level" of thought that springs from insight-intelligence. Disconnected from the holonomic order . . . however, brain-thinking tries to become (and thinks itself) all levels of thought and self-sufficient. This breeds a disoriented, semantic world, isolated from intelligence and the balance of the holonomic movement. From such an imbalanced thought-process only disorder and destruction can come, and in this artificial realm, only anxiety is permanent or stable.

The Pueblo chief Ochwiay said the whites were crazy since they maintained that they thought with their heads, whereas it was well known that only crazy people did that. Indians, he said, thought with their hearts. (This was many years ago, and Ochwiay was in his eighties.)

We have been conditioned to believe that that which *can't* be gripped by our ordinary thought is hallucination or illusion. We have been conditioned to believe that any incursion of the really great creative energies is pathological. So, for the culturally fragmented person, any move toward wholeness is interpreted as a threat, a final fragmentation or loss of coherence. When the instrument of body/brain becomes self-generative, anything not available to its weak energy must be interpreted as destructive. Thus our perceptions become inverted; we see things backward and turn heaven into hell.

Keys and Locks[6]

"Man is born like a garden ready planted and sown. This world is too poor to produce one seed." So proclaimed the visionary poet, William Blake, nearly two centuries ago. . . . An infant has an open-ended intelligence locked into his genes, but the key for unlocking lies with parent and society. Only intelligence can breed, stimulate, and foster intelligence. The medium for that fostering is culture. Culture is an artificial, man-made ambient for growing people, and every culture specializes in the kind of person it grows. Every culture fosters some particular potential at the expense of some other, defining itself by its own, arbitrary definitions.

An English group studying the Aborigine had one of their group travel a course of some one hundred miles covering a varied terrain of swamp, shifting sand, rock, forest, and so on, carefully marked on a map. One year later, when any possibility of a sign remaining seemed remote, they asked an Australian Aborigine tracker if he could follow the course. He replied yes, if they would give him an article of clothing worn by the man leaving the trail. Holding the item, the Aborigine went into dream-time. There he "got in touch with the Two Great Brothers who eternally, instant by instant, create the universe." In touch with this genius, he was automatically in touch with the man whose article he held and the event of laying down the trail. The Aborigine then broke into his loose, economical run, and followed the trail unerringly, without stopping to look for traces, if any could have conceivably remained.

A capacity can be lost to a culture, or never developed at all. Consider how we have lost a natural bonding to our infants at birth. Such a capacity can be regained or rediscovered and developed, only through outside intervention, or by some fluke of thought outside our developed worldview. Even then, maintenance of our culture's and its professions' definitions of itself can create a closed circuit blocking such intervention and enlightenment.

Many potentials are missed through failure of response from parents, who were in turn not developed in those potentials by their parents, and so on in infinite regress. Every capacity conceivable to imagination is inborn in us, since ours is an open-ended mind/brain, but any specific capacity must be brought forth and developed.

How then can a parent model for and stimulate personal power in a child unless that parent has such power to begin with? A double bind is inherent here, truly a case of don't go near the water until you can swim. This double bind can be broken, and the power of the bond established, however, by that parent finding a personal model of wholeness and at least *practicing* a discipline of wholeness. For the child will immediately model the parent's own example. (All of us did just this in our enculturation.) Fortunately, a total final "enlightenment" is not necessary, or the vicious circle could never be broken.

Form and Content[7]

The child, as a new content, continually signals his needs for formal structuring and screens his environment for the expected response to his needs. Should that response fail, he sinks into apathy. The unresponsive parent, like the devouring mother, indicates imbalance; like the rebellious child, she indicates a genetic system gone awry, one that expresses conditioning, not nature—something molded not created.

Both society's failure to respond to our needs and our corresponding antisocial acts indicate the unnatural. Form should be in love with content and vice versa, since each is really the other, their division only an assumption made for creative play. We should bond to our society at a point of our maturation, as we did with our parents (or should have). But the later bonding's success depends upon the earlier one. Bonding is the power that molds form and content into a unified work. Bonding must be developed—or allowed to develop. Once developed anything can be bonded, any experience molded into a unified work.

Intelligence is the ability to interact with possibility and "lift things into order." This takes a certain daring (which is why intelligence and confidence are almost synonymous). There is no anxiety when a developed, creative person sees chaos as the raw material for his own work of art, the art of creative perception. A developed or mature person should be able to create a form corresponding to the content of his creative desire and culture should provide for development of this ability.

A culture should automatically become obsolescent as its people-products mature. The successful parent is one whose child matures to walk away without a backward glance. Backward glances, either of obsessive love or hatred, show incomplete development, looking back to pick up missing pieces, to try to patch a broken system.

Ability is form, and creative imagination is content. Creative imagination is thought to be married to insight. The human is a form for content. When the form is considered the content, life leaves that form. When we identify with our body and brain, our possibility as a form for content is crippled and we end without content—truly hollow men.

So, once fallen into anxiety, a species can't raise itself. When our perception develops out of tyranny, we are fixed into a limited world and determined by the things we see. Determined by our cultural environment, we either maintain the fixity of it, no matter how awful it is, in fear of losing the little we have, or we try to engineer it mechanically, trying to make things in our head come out right.

"If the doors of perception were cleansed," Blake claimed, "everything would appear to man as it is, infinite." Neither form nor content exist as fixed items, but as events for and of perception. When the doors of perception are cleansed the world of frozen matter bursts and all is fluid and free. Consider for instance the Shaktipat experience of

Rudrani Farbman, of New York City, who, in 1974, took an intensive with Muktananda.

Baba pinched her hard on the forehead between her eyes. She felt: ". . . a sudden in-drawing of energy, a consolation of strength . . . then majestic, free of self-doubts." Riding her bicycle home that afternoon, everything ". . . began to turn into a sea of seething energy, taking form slowly and fluidly like slow waves in the ocean. Forms rolled and churned like cellular life, snakelike, extra-planetary." Rudrani began to see that the forms were ". . . tiny scintillating blue dots . . . dazzlingly beautiful. Everything sparkled, caught up in this radiance of dots. Forms dissolved . . . now all was dots." She became immersed in this ocean of blue dots, which gave ecstasy and peace.

"So this was what it all was, and always was," she thought. "Why had I not been told?" (Indeed, why haven't we all been told? But who has there been to tell us?) "I began to play with it," she goes on; she would focus and building sand people emerged, relaxed and all merged into blue dots and ecstasy. She knew then that it was up to her to either keep an arbitrary world together or let it go. Nothing was the same after this. Anxiety dropped away; she became fluid and free herself, her relations with her world changing.

Perception, like thought, is an end product. We, as perceivers, are recipients of that product. Thinking can't change the mechanics of our thought or perception any more than we can, by taking thought, increase our stature by a cubit. No thought generated by any brain in error can do other than replicate that error. Only insight can change the workings of a disordered brain. If the capacity for insight is lost to culture, that capacity must be given back from a source outside that culture or from a person plugged into a different circuitry, that is, a genius beyond the circle of that norm.

The Error—Correction Error[8]

There is a biological plan of magnificent proportions, a straight-line course of development that is built into our genes. The plan is flexible to accommodate an infinite number of variables, while its goal is specific and clear: a way for creating a new hologram out of the holonomic movement, a new representative of the whole; a new creator out of the creation. The plan is a way to develop thought out of consciousness as a tool of insight-intelligence. The plan depends on developing ability, which encompasses a certain amount of trial and error. In fact, the biological plan can accommodate error easily since error is only an aspect of experience, or the content that gives the form life.

Something happened to this grand plan, though, perhaps historically, and the happening is repeated anew in each of us. In the course of implementing the plan, we stumble occasionally, as is natural and to be expected. But we do not, as is natural and to be expected, correct our course; that is, we don't immediately follow our intent and maintain our alignment with our plan. We become engrossed in the nature of our stumble, our error of the moment, and try to correct the error instead of our course. And at this point we Fall.

The Fall takes place when we pay attention to the wobble and not our course; when we notice the wobble as a wobble, an isolated fact of its own; when we take our eyes off our straight-line course and shift our attention to the fact of our wobble. When we do that, we immediately feel anxious over our error, which we see not as course-deviation but as self-contained. Our anxiety is over being off-course, having shifted focus to the error, but we *interpret* our anxiety over having made an error.

So long as we are in line with our biological plan, everything is right—including wobbles and stumbles. Psychotherapist Jean Liedloff speaks of the "in-arms" period of infancy. When the infant is in the mother's arms, everything is right, and nothing much can go wrong. When "out-of-arms," or in abandonment, nothing is right and everything goes wrong. The one main signal of need is not being met, and none of the other signals then work. When we are in-arms biologically, development is smooth, playful, fairly effortless, and all energies remain coordinated. When we are out-of-arms biologically, uneasiness immediately sets in since the body and brain are looking for cues and responses expected from millions of years of development, and not getting them. Processes go out of synchrony and internal conflict begins to pile up. We fall into anxiety over our error and are impelled to correct that error.

In trying to correct our error, we have to take our eyes off our course of development and concentrate on the error. Then several things happen. For one thing, we are now off-course, going in a direction counter to our development. Our error has become our direction, and our pseudo-course. The error is not developmental of itself and the direction of error only leads to itself. We have stopped our growth in mid-wobble.

When anxiety arises as some thought in our mind, the "pressure" of it (to use David Bohm's term) immediately breeds another thought to try to ease that pressure. The novelty effect of each new thought brings us the feeling of some momentary relief of our anxiety, only to find anxiety immediately reinstated, inherent within that relieving thought—which calls for another. Anxiety can only breed anxiety. Anxiety is the one condition intolerable to us, and thought generated by anxiety—even though the impulse is generated to *escape* anxiety— will always relate to, and have inherent within it, that anxiety. Isolated thinking can't give unity, and only in unity are we free of anxiety.

When in sailing against the wind we shift our tack, we are guided by our course-direction. In the error-correction error, we *change the compass setting itself* away from its original goal over to the direction the *error is going in.*

With the wrong compass setting everything starts going wrong, and we are besieged by errors demanding correction. The problem with correcting error is that we become what we behold. With our eye on our course of development, it is impossible, regardless of context, to be off course. Regardless of how wildly we veer off or how complex and unruly the variables become, we are always on course and everything is all right when our eye is on the course. Our true course encompasses everything conceivable. When our compass is set correctly, and we know our relation to it, we can pile into choppy waters without qualm. The same arena of experience can be positive or negative according to our alignment or lack of it. Course alignment lifts order out of chaos. When our eye is on the error, though, we become that error. And like attracts like. Error produces error. When chaos is our orientation, we can't lift anything into order.

All the negative numbers in the world will not add up to a single positive one—although an unlimited negative-mathematics could be constructed. Thought, once it becomes self-generative, can only reproduce itself and maintain its disorder. Only insight can reorder and bring the brain's responses into alignment with the whole.

So error proliferates; each error breeds new ones like a tree that branches at every tip. (This is the bureaucracy-Pentagon syndrome.) Anxiety drives us to try to patch up each error, and we fall further behind until, locked as we are in the "magnitude of the problems facing our day," even the notion of development, a biological plan, of a meaning and goal to life, is lost to us.

Culture can't possibly be the vehicle for implementing the developmental plan when caught in error-correction. It becomes a taboo system of prediction and control, trying to organize the machinery for error-correction. Development is then bent toward a prediction and control that violates every facet of nature's design. With prediction and control the reigning passion and anxiety the normal state, the bulk of our energy goes to solve problems that continually outstrip us.

The solution is to turn our eyes away from the mass of errors screaming for correction and learn again to focus on the goal of development— that straight, simple line of the biological plan. The solution is to open to insight-intelligence, admit to our thought's absolute insufficiency, and allow our thought to be used as the instrument of the holonomic order within our head—as designed.

Now isolated thought, locked in its arrogant posture of prediction and control, fears the unknown, which always means the insight-intelligence realm. But, once the shift is made from error-correction to realignment with the plan, *error isn't something to correct anymore.* (How this baffled me!) Error is again only a deviation from the course, and the course is immediately the focal point of attention again.

Course-correction then replaces error-correction and then all that exists is the plan and its execution, which can encompass a multitude of errors.

To isolated and arrogant thought, emerging from a brain locked into escape from anxiety, such an observation is sheer gibberish. And strangely, such a simple turning maneuver is the prime sin against an error-correction society. One should devote one's life to mankind, give one's self for the welfare of others; live for the good of the whole of man (be general but never specific, abstract but never concrete). Not to do so is to be selfish, a shameful state. . . . Nothing *works*. Everything touched by error-correction turns to dust and ashes.

Every saint and genius has told us two things: we are not guilty of error nor called on to correct it; and the plan of life is built into us and its truth can never be removed. That truth in us can only be covered over, and that truth is our ever-present alignment with the whole; the truth of our real Self is God Himself, the perfection of our *own* divine being.

How the priests of culture hate this notion. How it embarrasses and threatens them, for their positions are founded on and maintained by error. . . . Nothing so disturbs the policeman as the idea that a person is essentially honest—no calamity would be so great as an absence of crime. The Pentagonian insists that human nature is warlike since any other position would disarm him. Were education to work, were children actually led forth to knowledge, educators would immediately disappear. Take away prediction and control, and bureaucracy would collapse. Take away separation from God, and the churches would empty.

In my early days of Siddha Yoga, I was often irritated that Muktananda seemed oblivious to the social crimes against humanity erupting all around us. Baba's presence itself had to bring about in me (by osmosis, I suppose) enough strength of mind, a certain clearing of error in my brain, for me to understand that he is not blind and deaf to the misery and terror about us. (Quite the contrary, only compassion could induce him to put up with our nonsense.) He sees the misery well enough, but only by a shift of viewpoint, an effort of unfocusing, perhaps. Otherwise he sees through error to the truth, which truth is our actual identity with God and perfection in Him. For truth can only see truth, it can't see error as legitimate fact. I wanted Baba to join with me in "getting those rascals" perpetrating these crimes. (And I certainly had my list, with medicine men at the top.) But Baba would have none of my craziness. He didn't even catch my fuzzy wavelength. I was asking him, in effect, to join me in error-correction. He invited me, on the other hand, to join him in truth.

The Great Vaccination[9]

As so often with genius, Jesus was at a radical discontinuity with his background. (Attempts to "unify" the four gospels with the Old Testament led to a hilarious logic.) If Jesus's "good news" of our identity with God and freedom from guilt were accepted, it would automatically abolish tyranny. To be free of guilt and at one with the universal system is to be free of anxiety—and you can threaten and control a man only through his anxiety. So the forces of social-political control must always induce and maintain that anxiety.

We vaccinate, you know, by injecting into our body dead or near-dead virus that cause a disease. Our body's defense system easily routs such a weak enemy, and, having learned that particular martial maneuver, can repeat the performance with ease and skill when the real enemy comes along. Great encounters of life and death can then take place below the level of our awareness.

In just this way, heresy concerning the "central point in history" proved the most potent vaccine in history. Most early religious education is a vaccination of classical proportions. We are injected with a dead or nearly dead form of the actual disease (the disease of God, this is) from an early age.

Our vaccination is against the most natural of all functions, our spirit. The word *spirit,* though, is almost meaningless, either over-filled with useless connotations or stripped and barren. Spirit is Shakti, energy, the particular aspect of energy that bonds together, that connects, that lifts order out of chaos as a unit in unity, with the whole of things. In the New Testament, the "Holy Spirit" was the energy or power that came with wholeness of self. Jesus spoke of the "Holy Comforter." *Holy* means "wholeness" (nothing more esoteric), and *comfort* means "with strength, or from strength," the power or strength that comes from being united.

Our vaccination, then, is against the bonding force within us, that design of nature that molds the disparate functions of body, brain, mind, personality, and so on into a coherent whole in harmony with the larger whole. A lack of spiritual development means that thought gets isolated from insight-intelligence and consciousness. A need for spiritual guidance means a need for restoring wholeness between thought and insight-intelligence, which can only take place through the power of consciousness.

It is against the insight function that we have been vaccinated. (That may be why we must make such enormous efforts to trigger insight-response along any line.) Thought is designed to be only a part of our awareness-existence. Consciousness and insight-intelligence should be equal or superior portions of our perception. Isolated in our thought we are seldom conscious and only very rarely experience insight. Were the "disease of God" against which we are now vaccinated allowed to unfold within us as designed, our full maturity would be that state, which is now either denied or projected, outside ourselves as something remote and unattainable.

All functions, including the overall function of coordinating wholeness or spirit, must follow the law of development. A corresponding stimulus must be given from without, from a developed capacity of the same order, to start development. And an ongoing developmental model must be given with a proper nurturing to sustain growth; the logical stages of growth must be honored. We must be allowed to crawl before we walk.

This need for a living model of wholeness is a qualification that nullifies most religions and nearly every preacher, priest, guru, or holy man. Wholeness means absolute unity, not almost—just as you can't be "just a little bit pregnant," you can't be almost whole and model wholeness.

Cant, dogma, theory, spiritual exhortation, philosophy, and so on are general expressions of the arrogance of isolated thought trying to create a semantic world that will be whole. Even piety, good intentions, and earnestness can never, alone, develop the process within us called the Spirit. Development must have awakening and modeling by a person who exemplified that which must be evoked from within.

For five decades I had wrestled with spirit in the vague, abstract semantic form of my inoculation, investing my energy in this search and getting only my own energy, slightly worn, back. My romantic idealism and emotional-sentimental love projected on the figure of Jesus (my only model) was reflected back into my life as romantic idealism and emotional-sentimental "love," but not as the power and transformation I so needed. The live and real spirit, however, once I had been exposed to it, moved into my life *through* the very symbols of my vaccination.

Inoculated against inner unity, we develop the true disease of alienation, which is separation from our Self. Cut off from our bonding-power in childhood, we spend our lives buying facsimiles of it in hopes of recovering something we know we have lost.

The God within—toward which Jesus pointed though historically projected out again as unattainable—is our inner process of development, our full and perfect maturation as designed; thought perfected as an instrument of insight-intelligence and open to the power of consciousness. "Be ye perfect as your Father in Heaven is perfect" was not some cruel jest, but a simple observation of what life is about. Perfection is full development not some divine abstraction of essence or quality removed from reality. Christendom made of perfection is a state devoid of humanness and so unattainable to us humans—which automatically creates guilt in us over our automatic and assured failure.

Muktananda insists that our perfection is already achieved, always present right here in us, that our job is to realize our true state—which means to push past our vaccination (rather as Saint Francis overcoming his greatest horror and kissing the leper fully on the lips—at which point all the bells of heaven rang).

Our split-mind projected wholeness onto a clockwork mechanical god-out-there, built machines to try to replace our corresponding loss of personal power, and we lost our identity to our own machinery.

As we project our longing for our whole Self onto something out there in "reality," we project our resulting inner terror and anxiety onto our social world. And the unforgivable sin of Western thought has been to break this double-projection, since the illusion of our whole world of folly would then snap, and its reigning priesthood would collapse.

Full development, for which we are genetically equipped, is pure creativity, which can only take place by thought being developed as an instrument of insight-intelligence, open to and capable of handling the awesome power of consciousness. Anything less is incomplete development, which will always (no matter how much gadgetry we pile around us) cause anxiety, because we aren't developing the higher levels of abstract or nonphysical thought we must have for "mental autonomy." Autonomy is the ability to create a perceptual experience not dependent on our given physical materials, even though our creative ability must arise out of those given materials.

The function of the great vaccination is to convince us that anything outside our self-generated thought and given physical world is "only imagination." Not only does this deny us a future beyond the physical, this limits present reality to the "objective"—that which is thought to be outside of and independent of us. Equally, our vaccination implies that the creative activity from insight-intelligence, should it be successful in breaking into our awareness, is an aberration, a harbinger of mental illness, leading to a collapse into chaos in our heads.

Nearly two centuries ahead of his time, Blake knew that reality *is* perception, and a creative act, with existence and perception identical. Consciousness, existence, and perception are the primal facts of the universal process, he insisted, the perceived object the particularized result of our perceptual process. We are centers of perception and our universe radiates out from our center. Our physical body is the outward extension needed by our perceiving center for its interactions with a resulting perceptual universe.

Indeed, there was no contest. We are now living in the pandemonium he foresaw should Newton, Locke, and company win the day, as they surely did. The "Enlightenment" proved no boon to man—just one more frying pan to switch into—and it may prove the final fire.

The priests who "stand at the narrow gate" and block man's entrance to life no longer wear vestments, but the thick-lensed spectacles of the smugly myopic, near-blind technician-bureaucrats who, because they see so darkly, deny light as a real phenomenon. Not only is our development blocked by such cultural models of despair, our true mental birth out of our physical matrix is blocked. (Do we turn on nature with such fury today because we can't get free of her?) We may be kept not just in infancy by the constrictions of a technological culture, but perhaps essentially in utero. The autistic epidemic may be but the first wave of far worse to come. We may be, after all, not so much a fallen race as an unborn one. A great imaginative energy is needed to burst us loose from this bind— an energy greater than the vast combine of isolated and arrogant thought now in control. The energy of freedom is being generated, too, out of our very need it comes, in the form of a "postulate-in-person"—lest we remain not just unborn, but go stillborn. The uterine infant can wait just so long past its delivery time, and we may be well past due.

Creative Imagination[10]

The dictionary defines *imagination* as "the ability to create images not present to the senses." One of the first capacities to appear for development, yet perhaps the least developed, is this ability to create, in a mental state, images that are not present in the physical state.

The Ugandan mother, "bonded" to her infant, knows when her infant is going to urinate and so "takes it to the bushes" ahead of time. Her brain registers that information and she acts on it. Bonding opens her to consciousness, which is the general field underlying both herself and child.

However, bodily senses are only a part of the perceptual spectrum available to the mind/brain. The Aborigine opens to the holonomic order when in dreamtime and can track an ancient trail since all time is "enfolded" in any single moment, and the trail's original "laying-down" is unfolded through dreamtime.

A child might see and respond to so-called extrasensory stimuli until he finds that such events upset his parents when reported, or that his parents do not share in his experience. Then not only does the child not get a name-label *for* the experience (which naming lifts order out of chaos and anchors new stimuli into the conceptual system), he gets negative feedback from his principal criteria for deciding what is *real*—his parents. A "selective blindness" toward such sensory stimuli will eventually take place. The child is in consciousness, but his adults and their world are in thought. When verbal thought begins, the child begins to identify with thought and *lose* consciousness. He does this because the adult world he *must* relate to is made of isolated thought split off from consciousness.

We adopt perceptual attitudes as infant/children to maintain our consensus or bond with our parents and later, society. We respond according to an aesthetic largely ready-made, which includes heavy doses of *samskaras** based on anxiety. Further, the visual system occupies the largest portion of the brain and incorporates and integrates all other senses. Thus, as the visual apparatus goes, so goes the whole sensory system and thinking itself—to the extent that we even refer to understanding as: "I see."

According to Blake, perception isn't something that happens to us through our senses; it is a mental act. To actively perceive, then, is to use imagination—the ability to create images not present in the senses. The more active one's imagination, the richer his perceptual experience, and the more real his world.

Surely our century has seen the emergence of a "normal" as the

---

*In Indian and yogic philosophy, *samskaras* are the mental impressions left by all thoughts, actions, and intents that an individual has ever experienced. They can be thought of as psychological imprints. They are below the level of normal consciousness and are said to be the root of all impulses, as well as our innate dispositions and karma.

standard of life, a norm, which has become the lowest common denominator of "objectivity"—seeing *without* imagination, pretending to be a mechanical camera reporting that which is inflicted on us by what we see. We have set up our *lack* of creative vision as our model and denied the vision of the poet, saint, or genius in general.

Creativity is a function that grows out of physical development. A developed intelligence is a developed creativity, one that can interact with a manifest order or un-manifest possibility and "lift chaos into order." A passive perception can't assume responsibility for what is seen and so never sees anything outside the Guinea Sun norm. "Satan never sees," Blake observed, "he always has to be shown."

Ron Resch, director of the Computer Geometry and Design Center at Boston University, attended Muktananda's Boston intensive in November of 1979. In his own words:

> Following Baba's touch I saw myself from a position up over my right shoulder. My body was composed of luminescent white light. I sat cross-legged, still as a statue, suspended in the blackness of outer space. Suddenly, like a rocket taking off, a small dense shaft of white light took off from the base of my spine and roared up through the top of my head. Streaking upward, it burst open to fill the heaven with stars. After some time the white light descended again in a kind of gossamer tubular form, settling over me like dew. The lower edge of the column was intense and rippled like a plasma ring being rocked on the surface of water. The ring and column enclosed me, undulating a circle of light around where I sat.

When Lightning Strikes[11]

A bolt of lightning arcs the gap of earth and sky in a two-part play: energy gathers over a large terrain and collects at some vantage point—a building, tall tree, a hilltop; while a similar gathering takes place in the clouds above. When the two collections come into proximity, the earth charge leaps up, the clouds charge down, and they merge in awesome exchange.

The cloud charge is by far the larger and discharges most of its energy into the earth. Some earth energy may end in the cloud, but the earth is much the richer for the encounter. (In addition, millions of tons of nitrogen are generated in this fashion each year, a principal way for renewing the earth's soil.)

As with lightning, so with genetic potential. Like attracts like. The lesser charge, built into the child, is receptive to and triggers a response from a superior or developed charge in an adult. The lesser charge is amplified in the exchange, and there is an overall renewal of nutriments for growth.

The nature of the superior force, which evokes the potential in the child, enters into the nature of the response the child makes. The awakening, the kind of development which then takes place, and the nature of the reality then experienced, are all of a part.

A certain trial and error enters into any learning, but no development is designed to be by trial and error alone. The human is meant for *continual* guidance and for constant discipline and self-control. So why should meditation and spiritual practice be any different? The induction of Shaktipat and guidance of Kundalini-awakening by Muktananda is a disciplined, intelligent response to our natural need—the response life has designed and provided. Just awakening Kundalini—rare as it is— doesn't bring wholeness. It's just the kindergarten. The diploma is no more awarded on Kundalini-awakening than is a youngster ready for the concert hall after a first piano lesson.

The Guru principle is designed to give this actual experience as the *starting point*—which makes eminently good sense. The Guru principle is designed not only to awaken our power and furnish a model for its development; he is also designed to *lend us his power,* precisely as a parent lends the child his power, both to give a clear demonstration of what development will give us and to get that development under way. Eugen Herrigel* tells how the Zen master would use the student's bow and so lend that bow his power, after which, for a time, the bow would

---

*[Eugen Herrigel (1884–1955) was a German philosopher and author who, through his writings, introduced Zen to the Western world. —*Ed.*]

respond equally for the student and let him know what to look for.

We learn from the concrete *to* the abstract, from the specific application to the broad application. The radical discontinuity between our spiritual goal and our ordinary locked-up perceptions is bridged through an initial grace. Having that bolt of lightning meet us (always *more* than halfway) gives us the vision to see where we are going.

My years of church going were like going to the tomb of a dead saint. Pilgrimage can be a great spiritual exercise. Just as there are "power spots" perpetuated by the American Indians, there can be power at the shrines of great saints. But spiritual awakening, guidance, discipline, and growth can't take place through shrines. You can't teach children music by taking them to the tomb of Beethoven once a week.

Muktananda is able to reach out and literally inject insight directly into a person's brain and life, and then guide the ensuing development, the reordering of that brain into creative coherence. This is possible only because the capacity is also within that other brain. Spark triggers spark, but the size of the one doing the responding to our small and feeble efforts is beyond our calculation.

Surely this Shaktipat effect is unique in history—as was Jesus. But surely the critical nature of our current history is equally unique. Extremes of crisis call for extremes of response. The passionate question of a mass driven to the brink of chaos triggers its response. We ask and we receive. We knock and the door opens to us. Whether we enter or not is up to us. This is a door, however, that doesn't hang around open, waiting for us to debate the issue.

Meeting of Minds[12]

Dr. D. K. Salunkhe, nutritionist of the Food Science Department, Utah State University, was in Istanbul, Turkey, as a consultant to a university there, setting up a department of nutrition. The doctor returned to his hotel room at midnight one evening, took two sleeping pills, and went to bed. He was awakened at 3 a.m. by a voice commanding: "Get dressed quickly and leave this hotel." The doctor ignored the intrusion, but the voice grew louder and finally imperious in its demand. Disturbed, the doctor got up, dressed, and stumbled down and out to the sidewalk. Immediately after he was outside a huge earthquake hit, leveling the hotel.

On his return home, Salunkhe confided this episode to his sister. Now his sister had met and become a follower of Muktananda's (the connecting link always must be there), and insisted her brother go see Baba. He undertook the journey and as he came up in darshan line for that first meeting, Baba's face lit up in recognition and he asked, an impish grin on his face: "So how was that visit to Istanbul?"

Eternity and Time[13]

William Blake said: "Eternity is in love with the productions of Time." Or, in less poetic terms the subtle orders of energy are in love with the gross physical; insight and consciousness are in love with thought; heart with head; God with Man; Shiva with Shakti.

The overall thrust of our personal development is for us to grow free of all physical processes, including world, body, and brain. What thought could power our mind or furnish its contents on death of the brain? . . . The answer is, of course, that which has powered things all along. The holonomic order is always a unity; and there is always only the one source, the energy of consciousness guided by insight-intelligence.

Development is so designed that by old age, we should have established a firm working relationship with, or *bonded* with, our upcoming nonphysical matrix, just as an infant bonds with its mother. Bonds are made of consciousness and should be developed throughout life, right along with the capacity for independent thought.

Life in the physical world is designed to build a matrix of physical experience out of which a nonphysical experience can be drawn. The acquiring of experience is the acquiring of the ability to handle that kind of experience. The *content* of experience is incidental to the *ability* gained for handling it. The content of perception gives existence its shape, but content is transitory, disappearing as it forms. The perceptual ability grows out of experience. Our ability to perceive is the lasting part of our personality—the instrument of mind that life on this earth is designed to develop.

Information is of the weak explicate order of energy and is expendable. The ability to *process* that information is of the subtle, implicate order of energy and is permanent within us. The shaping forces are the implicate forces, that which is shaped is explicate.

Ability may be the key to what happens to us in the next matrix, not some divine decree. If there is no capacity for nonphysical creativity, how could there be a successful matrix-shift to a nonphysical realm? For at death, when the physical body (and its world) collapses, instruments of the mind capable of relating to the nonphysical are needed.

Some people get upset by this observation, insisting that there are fixed, preset, and permanent "abodes" awaiting us after death. Perhaps there are, but even so, perception of that supposed realm, like any perception anywhere, would be a creative act, an ability of the instruments of the mind. The one thing that we can see from a study of infant/child development is the simultaneity of the development of intelligence and construction of the world.

Even should there be some fixed abode up-yonder, we must have the conceptual mechanism for perceiving it; which means, in effect, constructing it. Indeed, our perceptual development we make in the flesh almost surely determines that nature of the abode we finally perceive up-yonder (as it so seriously determines what we perceive down here).

The subtle body seems to be a mirror of the physical, an ability system that develops as we develop physically, and is subject to the limitations of that development. When I am in a subtle or causal state, I seem to perceive in an ordinary way (though what I perceive is seldom ordinary). Experiments by Charles Tart, Robert Monroe, and others clearly show that there are nonphysical stimuli, which our subtle body can receive and perceive. . . . The wonder is that something more is always forthcoming; for eternity can't fix itself in time.

Development requires that we fully experience each of the developmental matrices as we grow. To deny or restrict experience is to curtail development. Then there is an inadequate matrix-shift; capacity fails, death becomes a grim specter rather than the logical result of a growth process. Since all learning takes place from the concrete to the abstract, the creative process must be developed ahead of time to function after the death of the body. Learning can take place abstractly only when capacities *for* abstraction have been built up sufficiently out of concrete experience. Unless the strength of mind (i.e., the proper instruments of mind) is developed to handle creativity in the comparative weakness of the physical world, the far stronger forms of the subtle or causal will surely be beyond us.

Nature provides us with the bonds to each next matrix, for matrix-shift is the way of growth and development. There is a dynamic interplay between implicate and explicate orders, between thought and consciousness. Since consciousness is the energy giving birth to thought, thought and consciousness should bond and interact just as mother and child should. But thought gets split off from consciousness, and isolated into its own self-generation, from which it can't extricate itself. This is the Fall. Once fallen, only the power of consciousness can reinstate the union, as only the power of the mother can move for the helpless infant.

A successful birth can't take place from the womb unless uterine development has prepared for that exodus. In the same way, a true birth out of the physical life can't take place at death unless development is sufficient. Perhaps one is not stillborn, but the ongoing life is surely crippled and inadequate. The subtle body is the repository of the whole error-ridden mess of physical life. Rather than developed as an instrument of mind and Self, the subtle body usually remains a confused replica of the physical. If we haven't caught on and learned to be an instrument of our whole being while in the body, we certainly can't in the subtle state, since learning is from the concrete to the abstract.

Bob Monroe has given an account of the immediate after-death subtle state. That strange eighteenth-century genius, Emanuel Swedenborg, apparently managed to cross back and forth into the subtle state. The inhabitants there seem to continue to be their own undeveloped selves.

The mother of my children died when our fifth child was less than a year old. This child had cerebral palsy, as I mentioned earlier. The child's mother was completely locked in on her emotionally, unable to deal with the grim medical prognosis, which the severe cerebral damage indicated (and certainly bore out). After my wife died, she made five manifestations back into our life, all in regard to this damaged child. In two cases, she appeared in striking visual form, staring intently, over the crib, at the child. In another episode, the child's grandmother had the infant's crib next to her own bed. The mother appeared in the night, bent over the crib. The close proximity nearly froze the grandmother, literally drew the heat from her body, paralyzing her. Had the manifestation lasted longer than it did, the grandmother felt she would surely have died herself. In two manifestations, the mother manipulated the infant's body; in one striking case causing the infant to sit bolt upright, stare intently at a designated area, and give, very graphically, a symbolic sign that had been an "in joke," or closed private communication between my wife and myself. This was the first, and the very last, body movement the child was ever to make. (She lived for several years.)

Muktananda sees the creation as a great burst of love and joy. *Maya* is a Sanskrit term for our perceptual illusion that sees reality as an unalterable concreteness happening to us as fate. But Maya is not our delusion about an unreal world. It is our failure to perceive that the world is material for an ongoing creation. Maya indicates a failure of nerve, where we don't accept responsibility for what we see, but try to see a fixed matter for which we need *not* be responsible.

Muktananda says you either see the world in its frozen state or you see God. So every day, without fail, he exhorts us, over and over again, to "see God in each other." He challenges us to move beyond the frozen world of matter, which is always hell, into the fluid world of creation. It takes a powerful imaginative strength to burst beyond the bind of paranoia—which views the other person through the samskaras of hostility, fear, prejudice, envy, jealousy—and see that other person as God.

To create is to perceive in a fluid, dynamic state. When we die, the patterns of our physical world give way—for us they dissolve back into the subtle order from which they arose. Existence and perception being the same, for us to exist beyond life in the body, we must have a matrix beyond our physical world: a source of perceptual possibility; a safe space to explore that possibility; and a source of energy for that exploration. The subtle-causal realms offer this, just as they offered it for the construction of our physical world as infants. The problem doesn't lie with the matrix, but with our ability to shift into it.

Perception is creation and can use any source of materials for that creation: the world constructed from birth; the world of imaginative creation drawing *on* the world of experience; a consensus of imaginative creations shared with others; and the very implicate-causal order itself. All these are fluid states out of which reality may be lifted. We may "misplace concreteness" and miss the point of development if we assume that some ready-made given state after death is the point of life. The implicate-causal order is potential. To move into potential, we leave that which has already been realized.

There is, surely, an element of tragedy to the human race; not so much from the suffering and terror of so much of life as the uselessness of that suffering; not so much from the perceptual poverty and dullness of so much of our life as the unbelievable richness of experience that goes untapped. A negative whirlpool seems to pull us down into darkness, and surely it takes an enormous energy of imaginative creation to pull us out and free us from that negation. But, since Eternity *is* in love with Time, that energy is sent us, indeed is always present right within us, by which this freedom is attained. We must, however, first recognize the nature of our enslavement, and desire passionately, with all our heart, to be free.

4

♦

Evolution's End (1992)

Claiming the Potential of Our Intelligence

THE BACKSTORY FROM JOE

I was traveling and speaking for Siddha Yoga at that time, just living in airplanes and going from country to country. I got very ill and had to stay home. I tried finishing *Evolution's End,* but at that point I didn't have the energy for it. I couldn't walk across the room, a complete collapse of all my energy and very deep depression. I had this manuscript I'd been working on for a long time and it was a mess. I got a phone call saying that Gurumayi, the successor to Muktananda, wanted me to go on another tour. I had this huge manuscript, and I didn't know what to do with it so I sent it to Frank, a friend of mine in California. Frank owned a cable television distribution company. He had come to one of my workshops where I had ended with describing children's development and the damage television causes to children, and poor Frank was blown away. He sold his company, all of his business having to do with television. I said, "Frank, see if you can find somebody who would edit it and put it into some kind of shape because I probably won't make it back home and maybe my poor wife will have some benefit coming from the book if you would get it published." A month later I got a telegram from Frank saying that Harper had bought the book with a very large advance. Nobody had ever given me an advance like that before. By the time I got back home three months later it was in the mill with Harper and they had me slated for a nine-city book tour. Among other things they sent a copy to the distinguished professor Karl Pribram (1919–2015). I knew Karl, and he reacted to the book, saying that "it was full of half-truths and outright error." When Harper got the report from Pribram, who was a big wheel, they immediately canceled the tour. I went to see Karl, and he simply handed me his book and said, "You read this and every reference you have to all this silly nonsense about the three brains and evolution and so forth, take all that crap out and just use my outline and I will back you to the hilt."

As it turns out Karl Pribram and Paul MacLean, the famous neuroscientist whose book I had used, had been college mates and very close buddies. Pribram went to Stanford and MacLean went to the National Institutes of Health (N.I.H.), where he was the head of the whole brain department of evolution and behavior for years and years. When they asked Paul MacLean about Pribram's new book, he said, "I am a fairly well-educated person, a fairly well-read scientist. I have been in this for a long time, and I can't make heads or tails of Karl Pribram's book. I think it's really nonsense!" When Pribram heard, he wrote Paul MacLean out of his book, and never spoke to him again. That is the story of *Evolution's End*. I was carried away with the image of the evolution of the human psyche and how it's all locked right within our system and how the child's stages of development are going through those evolutionary stages along with field theory and how the brain accesses and translates nonlocal fields of intelligence and meaning.

EXCERPTS FROM *EVOLUTION'S END*

Introduction[1]

My work inspires such a variety of responses because it explores some very fundamental issues about the human mind and our development as a species:

- How our experience of the world and of ourselves forms within the "ocean of neurons" in our heads
- Why the very nature of our brain/mind leads us to "dominion over" the physical world and then beyond that world's boundaries
- Why we fail to develop and so feel victimized by the world instead
- What simple steps we can take as individuals to complete our natural development and achieve the potential nature intended

This book shows how a vague longing, which begins in our mid-teens, and our mounting personal and social problems are connected. Both result from a failure to develop our neo-cortex, or "new brain," the latest evolutionary achievement, which lies largely dormant within us.

The real thesis of this book, however, is the magnificent open-ended possibility our higher structures of brain/mind hold, the nature of their unfolding, why many of them don't unfold, and what we can do about it.

All of our perennial philosophies, spiritual paths, religions, dreams, and hopes have spun out of an intuitive knowing that these higher intelligences exist, that life is more than just an economic knee-jerk reflex, that we are not just glorified Skinner-box pigeons or naked apes. On the one hand we have divinized our potential, projecting who we are designed to be onto an abstracted cloud nine rather than fulfilling our evolutionary potential, and falling victim to the politics of that projection. On the other hand, and far more destructively, we have denied our evolutionary nature, grounding ourselves in the more primitive, physically bound modes of our brain/mind, and subjecting ourselves to the magician-priests who can best manipulate that physical realm.

Because nature builds new structures on the foundations of established ones, our huge "new brain," the one we seriously underdevelop, is built on the chassis of a quite ancient neural structure shared with all animals. This ancient chassis furnishes us with our physical experience of body and environment and has skillful drivers of its own, programmed for millions of years to maintain the physical system they inhabit.

If we develop the higher structure of our brain/mind, it

automatically integrates these lower ones into its service and employs the previous drivers to the best advantage of all.

If, however, we fail to develop the higher and just use it by default, we invariably employ its intellectual capacity in the service of our more primitive "defense" systems. This means that those ancient inflexible drivers have fragments of the new power infused into their old ways, which proves devolutionary. The new potential is lost and, to compensate, we employ the old system in nefarious ways and make awful creatures, behaving as no decent "lower" animal ever has or will.

Our personal awareness, with its ego-intellect, makes up an estimated 5 percent of the total intelligent energy of our brain/mind. (The rest provides the environment and maintains the conditions of this personal 5 percent.) Yet with this paltry percentage we try to manipulate universal forces of unknown magnitude and then wonder why everything goes wrong.

You will find a distinction in what follows between intellect and intelligence. Intelligence, found in all life-forms, strives for well-being and continuity; intellect, a human trait, strives for novelty and possibility.

Intellect is that impulse within us to solve problems, generally of its own making, and explore possibility. Intellect is evolution's gamble, and it attempts to both entice us toward and prepare us for a new realm of being. Intellect involves the brain while intelligence involves the heart. Intellect may be likened to a "masculine" side of mind, perhaps analytical, logical, linear, inclined to science, technology, the search for external novelty and invention; while intelligence is more a "feminine" side, open to the intuitive and mysterious interior of life, seeking balance, restraint, wisdom, wholeness, and the continuity and well-being of our species and earth.

A breakdown in male-female relations, epidemic among us, is a biological anomaly that has grown out of and is symbolic of the split between mind and heart in each of us. Intellect, trying to usurp nature and the wisdom of the heart for its own ends, has cut itself off from that heart. And like a child cut off from its mother, its entire development is at risk. Indeed, the mother figure is disappearing today, and an orphaned generation falls upon us. We humans do poorly without her. Matrix and guardian of our species, nurturer, source of strength and guidance for untold cycles of millennia, the mother has become the target of the male intellect, swallowed up as a dollar commodity, leaving all of us, male and female, motherless, bereft, and lost. All around us we see the breaking of the bond of heart and mind. From that of mother and infant, child and family, child and earth, young person and society, to the male-female bond upon which life itself rests, we tear at our living earth—our greater mother and life-giver—in an outward projection of our inner anxiety and rage. Should intellect win its battle with heart's intelligence, the war will be lost for all of us. We will be just an experiment that failed, evolution's end on a negative note. This book explains *how* this is so, why it *need not* be so, and how we might open to those dimensions within us as intended for us all along.

The Cerebral Universe: Idiot-Enigma[2]

Within that class of people called "idiots" there is a sub-group that used to be called idiot-geniuses, now called idiot savants, *savant* being French for "learned-one." Both terms are paradoxical since these people have an average I.Q. of 25. They are generally incapable of learning anything; few can read or write. Yet each has apparently unlimited access to a particular field of knowledge that we know they cannot have acquired. The identical twins, George and Charles, for instance, are "calendrical savants." Ask them on which date Easter will fall ten thousand years hence and immediately the answer comes, with all pertinent calendrical information such as the times of the tides and so on. Easter depends on both solar and lunar cycles and is a most difficult calculation, but George and Charles do not calculate, they simply respond to stimuli given, if that stimulus is resonant with their narrow spectrum of ability. Ask them for the date of some event before 1752, the year in which Europe shifted from Gregorian to Julian calendar systems, and their answers automatically accommodate to the appropriate system. They can range some 40,000 years in the past or future to tell you the day of the week of any date you choose. If you give them your birthdate, they can state the Thursdays on which your birth date might fall. In their spare time the brothers swap twenty-digit prime numbers, showing a parallel capacity not always found in savants. They can't add the simplest figures, however, nor can they understand what the word *formula* means. Ask them how they knew to accommodate to the change of calendrical systems in 1752 and they will be confused, since such an abstract question is beyond them as is such a term as *calendrical system.*

The twins, quite incapable of fending for themselves, have been institutionalized since age seven. Most savants are institutionalized, illiterate, uneducable, and male. (Eighty percent of all idiots are male, savant or not, which is not entirely beside the point though a separate issue.) During World War II, the British employed two mathematical savants who served essentially as computers. They were, so far as is known, infallible.

The issue with these savants is that in most cases, so far as can be observed, the savant has not acquired, could not have acquired, and is quite incapable of acquiring, the information that he so liberally dispenses. If we furnish the savant with the proper stimulus, a question about his specialty, he gives the appropriate response, but he can't furnish himself with that stimulus, can't develop the capacity as an intelligence, and can't move beyond his narrow limits.

A savant is predisposed to the intelligence of his specialty through some early infant-childhood experience that activates a "field of neurons" capable of translating from a "field of intelligence," within narrow limits. Just how this takes place is a major issue of the second section of this book. Walt Whitman furnishes us a clue to such predispositions:

> *There was a child went forth every day,*
> *And the first object he looked upon, that object he*
> *became,*

And that object became part of him for the day or
a certain part of the day,
Or for many years or stretching cycles of years.

Quantum physicists use the term *non-locality* for those organizing forces that are not "temporal-spatial," not in time-space, and this term offers a way to explain this aspect of the frequency-realm. We can't locate the potential, only our lived translation of it. Since the neural fields of our brain and the non-localized potential operate as a dynamic of resonant frequencies, our brain's neural-fields are obviously "quasi-temporal-spatial," both in and not in the time-space they give rise to. No research has been able to determine where in the brain perception actually takes place because perception isn't localizable, yet every response we make to the stimulus of awareness changes the field from which our awareness springs. Our lived experience is a dynamic between a non-localized potential and our particular localizing of that potential as our perceived time-space world.

Most creative people—scientists, artists, and spiritual geniuses agree that the Eureka! answer seems given, a grace they can only receive, not of their own doing. Gordon Gould, inventor of the laser in 1957, gives this report: "The whole thing suddenly popped into my head. . . . I was electrified. I spent the rest of the weekend writing down as much as I could and got it notarized. But the flash of insight required the prior twenty-years of work I had done in physics and optics to put all the bricks of that invention in there. . . . I think the mind is unconsciously churning away, putting all these things together like a jigsaw puzzle."

There are striking cases of simultaneous discovery of a new mathematical or scientific process occurring by unrelated people on opposite sides of the globe. The Eureka! seems to spring from a cauldron of inner ferment, a springing forth that is about the same in Einstein as the idiot savant. The savant, however, can only give information; the genius can create something new.

Translating intelligences from their potential state into our personal experience of them is what infant-child development, and indeed our entire life, is all about.

All the infant-child (and the adult as well) wants to do is what nature intended: learn and build those structures of knowledge. And all that is needed for this is an appropriate environment—being surrounded by a mature, intelligent intellect, open to mind's possibilities and tempered by heart's wisdom; recognizing that to the human all may be possible—but always asking, "Is it appropriate?"

Fields of Neurons[3]

According to research, our brain works by neural "fields"—groups of neurons operating in units. A neuron is a large brain cell that vibrates at a certain frequency and dies if this vibration ceases. It vibrates only in relay with other neurons with which it is connected through slender thread-like extensions called dendrites and axons. Dendrites meet other cell connectors at points called synapses where major exchanges of information-energy take place. In our neo-cortex, neurons are organized into fields of a million or so, relating through dendrites and axons. A single adult neuron connects with an average of ten thousand others to form such groups. The resulting networks create various forms of information-experience through exchange of frequency or "information" between neurons and fields.

Neurons don't contain information any more than the transistors or tubes of a radio contain the shows they play, nor can they store information. They "translate" potential frequencies with which they are resonant to which they have been "tuned" or keyed. Since neurons survive only as frequency patterns or vibrating units, they maintain a constant low-amplitude vibration at all times, even while we are asleep or unconscious, as do all the muscles of our body—interlocked as they are with the brain-dynamic that guides them. Like an engine idling, our neural fields are abilities ready to fire into action when called on, and they interact on levels of which we are seldom aware.

Nature's imperative, then, and her over-arching developmental rule, which has enormous consequences, is that no intelligence or ability will unfold until or unless given the appropriate model environment. Mind and environment give rise to each other through that newborn brain only if the environment is there. Even our primitive instincts require direct, close contact with the necessary corresponding environmental stimuli. We are born into the world like a garden that has been sown, but the seed must be nurtured and nourished by the appropriate environment. Further, the character, nature, and quality of the model environment determines, to an indeterminable degree, the character, nature, and quality of the intelligence unfolding in the child. That a French-speaking mama has a French-speaking child (or a German-speaking mother a German-speaking child, and so on), holds with all intelligences.

Our brain and the frequency realm it draws on are complementary, an interlocked dynamic. The nature of our cosmic soup is that every time we sample that soup, our sample itself enters into the ingredients we sample. Ours is a participatory universe; each participation enters into the possibilities for further participation, re-organizing relationships between potential fields and the brain-fields that translate them.

When we invented the automobile, a new category formed in the fields of potential. The more we use automobiles, the stronger the category becomes, as happens daily with mathematics or chemistry. As we did with the automobile, we are now doing with computers, an invention rapidly changing the whole set of our minds and shape of our society. Once set in motion any creative dynamic self-perpetuates, continually reinforced by its own output of events that dynamically feed back into their source, giving rise to a new display of the characteristics, which feeds back ad infinitum. The nature of our source is constant, its display infinitely varied. My mind maintains a steady image of my ego-self, while yet incorporating into it an inordinately complex new set of experiences, emotions, and thoughts. I have always been simply *me,* yet I realize that my five-year-old *me* and my current *me* have very little in common except that central agreement of always being *me*. . . ." These fields of potential shape us as we shape them—whether we are aware of it or not.

Mind and Matter[4]

Non-locality: in brief, under certain conditions, one particle of energy can influence measurements of another particle of energy at so remote a distance there is no possible way for a "message" to be sent from one to the other. In the same way, if we set up the proper conditions, two people in remote parts of the world can exchange information as such, when we know there is no way for a "message" to be sent. If mind and matter are two aspects of one whole, however, then the "whole" to which [physicists] Bohm and Peat refer is the "cosmic soup" itself, the nature of which should solve the enigmas of Bell's Theorem, the remote viewer, and our savant equally. The nature of that "whole" cannot, however, be a substance, thing, place, person, or god but, of necessity, only a function, a process. Since both physical matter and savant can be spun out of it, this process must unfold according to the nature of our interaction with it, our frame of reference, which then becomes our experience of the process. And that is the real and final nature of the function itself. Seeing, for instance, can be a creative act. The creative process is a dynamic that responds according to our participation with it. What we see is what we get—we can get whatever we can see, and we can learn to see in new ways.

If mind and matter are aspects of a whole, then the two fields must at some point converge. That convergence, I propose, occurs as neural fields of our brain translate such groupings of potential according to resonance. When the frequencies between neuron and potential-wave match, or can adjust and come into sync without too much trouble, then that potential actualizes. That actualization is our experience. We have a near-infinite number of neural fields available and no end of potential states to draw on.

Sooner or later, I propose, everyone will know that the neurons in his or her brain are the translating devices between this potential-wave and actualized-particle. . . . To perceive the wave is to experience its display of particles. Our act of perception translates wave into particle, our neural fields and their receiving senses are the means of that translation.

A brief layperson's explanation will provide the metaphors needed to pursue the nature of the "whole" of our mind-reality. Particles (and the universe built of them) being essentially light and variations on light, are subject to the speed of light as their ultimate limit of movement. On the other hand, the wave-fields from which they manifest are of a different state entirely, not "movement" of light but a frequency from which light itself springs—not in time-space, but the source of time-space. They are, in a word, non-localized, whereas the particles they display are localized.

Particle and wave are two different, though absolutely interdependent states as distinct as waking and dreaming. You cannot have one without the other, and you cannot have both at the same time, which is the nature of any complement.

Equally important is that even though the states are so different, what happens in time-space affects the wave-state giving rise to it, just as our being awake affects our dreaming and vice versa. So in the testing of Bell's Theorem, changing the condition of one particle group changes its wave-field, and the changed wave-field by default, instantly affects and changes its other displayed group of particles. Wave and particle are a complementary dynamic, and dynamics are a two-way affair, interchanging and interacting. There is no time lapse since the field from which the two displays are made is not in time; time is its effect. What happens in the physical world of form and time impacts the non-temporal state giving rise to that world.

A major proposal on which I base this book, one that seems to me strikingly self-evident, answers many puzzles concerning our brain and experience. The proposal, which I take as axiomatic from this point forward, is this: For our experience, neural fields of our brain are the median between wave-field and particle displayed. For us, a particle displays as we perceive it. Our perception is the particle-event "out-there" in our environment, exactly as nature designed. Our environment is the result of this "structural-coupling" between mind and its potential. That the resulting structure of our reality is an internal "self-organizing" system gives no basis at all, however, for assuming we "create" that world as it is to itself. Tree and stone in my backyard, bat in our church belfry: each is its own display, each its own dynamic drawing on, spinning out of, feeding back into the cosmic soup. As Nobel laureate and chemist Ilya Prigogine (1917–2003) observed, "Whatever we call reality, it is revealed to us only through the active construction in which we participate." The issue is not just a reality, but what is revealed to us.

A clear insight into the workings of our mind and reality has been offered for decades now by physicist David Bohm (if not a sage, as close to one as the scientific community can offer). In 1957, he published a work called *Causality and Chance in Modern Physics,* which, according to many, should have won him a Nobel Prize. His point of view established in that work led to his theory of the "holomovement," in which he describes the force giving rise to our reality as a conscious intelligence that can be expressed as matter or energy. He carries the well-worn paradox of the wave-particle dynamic into one of universal proportions, which he terms the "implicate and explicate" orders of energy.

According to David Bohm, the vast universe stretching out from us at every hand is but a "mere ripple on the surface" of the creative power inherent within the supra-quantum state. Creative energy is an unbroken holomovement resonating from a single source, though it is expressed as fields springing forth endlessly, giving rise to infinite expressions. Because of the indivisible nature of this energy, any of its "displays" (such as you and me) is at some point the totality of its order of energy, and of logical necessity, one with the unity of the whole; William Blake expressed this in his line "to see the world in a grain of sand."

Eastern philosophers have claimed that each of us contains the whole of creation within us. Thus in Kashmir Shaivism, an ancient psychology-cosmology, we find a striking parallel to quantum physics and Bohm's holomovement. In Kashmir Shaivism, the metaphors are not mathematical but stem from a "human metric." This theory states that all creation springs from a singular pulse of vibratory energy called a Spanda, which is the initial creative pulsation expressed by a non-moving point of consciousness termed The Self. The Self simply witnesses the moving creative energy springing forth from the Spanda. An even larger series of interweaving vibrations unfold, which eventually articulate as matter, a final irreducible state of contracted but stable energy. This creative power (the Kundalini Shakti in Sanskrit) radiates from that Spanda, the initial pulse of infinite energy, down to the gross finite world. For each of us, as a subtle energy wave stretching from the base of the spine to the top of the head at the fontanels, all of creation takes place therein.

The frame of reference through which we attempt to understand function determines the nature of what that function is for us.

Fields of Intelligence[5]

The more complex a brain structure and the more complete its development, the greater the portion of the soup it can access and experience. A portion of this soup source powers the worm in our flower bed through the few neural ganglia needed to do his worm thing, or bird on the wing to experience its world of delight. The source is both personal and universal; the process in my head draws on the same source as yours and all other forms.

Our lived experience grows out of and feeds back into the source, which changes continually, accommodating to our responses as we must then accommodate to our source's corresponding change. A wise man stated, some two millennia ago, "What you loosen on earth is loosened in heaven, and what is loosened in heaven is loosened on earth." "Heaven" is a metaphor for the cosmic soup, the frequency realm on which our brain draws for our lived experience, "earth" is that lived experience itself. Heaven and earth mirror each other yet are distinct, perfect complements as described in Humberto Maturana and Francisco Varela's "structural-coupling" between mind and environment.

This dynamic of complementarity underlies all creation, whether seen as structural-coupling, reaping-sowing, or quantum wave-particle. Inorganic forms such as stones cannot participate in the dynamics giving rise to them. Random collisions of atoms and molecules will eventually wear them away, their particles incorporating into other forms, participating in evolution in a slow, random way. Organic life enters into the dynamic of that wave-particle and speeds things up, at the cost of a stone's stability. The more complex that organic life is—starting with organic chemical molecules, moving on to microbes, and ending with such as you and me—the more complex are the wave-fields involved and the interactions possible between wave and particle. Unlike a stone, we humans can enter into and play with the dynamics creating us, but this open possibility is gained at the cost of permanence and stability.

Our brain encompasses myriad fields, specific constellates of neurons that can translate any number of fields of wave-potential into "particle form" or particularized experience, mixing these in an infinite number of ways.

Just as the particular frequency picked up by our television receiver determines what we experience on the screen, the wave-fields or frequencies, to which our neural structures of brain are tuned, determine the nature of what we perceive as our physical, intellectual, and emotional reality, the reality of our thought and awareness.

The "history" or expression of our individual experience feeds back into the general fields giving rise to that experience. Instant by instant we reap what we sow, individually and collectively.

Each field is a "unity" in that its potential holds all experience of a like order that manifests as the field's ongoing variable-diversity; this diversity interacts with that unified field from which it arises, changing that field's potential without changing its nature.

Triune Brain: The Mind of Three Brains[6]

When simple cells join . . . they exhibit organizing forces, in new
directions, which were impossible by any of the individual cells.

LUTHER BURBANK

All new Fields embrace lower-level morphic units that [already]
existed. . . . New patterns . . . contain the old within them.

RUPERT SHELDRAKE

When the higher flows into the lower it transforms the nature
of the lower into that of the higher.

MEISTER ECKHART

We have three distinctly different neural structures within what we once thought was a singular brain. Paul MacLean and his medical associates at the National Institutes of Health's laboratory of brain evolution and behavior derived this description of neural systems through a synthesis of research from their own and other major centers, such as those headed by Karl Pribram and brain surgeon Wilder Penfield (1891–1976). These three structures in our skulls represent the major neural systems developed throughout evolutionary history, through which we inherit all accomplishments that preceded and led to us, plus, may I add, a quantum leap of additional potential we have not yet developed.

MacLean calls these three structures of the reptilian, old mammalian, and new mammalian brains, in order of evolutionary appearance and placement in us. . . . This triune system demonstrates how nature builds her new and more complex structures on the foundations of previous structures. . . . The three are designed to act vertically as well, as an integrated unit.

These characteristics summarize the evolution of behavior itself, and exactly parallel the stages of child development. The reptilian brain, or R-system as MacLean calls it, encompasses our sensory-motor system and all physical processes that give us our wake state awareness in a body and world.

Incorporated into service of our two higher brains, the R-system gives us our explicate order. Nestled above it is our emotional or "old-mammalian" brain. This structure, with help from the temporal lobes and possibly other parts of the newest cortex, is called our emotional brain or limbic system (from *limb,* meaning "to wrap around").

All the crude instincts of the reptilian system are transformed into more flexible and intelligent forms of behavior when incorporated into this higher system. That simple reptilian aversion-attraction response, for instance, is elevated to a complex of "feeling-tones" that spin out a vast web of like-dislike, good-bad, angry-happy, sorrow-joy, love-hate polarities.

Here too is an intuitive intelligence to move for the well-being of the self, offspring, and species. . . . This emotional brain, or limbic system, maintains all relationships such as our immune system and our body's capacity for healing itself. Here lies the seat of all emotional bonds, from that of mother-infant, child-family, child-society, the foundational pair-bond of male-female, and so on. It is involved in dreaming, visions of our inner world, subtle-intuitive experiences, and even the daydreams and fantasies spinning out of its upper neighbor, the neo-cortex. This middle emotional system ties the three brains into a unit, or directs the attention of any one to the other as needed.

The third and highest member, our neo-cortex or new brain, is five times bigger than its two lower neighbors combined and provides intellect, creative thinking, computing, and, if developed, sympathy, empathy, compassion, love. Here we reflect on reports from those two lower neighbors concerning our life in the world and our emotional responses to that world. Here we scheme, figure ways to try to predict and control our environment of world and people; brood on our mortality and galloping morbidity; spin out poems of other climes and days; experience worlds within or beyond; hammer out restrictive laws for the behavior of others; invent religions and philosophies, pondering the destinies of man.

This highest brain can, if developed, access causality itself; through that potential we can radically alter those lower orders and alter the very nature of the environment given by our two primary systems.

Through this three-way, or "triune-brain," connection, those more primary instincts and intelligences take on a profoundly different character and have, as well, the intellect of our highest brain at their disposal in emergencies. Through operational development, which we will discuss later, our highest "causal brain" can also act on its patterning of those two lower systems and change them to varying extents, even, as Mircea Eliade* put it, "intervening in the ontological constructs of our universe." Our lower order intelligences become refined when incorporated into service of our neo-cortex.

If we get stuck in a defensive posture and focus the higher system on the needs of the lower, the bulk of that higher system must simply idle along until the coast is clear. If the emergency (or rage) persists, as in chronic anxiety or paranoia, that highest system can actually atrophy since so little of it is needed by or adaptable to serving our lower system. Thus we find highly anxious, insecure children at risk intellectually, and paranoid adults operating on minimals of intellectual power, subject to serious errors of judgment. . . . Were it not for our sensory-motor brain we could not speak or write. Were it not for our limbic system we could not communicate. Were it not for our highest evolutionary brain, we could not think as we do.

This growing belief that we use, at best, no more than 10 percent of our highest brain is contested by many neuro-scientists, and there is little way to test for it. Our mistake is in considering "use" rather than development.

In summary, our reptilian system registers physical experience but has no access to the formative fields giving rise to such experience. Our limbic brain, on the other hand, can access those formative implicate

---

*[Mircea Eliade (1907–1986) was a Romanian historian of religion, fiction writer, philosopher, and professor at the University of Chicago. He was a leading interpreter of religious experience, who established paradigms in religious studies that persist to this day. One of his most influential contributions to religious studies was his theory of Eternal Return, which holds that myths and rituals do not simply commemorate hierophanies, but, at least to the minds of the religious, actually participate in them. —*Ed.*]

fields of relationship and greatly expand on or alter the patterning of our physical body-world. It can't, however, access those causal fields that underlie everything; this is the job of the neo-cortex, which employs or interacts with the primary frequencies that cause the show. Through our access to these casual fields and the various hybrids between pure causation and implicate ordering, we can analyze any image or experiential formation taking place, intuitively sense the form-fields before they concretize, and intervene in our reality over a wide range.

The triune brain displays our universe, created within, projected without, and we enter into that creation, identify with it, lose ourselves to it, and become subject to it. Both fascinated and terrified, we plunge through it looking, till strength fails us, for some point of peace of mind or permanence. Since by its nature the vibratory universe unfolds in keeping with our movement, we perceive this as chaos or order depending on our state of mind, while the silent point of origin we seek, the Spanda and our Self silently witnessing it all, lies, of course, only within.

Images of Wake and Dream[7]

Our ordinary reality is, like our dream world, a "construction" the brain must make, and reality-construction calls on our totality of experience.

The Australian Aborigine lived in a state they called dreamtime, a perfect balance between implicate and explicate orders. (A few still do.) Their worldview was quite different from ours, leading to different capacities, perceptions, and ways of reasoning. The Kalahari !Kung also employ a state of consciousness different from ours, and can do things most of us in the West can't, such as heal serious wounds, sit in the middle of roaring fires, and other unlikely things. Carlos Castaneda's many volumes about his mentor, don Juan, hinge around a dream-state that our ordinary logic does not hold. The state is held by its own logical set, its "rule," which is also the way to get to that state (as is the case with fully developed yogis). The result is a non-temporal-spatial reality that gives a valid lived experience. Since this is an effect created from a subtle-causal dynamic it is a higher evolutionary achievement than our subtle-physical one. Apparently it hasn't been developed by enough people over a long enough period of time, and so is unstable, easily overwhelmed by the far more stable behaviors locked into our R-system with its ancient habituated, rock-like grounding.

In my earlier books I cited Charles Tart's research in mutual hypnosis, a phenomenon I now see in a new light. Two of Tart's graduate assistants, a young man and woman, were skilled in giving large-scale tests for hypnotic susceptibility and proved, as well, to be good hypnotic subjects themselves (a rare combination).

The man used the image of a golden rope ladder, which the woman could climb to the highest hypnotic state. When she reported herself at that high point, he suggested she find herself on a beautiful beach, and, from that position, put him into the same state. On gaining the same hypnotic height the pair found themselves together on a magnificent beach, with a champagne ocean, crystal rocks, and heavenly choirs singing overhead. The experience was both majestic and, again, fully tactile: they could taste, touch, smell, and hear as they could in everyday life. All such experiences were stable; phenomena did not shift, as such things do in dreams. (Either party could later go into self-induced hypnosis and find that beach intact, exactly as they had left it; something that can't be done with self-induced hypnotic dreams or ordinary visual-imagery.) On one occasion, they turned toward each other unexpectedly, occupied the same physical space, and their personal identities merged, each perceived his or her self as their combined personalities. This was unnerving. The man insisted on leaving the state and counting-down to normal. Tart conducted a series of these ventures; the woman eventually became quite at ease in her creative world-making while the experiments unnerved the man so severely he withdrew from the research. He could no longer grant himself consensus about what was real; the "non-ordinary reality" mutually created and shared had exactly the same tactile-sensory quality as their everyday experience.

No matter where imagery is finally placed, the inner or outer world, or in between, image-production is singular and draws selectively on every aspect of our brain, body, and mind.

"When the soul wishes to experience something," Meister Eckhart said, "she simply throws out an image, and enters into it." This throwing out is utterly simple as given us, awesomely complex when analyzed.

Sight [8]

When French writer, philosopher, and professor Jacques Lusseyran was eight years old, his eyes were completely destroyed by an accident at his school. When the boy's bandages were removed, his parents informed him that he had entered into a new kind of life, and that he must keep them informed of every discovery he would make in his new world. Children live in an open-acceptancy at that age, and within two weeks the first great event took place, his reports were ecstatic: the light he thought he had lost came flooding back in. But, and this was the far greater discovery, the light was within him. "All my life," he reported, "I have seen only the light reflected off of things. Now I can see light as it is directly." The light within, brilliant, awesome, and numinous, was a state as well as an experience; the light without was pale by comparison.

Then color came back, in a pristine, direct radiance of intense clarity unknown before; green was pure green, rather than the varied but weaker reflections of it off objects. Soon he could perceive the general presence of objects by a combination of his overall body-sensing and the subtle differences within the state of light itself. While he still couldn't run and play with other children, he never again bumped into objects and hurt himself as did most newly blind.

He found, further, that at the slightest hint of anger, irritation, sadness, or self-pity, the light within him dimmed. If he persisted in a negative thought, the light went out. Only then was he truly blind, which was terrifying. He quickly learned, from sheer necessity and direct feedback, to rule out negative thought. My meditation teacher once said, "No thought would dare enter my head unless invited." Would we be so mentally lazy and indulgent if we were to lose our sight at every negative thought?

Carl Jung spoke of the child living in the unconscious of the parent. The parent's implicit beliefs and expectations are decisive factors in the formation of the child's world-self-view, even when not spoken or expressed in any way.

Two centuries ago, William Blake claimed that he did not see with his eyes but looked through them as a pane of glass; we should learn to see creatively, he said, using active rather than passive vision. About thirty years ago the scientific community found that our eyes cannot convey light to our brain. The retina does not "collect light waves" and send them to visual receptors in our brain. Vision is a construction of the brain that we see with the help of our eyes when it refers to the outer world.

Research people claim that images are a primary part of thought. We think through imagery. Even congenitally blind people think in images.

Consider the scope of the self-fulfilling prophecies given children during those infinitely open years when the constructions of knowledge bring forth a world that is at its peak.

Sound[9]

French physician Alfred Tomatis found the labyrinthine nucleus of the inner ear's cochlea system, a principle congregating point for all our senses. Every neural process passes through or relates to this inner-ear complex. The ear is neurologically involved with the optic nerve (the second cranial nerve), the oculomotor (third cranial nerve), and the various cranial nerves involved in movement. All channel through the vestibular labyrinth of the cochlea, deep in the inner ear. Eye, head, and neck mobility have traditionally been associated with the optic nerve, but Tomaris found these functional structures under the control of the acoustic nerve . . . a major mechanism of reception and integration of perception.

By my participation in my world I place myself in the world that forms around my point of placement.

A rough sketch of the self-organizing nature of our brain, shows our sensory web to be our universe with ourselves at its center. . . . We are urged to recognize that the world everyone sees is not *the* world, but a world that we bring forth with others, a world that will be different only if we live differently.

States of Mind: Body to Match [10]

Hypnotists touch a hypnotized subject with a stick, tell him it's a hot poker, and he experiences a burn and raises a blister. Hypnotic suggestion depends on "concrete" language formed in childhood, where the word for a thing and the thing-as-itself are a single neural pattern. This language is retained by the right hemisphere of the brain, which, you may recall, has closer connections with the limbic system than the left, and can thus act on those limbic-R-system interactions giving rise to our physical experience. The left hemisphere, with its abstract logic and semantic language can, through the right hemisphere's direct connection with the limbic-R-systems, act on the named things in our primary world structure and change the dynamics between cause and effect, bringing about our physical experience. In post-hypnotic suggestion the hypnotist tells the subject they will experience the burn an hour later and they do. . . . We can ask, where was the blister during that hour?

Just as imagination is the ability to create images not present to the sensory system, phenomena that is not "present to the senses" can be created by our self-organizing structure, particularly private experiences such as in Tart's experiments or general hypnosis. When the creation is only within our own self-system, no universal fields have to be involved.

Once my meditation teacher told me to spend half my time in morning meditation sitting in the conventional cross-legged position, the other half lying flat on my back. The next morning, I dutifully sat as usual and then stretched out flat. Without warning or any of the usual transitions into an altered state, I felt myself rise out of my physical body and for a long period simply "lay" some six inches above it, my emotions, self-awareness, and senses intact so far as I could tell. I could hear my physical body breathing and feel my body heat coming up from beneath me; I was weightless, couldn't move about, had no blissful experiences, found the state uneventful, and wondered why I didn't travel to other realms as my friend Robert Monroe did. This happened for five straight mornings, however, and I finally got the message my teacher had intended for me: I knew that my self-sense was not limited to this body, and my subtle body was a very real experience, independent of context. My teacher later explained that one couldn't move into other realms in that subtle body until it was integrated into the "causal body." Only the causal system, he said, has the power to move our awareness beyond the physical.

New York University's Robert Becker studies electro-magnetic fields and claims that our body is a conglomerate of them, as is the body of our world.

One morning in meditation I experienced a "sphere of energy" resonating out of myself in vibratory waves extending about a foot, arching over and back into me. I perceived that this energy was my own consciousness "broadcast" out and coming back as my physical reception of what was being sent—my felt-perception feeding back into and becoming part of the arching "broadcast." All of this I knew to be the moving, vibrant power of creation itself. I could feel the power with my body and embraced its outer arc with my arms. I experienced it as an overwhelming love holding me in a cocoon-like vortex that constituted my universe. I knew that all creation unfolded within this cocoon. The screen of the world out there was the screen of my own mind and was out-there by virtue of this on-going dynamic. I knew that it was this cocoon of power to which Eckhart referred when he said the soul "throws out images to enter into." What is being "thrown out" is our universe itself.

Developing Our Knowledge of the World:
Heart-Mind Bonding[11]

Research on the heart is now where brain research was decades ago, but already our concepts concerning it are seriously challenged.

Our heart apparently plays a major if fragile role in our overall consciousness. Transmitters, which play such a critical role in neural behavior, have now been found in the heart and are connected in some way with the brain. Actions in the heart precede the actions of both body and brain. A key dynamic between heart and brain is centered in the limbic system. Years ago John and Beatrice Lacey, doing research for the National Institute of Mental Health, reported that our brain sends a running report of our environmental situation to the heart, and the heart exhorts the brain to make a proper response. We know now that the heart does more than exhort; it controls and governs brain action through hormonal, transmitter, and possibly finer quantum energies of communication.

Here, then, is the source of that intelligence, which keeps our diversity of body parts in functional wholeness, the "wisdom of the body" to which Harvard Medical School physiologist Walter Bradford Cannon (1871–1945) referred: a vital, yet primitive, cellular, chemical-hormonal kind of heart-intelligence that, through the limbic structure, maintains the integration and proper balance of the three parts of our triune brain and all body functions. The reason the heart can govern these physical processes is, I purpose, because it translates from its own non-localized "field of intelligence" just as the brain does.

Those heart cells communicate through their mutually non-localized base of relationship, a field of intelligence that is a larger, more universal, non-physical "heart"—creative consciousness as itself.

Two closely bonded people often share information across time-space, to which we attach occultist labels of various sorts, while all the time it is only true biology, the logic of our life system, the language of the heart. And, just as our physical heart maintains our body, the non-localized intelligence governing the heart in turn maintains synchrony with a universal "consciousness at large." So we have both a physical heart and a higher "universal heart," and our access to the latter is, as in all development, dramatically contingent on the development of the former. Just as the intelligences drawn on by the brain lead to specific abilities, the heart draws on the supra-implicate order and the realm of insight-intelligence. These higher orders don't articulate as specifics, but as a general movement for the well-being and balance of the overall operations of the brain-mind-body.

The three major stages of life are heart-centered in this sense: (1) the development of a heart-mind synchrony needed for physical life and observed in the various "Piagetian" stages; (2) a later "post-adolescent" development, which synchronizes the developed physical self and the creative process; and (3) a final "highest heart," which moves us beyond all physical-emotional systems. Two poles of experience lie within us, our unique, individual self-generating through the brain; and a universal, impersonal intelligence generating through the heart. The success of human life depends on the development of this heart-mind dialogue, in this complementary dynamic each profoundly affects the other and both are developmental. Since nature's model imperative always holds, even a supreme intelligence must undergo development within us if we are to access and benefit from it. Unfortunately, no academic concept or nurturing model-environment is provided for a "heart's intelligence," making our ignorance of it a dismal and crippling fact.

My meditation teacher once said, "You must develop your intellect to its highest possible extent, in order for it to be a proper instrument for the intelligence of the heart, but, only the intelligence of the heart can develop intellect to its highest level." This describes what evolution is about and what our personal evolution must be, an issue that we will clarify as we examine development itself. But again, remember that the intelligence of the heart must itself be developed, and it does so through the conventional methods nature employs, according to the nature of the models provided. Given the appropriate environment, that intelligence will flower; without it the heart will function on a straight cellular, hormonal level maintaining life only on a "reptilian-mammalian level."

Saints and sages have always claimed that the true seat of the mind is in the heart. In 1932 an American Indian medicine man told Carl Jung that white men, with their wrinkled faces and constant anger, were insane and killed so wantonly because they thought in their heads. Whole people, he explained, think in their hearts.

Intelligence is the ability to function for our well-being, a capacity not a content. Just as a multi-cellular organism has incorporated the single cell into its higher evolutionary possibility, intelligence is designed to incorporate intellect into its service. To do this, that intellect must first be developed. The intelligence of the heart must not only be developed as itself, it must in turn have something to "operate on," something to respond to. Without a brain system to function in synchrony, the universal intelligence of the heart is stillborn.

Since all intelligences are coded to unfold within nature's timetable, intellect opens on target whether an intelligence of the heart has developed or not (just as sexuality unfolds at puberty whether we are ready for it or not). And therein lies the problem. The dynamic of the heart and brain is the dynamic of intelligence and intellect, the principle dynamic on which our life is based. If we develop intellect and fail to develop intelligence we are then subject to a novelty-seeking mind that operates without regard to our own or others' well-being. Anything is possible to us, but what is appropriate.

Play[12]

Play is the foundation of creative intelligence, but, like any intelligence, it must be developed in keeping with nature's model-imperative, the child who is played with will learn to play. The child who is not played with will be unable to play and will be at risk on every level. One of the foundations of play is storytelling. Even before they can speak, infants will listen raptly to adults speaking or telling stories. Understanding the words is almost incidental in the beginning; it's the sound of those syllables that fascinates. In his memoirs one gentleman recounted how as a toddler he loved to snuggle into his grandfather's lap and listen to him read the great philosophers, lofty words that predisposed that young mind toward higher things.

Time-honored children's tales are equally vital to the child's development. The child listens to the storyteller with total entrainment; he grows still, his jaw drops, his eyes widen, and he stares fixedly at the speaker. His vision, however, turns within where the action is, for the words of a story stimulate the creation of corresponding internal images. A little girl told me she liked radio more than television because the pictures were so much more beautiful. The radio words gave the stimulus; the beautiful pictures were her own creation. This imaging is the foundation of future symbolic and metaphoric thought, concrete and formal operational thinking, higher mathematics, science, philosophy, everything we consider higher mentation or education.

Recent research suggests that all thinking involves imagery. The dream world the early child lives in is a hybrid between the transitional implicate order and the explicate order of her or his environment. The limbic system, on which all this centers, must adapt and transfer physical signals to the neo-cortex as well as interpret and transfer its concepts back to the R-system. For example, written symbols, such as those used in alphabets and mathematics, are perceived only as physical images, contrasts of dark and light, chalk on a blackboard, print on paper, by the R-system. To be *conceptualized* and meaningful, these perceptions must be transferred to the neo-cortex. The translator and transference medium is the limbic system.

The foundation of this metaphoric-symbolic capacity is the principal task of early childhood and is established through play. In this, storytelling plays a major role; the spoken word has played a vital role since the child was in the womb. At the appropriate time and place the right words stimulate the brain to create a corresponding flow of images. This creative act is an enormous challenge to the brain and involves virtually every neural field; this is why young children seem "catatonic" while listening. The entrainment needed for this flow of images is so total that no energy is left over for anything else. After age five or so, children become more active listeners because their capacity to create images in this fashion has developed well enough to operate on much less energy. Since each new story requires an entirely new sequence of neural field interactions, children want to hear the same story over and over again, not to "learn" it—most children remember a story after one hearing—but because repetition causes the interweaving neural fields involved in the image-flow of each story to myelinate. Each new story requires an entirely new set of connections and new fields of response. Thus, the more stories and their repetitions, the more neural fields and connections between them are brought into play. The stronger and more powerful conceptualization, imagination, and attentiveness become, while the scope and flexibility of neural capacities in general increases. (Waldorf schools wisely repeat all stories a half dozen or more times, or even "live with" a story for days before moving to another.)

Once the imagery fields of a new story have stabilized, children, no longer embedded in the action, can stand back from this function and take charge, as in the cycle of competence. They are ready to reverse the process: take the internal image-flow of their own making, and overlay it on an appropriate external stimulus. They want to modulate their outer world with an inner image, a first step toward creation itself. (And think how early this begins.) We tell our toddler the story of "The Three Bears" over and over as she sits glassy eyed and still. One day, however, we sit down to dinner, and our little bear says, "Oh, it's too hot," pushing away her "porridge." "We must go for a walk in the forest." And she insists that we take part in her play, leaving the table and going for a walk, real or pretend. Or, following the story of "The Three Pigs," a knock at the door elicits, "Oh, it's the big, bad wolf. Run and hide." Each of us becomes the target of imagery overlay, taking our part in the outer casting of her internal production.

She has created an inner world around the story, extracted its essence, and applied it to a different situation. This completes the dynamic. Her outer play feeds its concretization back into her creative world. Her implicate has been made explicate. "Inner world" means the limbic-neo-cortical dynamic, "outer world" means the limbic-R-system dynamic. In play the R-system responds to orders coming from higher upstream—patterns that will integrate the triune system and ego-self—and through such actions she learns that her own thought and imagination can make a difference in her world.

Each and every form of play is an exercise in metaphoric-symbolic thinking, the foundation of all literacy and higher learning. As abstract mathematical formulas such as $E=MC^2$ has no meaning at all in itself. We "see" what something stands for only if we can manipulate that imagery on a mental level. Metaphor and symbol can operate vertically and laterally, linking the three realms of mind or operating within any of them individually. Metaphor can be in the service of the causal level, building lateral connections between geometrical-archetypal images, as in the imagery in Dante's *Paradiso*. Symbolism in its highest sense usually has a causal aspect and can become one with a numinous source—that is, participate in creation.

After age seven, stories shift, as does play. Animals are just animals to the middle child, and they want stories of animal and human relations. Stories of magic, mystery, and extraordinary people are equally powerful, and the child plays at being the fantasy figure or acting out the hero model. To a child, reality is whatever one makes of it. At age nine, with a battered old cowboy hat, a homemade six-shooter sawed out of a wood shingle with a split spool for a cylinder, and a gun holster made from a scrap of old car seat leather tied about my waist, I was transformed into the likes of Buck Jones or Tom Mix, the cowboy giants of the screen before whom I sat in awe and wonder on those Saturday afternoons when I had been lucky enough during the week to earn the huge ten cent admission.

Competitive team games have nothing to do with middle child play. Everyone wins in child play, and, as Bruno Bettelheim has made clear, no child *should* ever have to lose. All the middle child learns from losing is to be a loser. Winning and losing appear spontaneously later and serve different functions.

This play of the eleven- and twelve-year-old is based on one overriding principle: self-restraint. The wide-open possibilities of the middle child give way to the constricted, rule-ridden organizations of the late child because puberty looms ahead: adolescence, leading to becoming a functional member of society; sexuality, with its possibility of becoming the parent—responsibilities requiring maximum self-restraint.

At age eleven we can no longer afford the luxury of anything and everything being possible. The open parameters of childhood close to the disciplines of formal operations: learning the "body of knowledge" of one's culture, the selective, disciplined learnings we call higher education. Nature prepares us for this through childhood play, which enables us to enter the next phase with excitement and joy.

Play's End[13]

[*Note: Evolution's End* was written during the late 1980s and published in 1992, fifteen years before the first so-called smart phone arrived in 2007. All the issues Joe describes regarding the impact of screen technologies apply equally to computers and mobile devices, even more so given the designed interweaving of the child's personal identity implicit in social media now carried by the child everywhere he or she goes along with the forced and pervasive use of these technologies in early childhood education.]

Play develops intelligence, integrates our triune nature, prepares us for higher education, creative thought, and taking part in and upholding a social structure, helps us prepare for becoming an effective parent when that time comes. Play is the very force of society and civilization, and a breakdown in ability to play will reflect in a breakdown of society. We are a tough, resilient species; our capacity to compensate for damage is enormous. Our children could compensate for hospital childbirth and the ensuing separation anxiety of day care and its abandonment, but children can't compensate beyond a point, and we went beyond that point years ago. Some ten years after we began to systematically separate infants from mothers in hospitals, eliminating bonding and breaking down development of the limbic-heart dynamic, we introduced television. The major damage of television has little to do with content: its damage is neurological, and it has, indeed, damaged us, perhaps beyond repair.

First, television replaced storytelling in most homes, and it changed the radio from a storyteller to a music box. When television is criticized, its apologists point to similar warnings made when radio burst on the scene early in the twentieth century, but radio as an endless storyteller sparked the imagination of and helped give rise to a generation whose creativity changed the face of the earth (for better or worse). Television, on the other hand, has now been with us far longer than radio was before television's introduction, and its programming has deteriorated at an astonishing rate for the same reasons that it damages us.

Television also replaced family conversation in general. The TV tray replaced the dinner table and its captivating table talk. Carol Gilligan points out that grandmothers used to sit and relate their childhood stories to a rapt audience of grandchildren. That remarkable series of books by Laura Ingalls Wilder grew out of her parents and grandparents "telling their stories." Gilligan saw this as a primary need that grandmothers had (a recapitulation that rounded out their lives), but grandmother tales filled many needs: they provided continuity between generations, gave children a sense of history, and established a continuum of meaning to life. I heard both my grandmothers' and grandfathers' stories either directly or indirectly through my parents. And I knew my mother's childhood, as I did my father's, by their reminiscing, which would hold us spellbound on a winter's evening or at the table. . . . We knew who we were and where we came from, our lives had significance, drama, meaning. "Tell me about when you were a little boy," my daughter begs, and never tires of listening (even to my repetitions and elaborations).

Second, with television on the scene, parents rarely played with children. All sat around the box, and even playing among siblings disappeared. Thus no capacity for play and its internal imaging developed. Nintendo does not and cannot replace imaginative play.

Third, and perhaps most critical, television floods the infant-child brain with images at the very time his or her brain is supposed to learn to make images from within. Storytelling feeds into the infant-child a stimulus that brings about a response of image making that involves every aspect of our triune system. Television feeds both stimulus *and* response into that infant-child brain, as a single paired effect, and therein lies the danger. Television floods the brain with a counterfeit of the response the brain is supposed to learn to make to the stimuli of words or music. As a result, much structural coupling between mind and environment is eliminated; few metaphoric images develop; few higher cortical areas of the brain are called into play; few, if any, symbolic structures develop. $E=MC^2$ will be just marks on paper, for there will be no metaphoric ability to transfer those symbols to the neocortex for conceptualization, and subsequently, no development of its main purpose—symbolic conceptual systems.

An equally insidious effect is habituation—the natural condition of our two animal brains with their hardwired response to "concrete information." Unable to adapt to novelty, these primitive systems avoid it. They seek out compatible stimuli and feel "comfortable" with familiar input unless moved by the novelty seeking of the neo-cortex. Recall how a new story told to a child ties up a majority of the neural fields and locks in all three systems to create a flow of new imagery matching the new stimuli. Repetition brings myelination and stabilizes the creative action. That imagery pattern becomes an integral part of the neural system and is then played out on the external world, part of the general reference maps called on in an expanding world. Note that each new story requires a whole new set of patterns to accommodate the new stimuli, requiring entrainment of all three brains over and over. The brain is challenged anew and continually enlarges the number of neural fields involved in new image-pattern flows.

Television, as a source of paired image and sound, can be assimilated by a single set of neural fields. The same neural field, initially worked out to handle such a paired stimuli-source, fires in and that singular field responds. Note that we *habituate to television within a few minutes of viewing*—from the very first exposure on—since no creative response to such stimuli need or can be made. That response is already part of the stimuli coming in. This means, in effect, that those six thousand hours of television the average child in the United States sees by age five might as well have been all one program.

Recently groups of five- and six-year-olds were shown a number of regular television shows designed for their age group. For this experiment, the sound tracks were switched so that the sound did not match the imagery on any of the programs. The children did not recognize the discrepancy. The reason is that the brain habituates to the single source of stimuli; primary autonomous processes take over at any repetition of that stimulus, regardless of its apparent variety. So the nature of the stimuli, the program, is beside the point, and so much for the wonderful information and learning programs often proposed for those six thousand hours.

Habituation also pacifies the brain, puts it to sleep, since the stimulus includes the brain's own response and so demands almost no output of energy from the brain, while it occupies the mind so that no other stimuli are sought. This again indicates that habituation is a primary reptilian response. Paul MacLean shows that the R-system takes over all learned physical patterns of the neo-cortex. Once the R-system can handle a source economically, it doesn't need to carry the signals higher. With the rapid turnover of imagery, the apparent novelty of the programming fools the novelty seeking aspect of the neo-cortex. Combined with the habituation, we have difficulty turning away even when we hate the program playing.

Failing to develop imagery means no imagination. This is far more serious than not being able to daydream. It means children who can't "see" what the mathematical symbol or the semantic words mean, nor the chemical formulae, nor the concept of civilization as we know it.

They can't comprehend the subtleties of our Constitution or Bill of Rights and are seriously (and rightly) bored by abstractions of this sort. They can sense only what is immediately bombarding their physical system and are restless and ill-at-ease without such bombardment. Being sensory deprived they initiate stimulus through constant movement or intensely verbal interaction with each other, which is often mistaken for precocity but is actually a verbal hyperactivity filling the gaps of the habituated bombardments.

The average child in the United States sees six thousand hours of television by their fifth year, at which point, in the midst of what should be the high point of their dreamlike world of play, we put them in school, prevent bodily movement (most purposive learning is sensory-motor at this age), and demand they handle highly abstract-symbolic systems (alphabets and numbers) for which most of them have no neural structures at all. Driven by nature to follow their models, they try and can't. Their self-esteem collapses and failure and guilt give rise to anger. Even after beginning school, they continue their time-percentage of television viewing unabated. They spend more hours looking at television than attending school, and our national daily viewing time grows year by year.

Having no inner imaging capacity leaves most the brain unemployed, and a child who can't imagine not only can't learn but has no hope in general: He or she can't "imagine" an inner scenario to replace the outer one, so feels victimized by the environment. A recent study showed that unimaginative children are far more prone to violence than imaginative children, because they can't imagine an alternative when direct sensory information is threatening, insulting, unpleasant, or unrewarding. They lash out against unpleasantness in typical R-system defensiveness, while the imaginative child can imagine an alternative, that is, create images not present to the sensory-system that offer a way out. True playing is the ability to play with one's reality. Thus imagination gives resiliency, flexibility, endurance, and the capacity to forego immediate reward on behalf of long-term strategies.

Forty years ago, along with the epidemic of daycare and television, a new phenomenon burst on the American scene: the toy store. Until that time, the average American child had a maximum of some five toys. I can recall each of mine; they were precious. Christmas, the only time we ever got a toy, was a time of near unbearable excitement. My Flexible Flyer sled was secondhand, but lasted my whole childhood. My Radio Flyer wagon was new when I got it and lasted from my fifth year until my twelfth year as a major item. My Rollfast skates were new and lasted until my fourteenth year. I used them hard. (A new pair cost 79 cents, no small sum.) I bought, for $2.87, my bicycle at age eleven, an ancient relic for which I saved for two years, and it lasted till I left home at fourteen. I never heard the word bored until I was in the armed service in World War II. I never knew a bored child in my own childhood. There was far too much to do, yet we had only a few toys.

When today's toddler sees her mother making cookies and wants to take part, she need not resort to jar top, stick, and mud, like some primitive. She probably has a complete miniature kitchen, scale-model perfect with battery-operated appliances. When a five-year-old sees the road-roller he doesn't need to find an old spool: The massive toy industry provides a complete road-roller, exact in detail, battery powered so that the child can watch passively as he does when the same item is advertised on television. Children are inundated with objects that don't stand for something but already are. A clothespin need not be draped with an old rag to make a doll; our daughters have shelves bulging with dolls of every description—life-like, sexy, indeed complete with all the organs for real precocious sophistication if you like. Where is the metaphoric-symbolic learning or the dreamworld of play-acting the adult?

The electronic toy does everything at the push of a button that itself habituates. Boredom sets in immediately; what's next? Even playing with such objects children often merely act out the images advertised on television. When they identify with the television children playing with the same toy they feel some group authenticity, a belonging not found elsewhere. Television, of course, is the way to sell those toys that then represent the television images flooding the young brain, reinforcing the television stimulus when that stimulus is absent.

The 30 percent or so of our children still capable of learning in school have been read to and played with by their parents, generally in addition to television and mountains of plastic junk. This shows how little attention is needed to nourish the brain and get its creativity going. While the screen itself prevents neural development, its content affects behavior. By 1963 studies had shown a direct one-for-one correspondence between the content of television and behavior. Violence on television produces violent behavior in young people. Everyone knows that. Once one has habituated to violence as a way of life, however, anything less is boring. There are sixteen acts of violence per hour on children's programming, only eight per hour on adults'. By the time our children become teenagers, they have seen an estimated 18,000 violent murders on television, their primary criteria for what is "real." Life is shown to be expendable and cheap, yet we condemn them for acting violently.

One final point that needs mention in this parade of intellectual interference with the intelligence of childhood is minor but has its effect too. I have discussed how play in the pre-puberty and early adolescent period centered around the concept of *us*, group action, and the need for self-constraint on behalf of us, the team, club, or organization. My concern here is over our sandlot football, baseball, and street games. Sometime after World War II, society suddenly had no room for children, our quiet childhood streets filled with speeding autos, many new communities had no sidewalks; yards were status symbols, and children's play was relegated to playgrounds with professional playground supervisors. Child safety became a paramount concern. Supervised play replaced child play. Adult rules, regulations, and decisions began to replace our passionately defended personal criteria and judgments.

The high point of this adult intrusion on childhood is centered in Little League. Gone were the choosing up of sides, the striving for fairness, arguing the rules and infringements, the heated hammering out of decisions. Everything was managed by adults. They created the teams and provided the uniforms, which of course soon carried advertisements of "sponsors," adults made the rules and regulations and enforced them; adults called the shots, children stood, grim-faced and serious while parents on the sidelines shouted invectives for victory at all costs. This new child carried the team, sponsor, parents, and social image on his or her shoulders into victory or defeat. Insidiously, Little League targeted younger and younger children, until even the little tots were dutifully marching out in full advertising array to do battle with the enemy. Whatever might have been left of play after television was killed by Little League and other organized sports leagues, substituting a deadly serious adult form of win-or-lose competition for what had been true play. Gone are the invaluable social learnings, self-restraint, and ability to decide.

There are many other facets to the current collapse of childhood. I have touched on the issue only briefly, but one thing is clear, our schools have deteriorated because they must deal with damaged goods. Most responsible for this damage is hospital childbirth; second comes television. Next comes daycare, which fosters television and is a result of hospital childbirth. Premature schooling runs fourth. And as our damaged children grow up and become the parents and teachers, damage will be the norm, the way of life. We will habituate to damage. Nothing else will be known. How can you miss something you can't even recognize, something you never had?

Formal Operations[14]
[*Note:* Formal operational thinking, the ability of the mind to operate on and change information in its own brain is the first stage of causal thinking. The thrust of the biological plan during this period is for the mind-brain to become its own source of possibility. Through formal operations, the mind can experience information and perceptions from its own creative thought alone. Out of its vast pool of knowledge, the brain can then create its own stimuli and experience perceptions from

its own abstract conceptions. Thus, suggestibility will eventually be phased out as a tool.]

Around age eleven some momentous events take place: the brain releases a chemical that dissolves all unmyelinated neural fields, removing 80 percent of the brain mass available at age six. Formal operations begin that, in turn, depend on a semantic language that unfolds parallel to it.

Just as concrete language participated in physical object-events, semantic language participates in thought. A word can now be an intermediary between ourselves and our own thought and can allow us to look at it objectively. From this we develop a self-awareness through which we can see others' points of view, stand in their shoes as it were. Even greater, through this way of thinking we can discover levels of awareness beyond physical reality.

Our capacity to grasp and describe abstract concepts or states of mind, can, if we receive the right stimulus and guidance, be the very instrument to lead us beyond our natural "embeddedment" in word thoughts. The quiet mind, free of "roof-brain chatter," is rare since it comes with a high level of maturity.

Intellect, a variable of intelligence, undergoes its greatest development now and can detach from and then dominate the physical intelligences leading to it. If developed, we can intellectually modulate our earlier animal emotions and be a bit more reasonable, humane, and civilized. Fully developed, intellect can move us beyond our embeddedment in all the structures of knowledge built up to this point.

With an abstract, semantic language we can create thoughts "out of the blue," thoughts that arise from the act of thinking, rather than from response to objects themselves. Walking on beds of fire is a concrete operation, but the idea originated in our ancient past from a formal operation of mind. Fire in itself could never suggest that it's not burning. We can extract information out of context and operate on it with self-created ideas that are discrete and self-referring, rather than balanced within a larger frame of reference.

At age eleven, an intelligence opens that can, if developed, stand outside this capacity and operate and change the structures of thought. . . . Formal operations, incorporating concrete operations into their service, could bring us dominion over the physical world so that we could use that world as our launching platform to go beyond it. We get caught up, however, in using the capacity only to dominate our world and so lose sight of anything more. Formal operations can lead us to causality and give us our foothold in creation, a way of becoming one with creative intelligence. This process alone can integrate us and our intellect into a higher form of well-being and counter the destructive tendencies of an immature intellect.

At age eleven, when nature cleans house by dissolving all unmyelinated neural connections, she clears the decks for a much more refined and apparently restricted but more powerful level of operation. Yet, loss of 80 percent of our neural mass is disturbing because we end up, neurologically, with what we had at age one. Overproduction is nature's way, but such a massive neural loss is not; the only other comparable losses are immediately replaced by brain growth spurts. This loss is a culturally induced phenomenon, both the direct result and direct cause of our dysfunction and cultural disease. Perhaps such a loss has long taken place, indicating an ongoing failure to become what evolution intends, which is all the more reason to look for a way beyond. The causes of our breakdown, technological childbirth and day care, for example, become self-replicating fields of potential, rapidly taken for granted, with the resulting fear, anger, and general helplessness accepted as our natural condition. The causes of our grief become our frames of reference.

For whatever reasons, we enter into our formal operational stage with 20 percent of the neural structures available four years before. And that 20 percent was almost surely established before age seven, with only minor elaborations added thereafter. Instead of building new structures of knowledge during the intuitive and concrete operational stage, the child seems to only expand on earlier learning, filling in the gaps. No learning that demanded new neural structures *could have been* introduced during this middle period or we would not end up with the "neural weight" we started with in infancy. Surely there is a general "tightening up" of neural fields, eliminating redundant connections, making greater use of remaining ones, as happens in maturation. In no way, however, can this account for an 80-percent reduction, but rather the opposite. Nature wouldn't add huge volumes of neural mass only to help tighten up and make more efficient the fields already in operation. Neither of the growth spurts at ages four and six produced very much. Surely our worldview is far more sophisticated by age eleven, but with no more neural circuits than we had when we entered early sensory-motor development. The implication is that we added nothing significant beyond physical-sensory emotional experience and left the higher system largely dormant.

I presented recent research suggesting we develop only a fraction of our neo-cortical potential. The prefrontal lobes are a very recent evolutionary addition and are the last to be developed in children. Researchers suggest that our intellect is developed for and devoted to manipulating our physical environment. Even science, no matter how rarefied its mathematics and hypotheses, is oriented to strictly physical processes. The character and nature of everything taught to us between seven and eleven (and indeed beyond) directly relates to our consensual world of outer objects, events, and processes, for which we already had made our constructions of knowledge *by* age seven. Since the unquestioned assumptions of our culture has been that no dynamic exists between mind and environment, every aspect of that learning from age seven to eleven could, as a result, be assimilated to previously developed neural patterns, those of our concrete thinking.

Jean Piaget was intrigued with the discontinuities between each of the child's stages of growth in the first fifteen years. Each new stage opens capacities beyond those of the previous stage. Although in retrospect we can see clearly how everything in a previous stage prepares for the next, no period in itself suggests the powers to come. Nothing in the first four years would in any way explain intuition; nothing in the first seven years suggests the stunning capacity of operational thinking;

concrete operations in no way suggests the richness of formal operations. These discontinuous leaps, each one opening new vistas of possibility beyond the reach of its predecessors, follow a king of Richter scale exponential increase. If we started with the infant mind, compared it with each successive stage computing corresponding increases in ability all the way to adulthood, and then computed on a like increase beyond, we might gain some indication of the power inherent in us. The nature of such a new form of intelligence couldn't be known other than by being it, and nothing we are doing now indicates the nature of such a quantum leap of creative being. Even if we had models to demonstrate it, who could grasp what was offered? A four-year-old can't understand the law of conservation, nor an eight-year-old formal operations, nor the average adult anything of post-operations. As William Blake observed, cups can't "conceive beyond their capaciousness."

Our current use of intellect is proving destructive to our life and planet and creating problems, which that intellect is hopelessly incapable of solving. Since the higher transforms the nature of the lower into that of the higher, it should be obvious that the intelligence inherent in our undeveloped neo-cortex is one that would incorporate and use this astonishing intellect of ours, transforming it automatically in the process, leading us to a lifestyle in which our current problems would not exist. Intellect, driven by novelty, asks only, "Is it possible?" Intelligence, driving for our well-being and fulfillment, asks, "Is it appropriate?" A fully developed and integrated intellect could not, by its nature, make any move that was not for the well-being of self, society, and world. We would, by the very nature of our minds, be incapable of even considering dumping 100 million tons of violently toxic chemical waste on our own nest, or spend enough on armaments in one day to adequately feed the seven million or so children who starve to death each year.

Access to the Field [15]

There are two main paths to the witness state—that of Eastern meditation or Christian contemplation. They are structurally parallel but texturally quite different. Bernadette Roberts* achieved the highest state through the contemplative path and experienced nothing similar to accounts of Eastern saints. She points out that we can only enter this journey from a "frame of reference," a path, or means for accessing the goal. Yet, Roberts also points out that the goal toward which we move must always, of necessity, fall outside any frame itself. Our goal lies beyond our "cosmic egg," yet only from a cosmic egg can we find the crack that leads to the goal.

The frame of reference becomes its own field perpetuating itself, and, while the rewards of the relationships unfolding can be immense, the goal of evolution can be lost. "I must create a system of my own," cried poet Blake, "or be enslaved by another man's."

Those who break through the "fast-binding" of a system are generally suspect within their own tradition. Nothing so upsets the bishop as the rumor of a saint in his parish. William Blake, having no sectarian ties, was considered mad by his social peers. Jesus broke with his frame of reference and so literally outlawed himself in the eyes of his society and was hung as a common criminal. Bernadette Roberts, as her predecessors Eckhart and John of the Cross, inadvertently broke with her Catholic frame of reference in order to fulfill her longing, but she fulfilled that Catholic frame in so doing. We would have no Eckhart, John, or Bernadette Roberts were it not for their Catholic frame though each of them had to struggle with and go beyond that frame to fully express it.

For centuries people have foolishly speculated on "where" Jesus went to "learn" all his tricks. Everything is within each of us, and, if conditions are right, our perfection "throws out an image" and invites us to enter, each according to some destiny over which we have neither control nor the slightest notion of where it leads. "He" or "it," evolution herself, is continually trying to break through into our human psyche. Evolution's end was clearly articulated at the first instant of creation.

---

*Bernadette Roberts (1931–1917) was a former Carmelite nun and contemporary Christian mystic.

The end was in the beginning and has already taken place in that non-temporal realm. But the workings-out in time of evolution's intent is another matter, subject to any number of random factors including the whims of our individual egos and wills.

Evolution's intent gives no guarantees, no resting place to "lay one's head" since the goal is in an unknowing. . . . The statement: "God cannot turn out to be anything other than your own self" represents different aspects of our journey. First is that we are each a definition of God, a definition that could come only "after this creation." God in this sense has no other definition than us—for or to us—so we find him only within. The field of compatible-variables is both never changed by its variables, yet, having no being except through such variables, the field infinitely reflects each variable equally. The question of God and our relation to him has arisen in our minds throughout the ages, but in fact we are God asking that question, the creation has given rise to this capacity to question itself; we are the only way by which such a question could arise; and we are the only answer to that question only we can ask, the real payoff of the novelty factor built into us. And God will "exist" for us to the extent of our definition, and we define God according to the nature and character of our models.

As Blake said, anything possible to be believed is an image of truth. Truth is function, not a thing, idea, event, or semantic slogan. Truth is how the creation works. Understand function and you are home free. The opposite of truth is delusion, the non-functional.

So even this rug, the union of individual and God, will be pulled out from under us sooner or later. A further stage will open. We will have to leave the safe harbor of even this highest knowing, since, as Eckhart put it, all known things must be left behind. Only then will we express evolution's end that was in its beginning, which is the opening of a new evolution.

5

◆

The Biology of Transcendence (2002)

A Blueprint of the Human Spirit

[*Note:* Each year Joe spent months exploring Eastern meditation practices: Siddha Yoga, Kundalini Shakti, Vedanta, and Kashmir Shaivism in retreats in India. Here his meditation teacher Muktananda described how the energy of the heart was universal and connected us to universal fields of meaning of a completely different order than our personal thoughts, intellect, and conditioning. A century earlier Rudolph Steiner declared how the human heart is much more than a pump, that the entire body is electrified, something evolutionary scientist and geneticist Mae-Wan Ho explored, referring to the liquid crystal structure of the water in each cell. During the years after publishing *Evolution's End,* these themes exploded in Joe's mind. Often he traveled to California to meet with the founders and researchers at HeartMath, an organization born out of a deep sense of caring for people and our planet. Founded in 1991 by Doc Childre, HeartMath developed a system of tools and technologies to bridge the intuitive connection between heart and mind and deepen connections with the hearts of others.]

THE BACKSTORY

Each successive book was an attempt to correct or improve the previous, and to push forward, and more deeply, into new challenges. Completing one book naturally flowed into beginning the next. During this time the *intelligence of the heart* and the *heart-brain connection* became the focus of Joe's lectures. What we call human consciousness is a symphony, with multiple intelligences singing their unique songs together. In *The Crack in the Cosmic Egg,* the causal-creative nature of mind or spirit entered into the ontological creation of our physical reality. In *Bond of Power,* the model imperative took center stage where both physical and telepathic modeling opened new possibilities for evolution's ever-present journey forward. *Magical Child* often focused on the failure of the model and how this created a strange-loop with impaired inner capacity being reflected in the outer society and culture. In *Evolution's End,* we discovered how access to universal fields of meaning can inspire and inform. Now, the universal energy of the heart is center stage in Joe's life. He insisted that, rather than abstracted mind being our salvation, transcendence is the very center and central force of life itself. Vast capacity is innate, but always, development is the challenge, and development demands a model.

Like fraternity drinking buddies, a generation apart, Joe and I would share long conversations driving from airports to engagements. Physicist Fritjof Capra and the Center for EcoLiteracy, a nonprofit organization dedicated to education for sustainable living, hosted an invitational symposium in Berkeley, California, with twenty international experts—educators, computer scientists, and media experts—on the use of computers in early childhood, at a time when Silicon Valley was pushing trainloads of technology on schools. Joe was invited, and I tagged along. The event was memorable for several reasons. After previewing all the latest "educational programs" for children, Joe wept. He understood, no matter how many times *Sesame Street's* flashing screens appeared, the screens themselves were dead and that dead screens would increasingly suck the life out of millions of children.

That is, after all, the model imperative. After several informative and passionate days, it was agreed by all that the less screen time, up to age eleven, the better.

After age eleven, let them have it. Why age eleven? At approximately age eleven, nature assumes the developing brain has encountered all the models in the natural environment. Hormones are released that dissolve the unmyelinated neurons in the brain, a process called neural pruning, bringing the house to a new and more effect order. But wait, what if, instead of living models, the brain is drenched in dead counterfeit images that displace lived experiences, what kind of brain is left?

After the symposium an admirer of Joe's, who worked for a state senator, arranged for Joe to speak to California legislators, again at a time when the state was considering investing millions in early childhood educational technologies. Of course, Joe shared the findings of the international symposium. Several days later the colleague who invited Joe to speak to the legislators was terminated.

All Joe's works imply and involve modeling, and modeling is the true heart of education, real education, not conditioning. Intellect, as wonderful as it is, is crippled when informed by the other intelligences when those intelligences are malnourished or, worse, not acknowledged, opened, or developed. The essential key to human development, and our survival, is not in abstractions but rather in the full and rich understanding of the transcendent spirt that radiates every cell of our body. From the beginning of our life, the characteristics of each new possibility must be demonstrated for us by someone, some thing, or an event in our immediate environment. . . .

Machines and machine-learning systems can calculate much faster and more accurately than the human brain. What machines cannot do is experience empathy, altruism, compassion, to feel directly that the human body is itself an interdependent ecology, entangled with all other life forms; machines cannot live in beauty, be guided and inspired by innate curiosity and wonder. No machine can model these intrinsic states and we know that as intimately as we feel the blood flowing in our veins. The transcendent spirit of our own biology is the key.

M.M.

EXCERPTS FROM *THE BIOLOGY OF TRANSCENDENCE*

Introduction[1]

"The ability to rise and go beyond" is the definition of *transcendence* and the subject explored in the following pages. While this force constitutes our nature and fires our spirit, an honest exploration of it must contend with this counter question: Why, with a history so rich in noble ideals and lofty philosophies that reach for the transcendent, do we exhibit such abominable behaviors? Our violence toward ourselves and the planet is an issue that overshadows and makes a mockery of all our high aspirations.

Sat Prem, a French writer transplanted to India following World War II, recently asked this question: "Why, after thousands of years and meditation, has human nature not changed one iota?" In the same vein, this book asks why, after two thousand years of Bible quoting, proselytizing, praying, hymn singing, cathedral building, witch burning, and missionizing has civilization grown more violent and efficient in mass murder? In exploring the issue of transcendence, we explore by default the issue of our violence. The two are intertwined.

Neither our violence nor our transcendence is a moral or ethical matter of religion, but rather an issue of biology. We actually contain a built-in ability to rise above restriction, incapacity, or limitation and, as a result of this ability, possess a vital adaptive spirit that we have not yet fully accessed. While this ability can lead us to transcendence, paradoxically it can lead also to violence; our longing for transcendence arises from our intuitive sensing of this adaptive potential and our violence arises from our failure to develop it.

Perennially our pleas to cloud nine go unheeded, our struggles against principalities and powers are in vain, and we wander in a self-made hall of mirrors, overwhelmed by inaccessible reflections of our own mind. Handed down through millennia, our mythical and religious projections take on a life of their own as cultural counterfeits of transcendence.

Culture has been defined by anthropologists as a collection of learned survival strategies passed on to our young through teaching and modeling. We will explore how culture as a body of learned survival strategies shapes our biology and how biology in turn shapes culture. Religious institutions, cloaked as survival strategies for our minds or soul, are the pseudo-sacred handmaidens of culture brought about through our projections of the transcendent aspects of our nature. Thus this trinity of myth, religion, and culture is both the cause and source of our projections. Each element of the trinity brings the other into being and all three interlocking phenomena—myth, religion, and culture— are sustained by the violence they generate within us.

That we are shaped by the culture we create makes it difficult to see that our culture is what must be transcended, which means we must rise above our notions and techniques of survival itself, if we are to survive: thus the paradox that only as we lose our life do we find it.

A new breed of biologists and neuroscientists have revealed why we behave in so paradoxical a manner that we continually say one thing, feel something else, and act from an impulse different from either of these.

A major clue to our conflict is the discovery by these new scientists that we have five different neural structures, or brains, within us. These five systems, four of them housed in our head, represent the whole evolution of life preceding us: reptilian, old mammalian, and human.

As long intuited by poet and saint, the fifth brain in our system lies not in our head, but in our heart, a hard biological fact (to give the devil of science his due) that was unavailable to the pre-scientific world. Neurocardiology, a new field of medical research, has discovered in our heart a major brain center that functions in dynamic with the fourfold brain in our head. Outside our conscious awareness this heart-head dynamic reflects, determines, and affects the very nature of our resulting awareness even as it is, in turn, profoundly affected.

From this background I make two proposals here that are necessarily hypothetical. First, the crux of our ever-present crisis hinges on failure to develop and employ both the fourth and newest brain in our head (one added quite recently in evolutionary history) and its dynamic interactions with our heart-brain. Second, the great saints and spiritual giants of history (even though overlaid with myth and fantasy by cultural counterfeits) point toward, represent, or manifest for us our next evolutionary step, a transcendent event that nature has been trying to unfold for millennia.

From the beginning of our life, the characteristics of each new possibility must be demonstrated for us by someone, some thing, or an event in our immediate environment—but the same chicken-egg paradox will always emerge if we try to determine or bring closure to the riddle of an origin.

This need for a model is acutely the case with a new and unknown form of intelligence such as that offered by our fourth brain and heart-brain. The striking contrast between our ordinary human behavior and the actions of the great beings of our history (Jesus, Krishna, Lao-tzu, Buddha, Eckhart, George Fox, Peace Pilgrim, and a long line of like geniuses) is what makes these figures stand out in time, even shifting or warping history itself.

In every case, however, rather than developing the capacities these great models of history have demonstrated, humankind has projected both the capacities and the image of the models demonstrating them. That is, we invariably build religions around our spiritual giants or use them to support a religion in order to avoid the radical shift of mind and disruption of culture these rare people bring about, shifts we interpret, ironically, as threats to our survival and thus instinctively reject. Bio-culture effects, once initiated, tend to self-generate. Projected by us, we perceive the behaviors demonstrated by our great models as powers out there to which we are subject, rather than as potentials within ourselves to be lived.

As model of a new evolutionary intelligence, Jesus met and continually meets a grim fate at the hands of this cultural effect. But the cross, the

182 ♦ The Biology of Transcendence

instrument of his execution, symbolizes both death and transcendence for us—our death to culture and our transcendence beyond it. If we lift the symbol of the cross from its mythical shroud of state-religion and biblical fairy tale—which is to say, if we can rescue Jesus from the Christians— then the cross proves to be the "crack" in our cultural cosmic egg.

It is toward this crack that this book points, as did my first book half a century ago. May this new one throw more light and help us to open ourselves to nature's new mind, wherein lies our true survival.

Evolution's Latest—The Prefrontal Lobes[2]

Immediately behind the ridge of our brow lies the prefrontal cortex (the prefrontal lobes), the largest and apparently most recent of brain additions. Behind the prefrontals lies the rest of our neo-cortex. While our reptilian brain has modules or parts that are hundreds of millions of years old, indications are that only about 40,000 years have passed since our prefrontal lobes appeared in their present size and with their current significance.

Neuroscientists have a variety of viewpoints on this comparatively new portion of our neural system, which was once called "the silent area" of the brain because its function was largely unknown and no activity was indicated there. Paul MacLean considered the prefrontals a fourth evolutionary system, however, and called them the "angel lobes," attributing to them our "higher human virtues" of love, compassion, empathy, and understanding, as well as our advanced intellectual skills. Neuroscientist Antonio Damasio considers prefrontal function the source of all higher intellectual capacities such as our abilities to compute and reason, analyze, think creatively, and so on.

The Stages of Prefrontal Development[3]

Significantly, the prefrontals unfold for development in two stages I refer to as primary (meaning early) and secondary (meaning late). Primary prefrontal growth and usage develops rapidly after birth, in parallel with the rest of our brain. At about age fifteen the majority of the threefold brain completes its development and stabilizes. Only then does the secondary stage of prefrontal growth begin, opening with a major growth spurt, or outpouring of new neural material. Because it was discovered only recently—in the late 1980s—this aspect of development has not yet been acknowledged on a broad academic level.

It is this secondary stage of prefrontal growth, about which we are only beginning to learn, that relates to the two roads we as humans may take—both the path of violence and the path of transcendence.

Primary Prefrontal Development and the Orbito-Frontal Loop [4]

In their early primary stage, then, the prefrontals unfold not so much from their own inherent capacity for development, as the older brain systems do, but more through their influence on the unfolding of these earlier evolutionary systems. The prefrontal lobes parallel the growth of the other systems because they have an important task at hand. Their main objective at this time is to govern each module or lobe of the three-fold brain in its sequential unfolding in such a way that each older system forms according to the needs of the prefrontals in their secondary stage of development during the child's mid-adolescence. The task of the prefrontals is to turn the unruly reptilian brain, old mammalian brain, and neo-cortex into one civilized mind that it may access later. It is only when this has occurred that the secondary prefrontal stage can unfold as designed.

All primary and secondary prefrontal functions having to do with our relationships and our control of the R-system instincts (survival, protection, sexual drives, appetites, and so on) center on the orbito-frontal link with the emotional-cognitive brain. And further, the "affective tone," or emotional state, experienced by the toddler during the exploratory period after age one determines the nature of the orbito-frontal loop and its ability to function. Psychologist Allan Schore explains why it is that a toddler's emotional state during this time of world exploration determines whether or not the orbito-frontal connection is established and used or largely lost: He describes how the orbito-frontal linkage is entwined with the care a toddler receives and how this, in turn, determines the lifelong shape and character of that child's worldview, mind-set, sense of self, impulse, control, and ability to relate to others. With this explanation in mind, it's impossible to overestimate the importance of the orbito-frontal function.

Other Stages of Brain Growth Development during Primary Prefrontal Development[5]

Beyond the growth that leads to the development of the orbito-frontal loop, a number of other neural growth spurts occur in other parts of our brain at birth, age one, age four, and age seven, with additional shifts of function taking place age ages nine and eleven. These shifts coincide with the developmental stages of childhood called "windows of opportunity," during which particular blueprints for intelligences and abilities unfold relative to the neural modules or parts of the brain ready for development at those times.

In "building" a child's brain and corresponding capacities, each window of opportunity closes as the next one opens in its appropriate evolutionary sequence—though perhaps it's more accurate to say that a developmental stage doesn't close so much as the energy and attention of growth simply shift to the next module or portion of the blueprint waiting to be read and made real. According to this pattern, our neural structures are printed and ready for stimulus and response in their sequential evolutionary order. At each shift from one developmental period to the next, the child's energy and attention also shift, looking for that next window of opportunity.

The Role of Experience in Prefrontal Development[6]

All of this sequential development takes place in our first fifteen years of life as preparation for the mid-adolescent prefrontal growth spurt that allows us to rise and go beyond the limitations, constraints, and shortcomings of the earlier neural system.

Miss one sequence and the entire structure is at risk. Try putting a roof on a house with no walls, or framing walls with no foundation! To do her part in making certain no step is missed or shortchanged; nature provides us with genetic blueprints, but only as bare outlines for possibility and action. It might be assumed that these generic blueprints within a child will suffice as the stimuli for neural development. Those genes, however, must be stimulated by the child's interaction with the actual expression of the capacities they imply at the time when those capacities within the child are ready for development. This is why one infant or child can't model for another. Someone who is fully able to do something or behave in a certain way must perform the role of model if a similar ability is to be awakened in that child.

If, however, a child's environment does not furnish the appropriate stimuli needed to activate prefrontal neurons—the model imperative has not been fulfilled—the prefrontals can't develop as designed. Their cellular growth itself becomes compromised and faulty.

Overall, nature's blueprint unfolds regardless of the success or failure of any individual stage of development. If the window of opportunity offered by a particular stage is missed, she blithely opens the next one on schedule as though all were well. Despite the fact that each stage of development depends on the success of the previous one for its own success, the stages keep coming. Nature's schedule, not our response, is at the controls. She doesn't call a time-out if a child's nurturing environment fails to respond to his needs.

Neuropsychologist Elkhonon Goldberg refers to the prefrontal cortex as giving us our civilized mind. At least, we are given the chance to develop civility through the prefrontals, and it is this civility that is a prerequisite for the development of our capacity to transcend, to fill our role in evolution as well as curb our suicidal violence, and to survive.

Secondary Prefrontal Development[7]

Each major stage of development offers a window of opportunity distinctly different from anything that has come before. When a higher neural form in our brain completes its growth and begins its full function, a new form of reality and a larger world unfold to us and distinctly new behaviors and abilities fill our repertoire. As we grow from birth to age twenty-one, the strength and complexity of these stages increases exponentially. The fifteen-year-old brain is as different from that of a five-year-old as are the body sizes and behaviors of the two. Logically we could expect that on the completion and maturation of nature's latest, largest, and highest brain at age twenty-one, we would possess capacities more dramatically different from and more powerful than anything previously experienced. . . . But, in fact, nothing much happens at all.

The Missing Stage[8]

In 1988, Oxford University Press published an intriguing work edited by physicists C. N. Alexander and E. J. Langer titled *Higher Stages of Human Development: Adult Growth Beyond Formal Operations.* Even though this work was compiled before discovery of the late-prefrontal growth spurt, two items stand out in relation to what we now understand about this developmental stage. First, the editors showed how the increase of intelligence at each stage of development is disproportionately greater than the increase exhibited in the previous stage, similar to the order of increase found in the Richter scale for measuring earthquakes. Thus the intelligence increases in the stage designed to open at late adolescence is an order of magnitude vastly beyond that of the previous stage, suggesting an intelligence in no way related to anything coming before. Adding up all experience and knowledge gained to that point gives no hint of the possibilities ready to unfold somewhere around age twenty-one. A similarly massive gain in intelligence can be found when the six- to seven-year-old shifts into operational thought.

Second, as each developmental stage offers a more advanced intelligence, a significantly smaller percentage of our populace achieves that stage. The more advanced the intelligence that unfolds through evolutionary process, the fewer the people who develop it.

For most twenty-one-year olds, when the infrastructure of evolution's newest brain is complete and the neural form is ready for full functioning, nothing seems to happen that is in any way commensurate with the newness, size, and long, drawn-out formation of the complete prefrontal cortex.

On the contrary, evolution's latest neural addition seems to lie largely dormant within us despite the fact that it seems it should offer a discontinuously new potential, a new reality—a whole new mind. The primary prefrontal function, formed in the earliest years, continues, but there is little to indicate an evolutionary shift of function and behavior, or revolutionary change in life, as can be rightfully expected.

A Trinity of Great Expectations[9]

Consider three characteristics of adolescence: a poignant and passionate idealism arises in early puberty, followed by an equally passionate expectation in the mid-teens that "something tremendous is supposed to happen" and finally by the teenager's boundless, exuberant belief in "the hidden greatness within me." A teenager often gestures toward his or her heart when speaking of these three sensibilities, for the heart is involved in what should take place. Recall what Eckhart said: "There is no being except in a mode of being." The teenager's gesture toward the heart when expressing these great expectations shows that the heart is involved in these feelings and thoughts.

The brain is the heart's modus operandi, or means, for transcendent experience, and nature intends this highest stage to be ready to unfold fully at twenty-one. Development of this new stage would be life-long if that stage were to unfold. Rudolf Steiner* clearly describes these higher stages, pointing to age thirty, for instance, as the time of another step toward transcendence.

Operating to this mature developmental sequence is the adolescent's great expectation. We might think the intelligence of the heart is present all the time and permeates all being, but the heart's latent capacity for deep universal intelligence must, like the brain, be provided with models

---

*[Rudolf Steiner (1861–1925) was a philosopher, social reformer, architect, esotericist, and clairvoyant. —Ed.]

for its full growth and development. If no nurturing or modeling is given, the powers of the heart can't unfold—they will be dormant for life.

A Dialogue between Brain and Heart[10]

Over many years of research under grants from the National Institutes of Health, John and Beatrice Lacey traced the neurological connections between the brain and the heart. Their discovery of these connections and the ongoing heart-brain dialogue was largely ignored by academic science. Today the new field of neurocardiology has verified and validated the Laceys' work, which means that, in time, acceptance will follow.

The heart certainly has an intelligence, though this calls for a new definition of the word to differentiate it from cerebral intellect. The heart's intelligence is not verbal or linear or digital, as is the intellect in our head, but rather is a holistic capability that responds in the interest of well-being and continuity, sending to the brain's emotional system an intuitive prompt for appropriate behavior. Intellect, however, can function independently from the heart—that is, without intelligence—and can take over the circuitry and block our heart's more subtle signals.

The following, then, is a sketchy summary of the hypotheses regarding the heart-brain-body dynamic:

1. The heart's electromagnetic field is holographic and draws selectively on the frequencies of the world, our solar system, and whatever is beyond.

2. Through glial action, our neural system selectively draws the materials needed for world-structuring from electromagnetic fields as coordinated by and through the heart.

3. Our emotional-cognitive brain makes moment-by-moment qualitative evaluations of our experience of the resulting world structure, some of which we initiate in our high cortical areas and others of which form automatically and instinctually in the old mammalian brain.

4. Our emotional-cognitive brain has direct, unmediated neural

connections with the heart. Through these neural connections the positive and negative signals of our response to our present moment are sent to the heart moment by moment.

5. The heart's neural system has no structures for perceiving or analyzing the context, nature, details, or logic of our emotional reports. Thus, the heart can't judge the validity of or reason for these reports and responds to them as basic facts. The heart responds on all levels: electromagnetically, through the unmediated neural connections to the limbic brain, and through neural connections to a myriad of body functions. Additional responses include hormonal shifts between the heart and the body and the heart and the brain, and perhaps shifts on sound and thermal levels. In response to a negative signal, the frequency realm of the heart drops from coherent to incoherent. This is a survival maneuver that opens the heart spectrum to an indefinite or variable state. In this fluid situation our body, brain, and heart can respond in new ways to an emergency, if the old survival responses initiated by our lower brain systems are insufficient.

6. When the heart makes such an adaptive shift, suspending its stable norm, our perception changes accordingly. The world we see and experience in a state of fear, rage, dire emergency, competition, or struggles is quite different from that which we experience in a state of harmony and love.

7. During an initially negative response, our brain shifts from the slower reflective intellect of the frontal lobes and neo-cortex to the quickly reflective reptilian brain and its links with the emotional-cognitive brain's survival memories and maneuvers. This shift from forebrain to hindbrain is not voluntary or within our awareness—it just happens and always appears as logical, practical, common sense.

8. The dialogue between our heart and brain is an interactive dynamic where each pole of our experience, heart and brain, gives rise to and shapes the other to an indeterminable extent.

No cause-effect relationship can be implied in such an organic, stochastic, and infinitely contingent process. This mirroring is another vital example of the creator-created dynamic.

Evolution and Devolution Again[11]

Our potential can't be utilized and our dilemma can't be resolved by either intellect or moral and ethical effort alone (if at all). But we have within us this other link, the three-way connection among our emotional-cognitive brain, our prefrontal lobes, and our heart. Here in this connection lies our hope and transcendence—if we can break from the madding crowd. Through understanding and using our heart's intelligence along with our brain's intellect we can resolve our dilemma. Whatever language or rationale it might take, our task is to discover—or rediscover—these two potentials, align them, and come into transcendent dominion over our life.

Fields within Fields: Of Frequencies and Neurons[12]

Our heart participates in electromagnetic fields within fields nested in hierarchies that are holographic, the whole existing within any part, and all functioning as an integrated dynamic. Mae-Wan Ho, Ph.D., a reader in biology at the Open University in England, studies the coherence inherent in each living creature. "[B]ased on empirical findings from our own laboratory, as well as from established laboratories around the world," she writes, "the most suggestive evidence for the coherence of the organism is our discovery, in 1993, that all living organisms are liquid crystalline."

Coherence, in this context, refers to the fact that the trillions of cells and the myriad parts comprising them function together as a unit to produce the mysterious, unified, and magnificent whole called *me.* I must remind myself, as a layperson, and my reader as well, that by this word *organism* biologist Mae-Wan Ho means me, this person sitting here at this keyboard, and you, there reading, and that we are not just specimens of research material on the microscope's slide but are, in fact, what all this research is about.

Mae-Wan Ho continues:

> In the breathtaking color images we generated, one can see that the activities of the organisms are fully coordinated in a continuum from the macroscopic to the molecular. The organism is coherent beyond our wildest dreams. Every part is in communication with every other part through a dynamic, tunable, responsive, liquid crystalline medium that pervades the whole body, from organs and tissues to the interior of every cell. Liquid crystallinity gives organisms their characteristic flexibility, exquisite sensitivity and responsiveness, thus optimizing the rapid intercommunication that enables the organism to function as a coherent whole.[13]

When coherent, this polyglot of flesh, blood, sweat, and tears has dominion over the world, naming animals and stars, the parts of our own innards and atoms, and is the source of poetry and song. Mae-Wan Ho observes:

> The visible body just happens to be where the wave function of the organism is most dense. Invisible quantum waves are spreading out from each of us and permeating into all other organisms. At the same time, each of us has the waves of every other organism entangled within our own make-up. . . . We are participants in the creation drama that is constantly unfolding. We are constantly co-creating and re-creating ourselves and other organisms in the universe, shaping our common futures, making our dreams come true, and realizing our potentials and ideals. [14]

A radio receiver is a critical part of the radio world—without a receiver the rest of a broadcasting system is worthless. The receiver alone gives those invisible waves their being throughout that broadcast field. But the receiver is neither the sending station nor the field itself. The same is as true in the labyrinths of our brain-mind as in the world of radio. A field effect might be registered by a particular brain-body receiver, producing a corresponding experience, but that brain-body, while one of an infinite number of possible loci, is not then *the* locus, genesis, or possessor of that field.

"Not I but the Father within me does these things," said Jesus of his miracles. But without Jesus, there is no Father and there are no miracles. "Without me, God is helpless," was Eckhart's audacious claim.

The Anatomy of Evil: Why Nature's Plan Breaks Down[15]

One of Paul MacLean's most valuable contributions was his insight into what he termed *the family triad of needs:* audiovisual communication, nurturing, and play. As with all mammals, our human nature rests on these three interdependent requirements, without which we could not long survive as a species. These needs bring about and sustain human development from birth and are, I would add, the springboard to transcendence itself. Our failure to provide all three disrupts intelligence and social development but at the same time supplies the means for enculturating us, thereby sustaining culture.

The Model Imperative[16]

The family triad includes by default nature's imperative that a model be given for all aspects of development. Recall that a model is the living embodiment of the child's inherited capacity or talent and that its stimulus—a possibility demonstrated by the model's presence—brings about a like response in the child, building a structure of knowledge or imprint within.

There are no exceptions to this necessity for modeling, and three examples are presented here: our capacities for language and vision and intelligence of the heart. These three unfold as naturally as breathing, are neural imprints or constructions of knowledge we automatically make, and their need for ongoing model stimuli is exemplary of all of our capacities.

The importance of the model imperative in an infant's initial development; the mother's voice is the model stimulus in utero, which activates the infants language and sensory-motor system. In the same way, presentation of the mother's face at birth acts as a stimulus to which the infant responds with awareness and the initial development of vision. (In the case of congenital blindness, nature compensates, as always, as best she can.) And so it goes with all forms of human capacity whether sensory-motor, emotional-cognitive, or intellectual. Outer stimuli bring inner neural-muscular responses and eventual growth of a structure of knowledge or learning. And in all development, given the appropriate model environment, functions unfold automatically, as nature designed. Denied the model, nature must compensate and the function is compromised.

Undermining the Family Triad of Needs[17]

The one aspect of humans that nature couldn't anticipate or prepare for was the development of a male intellect that encroached upon and finally threw monkey wrenches into every aspect of this wonderfully designed birth-and-bonding procedure. This encroachment was slow, devious, and deceptive, but thorough. During the Middle Ages and the emergence of the Inquisition, a growing fanaticism concerning witchcraft centered on the crone, the elderly midwife who passed on to the young women whose infants she delivered the general background of female wisdom handed down through the ages. The crone became a major target of the Inquisition and her body of knowledge suspect.

Among many issues that rankled the cloth was the crone's notion that childbirth was neither a painful nor a dangerous ordeal (and indeed, under the crone's skillful hands it seldom was). After all, churchmen reasoned, the Bible itself said that pain and suffering in childbirth was a sentence pronounced on womanhood by God—of course the crones had to go. Thus their demonization as preparation for their complete elimination became doctrine, and even today the term *crone* brings to mind the archetypal witch, a toothless hag hunched over a fire, stirring a pot of evil brew.

From the late Middle Ages on, as detailed by Suzanne Arms in her remarkable book, *Immaculate Deception,* medicine men in general horned in on this mother-child bonding domain. Following Bacon's proposals, dominating nature in all her roles had become the scientific passion (oddly fitting the church doctrine from which the notion arose). After centuries, the practice culminated in modern times in which doctors in twentieth-century America eliminated some 97 percent of breast-feeding and thus the central function around which the multifaceted bonding procedure unfolded. Bonding became the butt of jokes in academic and sophisticated circles and was viewed as a notion adhered to only by hippies and new agers.

In America the disruption of bonding through the elimination of breast-feeding and the separation of mothers from infants during the long hospital stays that were often required through much of the last half of the twentieth century set the stage for Madison Avenue to turn the breast into the hottest sales gimmick ever discovered, an unconscious cultural collusion between two destructive forces: medicine men and advertising men. If denied the breast at birth and during infancy, a male can become obsessed with breasts. Assuming that marriage assures him permanent rights to a pair, he can become unhinged when an infant comes on the scene and takes over, particularly if the mother breast-feeds. Some fathers object to breast-feeding, which is hardly supportive for the mother or surprising for males, who were not breast-fed and nurtured themselves. And some of these men, feeling abandoned yet again, may in turn abandon their families—another cultural double bind wherein everyone loses.

Since separation of mother and infant became *de rigueur* practice throughout most of the twentieth century, many of our infants, to say the least, were not given appropriate nurturing or provided appropriate models and stimuli at birth or in the critical first year.

Statistically, infants deprived of early face stimuli and all the attendant benefits showed no signs of visual awareness or consciousness until ten to twelve weeks after birth. This contrasts sharply with the two to three minutes it takes to display these capacities when nature's model imperative is met.

When we look at the mounting crisis in the lives of young people today—the crises in family, education, social structures, deteriorating health and well-being, increasing violence in all its forms—all spilling over into the adult world in ever greater quantities, we must factor in our long century of disruptions of natural process on every level, starting with childbirth, bonding, and early nurturing. Our intellectual high brain can rationalize whole volumes of reasons and causes for our mounting disease, but our ancient brains, the foundations on which we stand, are subject to natural process unadorned and have no access to our rationalizations for breakdown as substitute for function.

On many levels contemporary life undermines the family triad of imperatives for development. In so doing, the way opens ever wider for enculturation on ever more stringent levels. The results are not encouraging.

The New Indifference[18]

Back in the late 1960s, professors at the University of Tubingen, Germany, noticed a serious drop in sensory perception and general awareness in their students. (The same drop was noted in 1966 in the United States.) Students didn't appear to be as aware of information from their environment or schooling or didn't seem to register it as young people had previously. A corresponding deterioration in learning patterns was also evident. The German Psychological Association joined the university in a research project to determine if such a shift could be quantified. Tests involving some four thousand test subjects—young people in their late teens to early twenties—were carried out over a twenty-year period. The conclusions can be summarized thus: "Our sensitivity to stimuli is decreasing at a rate of about 1 percent per year. Delicate sensations are simply being filtered out of our consciousness." In order for our brains to register it, ". . . especially strong stimuli" are required. (The translation of the German reads that in order for our brains to register it, "brutal thrill" stimuli are necessary.)

Most noticeable was this elevation of what is termed the *gating level of the ancient RAS,* or reticular activating system, where sensory input from the body is collected, collated, synthesized into basic world information, and sent up to the higher brain centers for processing. The high-intensity stimuli to which these young people were subjected from birth along with the corresponding lack of appropriate nurturing and natural development resulted in a high level of stimuli that must be received in order for cognizance to form. Sensory information below a certain level of intensity or weight was not registered because it was not of sufficient strength to cross the high RAS threshold into conscious awareness and perception.

According to Dr. Harald Rau of the Institute of Medical Psychology at the University of Tubingen:

> It is apparent that the cross-linkages [networks for sensory synthesis and associative thinking] have been reduced, and that the capacity [to screen out stimuli] has been enormously increased using direct stimulus carriers working parallel to each other.
>
> . . . Previously, an optical stimulus would be directed through various brain centers and would also activate the olfactory center, for example. Today it appears that entire brain areas are being skipped over. The optical stimulus goes directly and exclusively to the visual center . . . the stimuli are then processed faster, but the stimuli are inadequately networked [not integrated by other stimulus centers] and not enhanced with emotional input.

There is no effect—no emotional intelligence. Information is processed without evaluation, thus without reference to areas of knowledge or meaning and without emotional response. The claim of the research people is that those born before 1949 show "old-brain" reactions—that is, the norm of the time. Those born between 1949 and 1969 show modified brain action. Those born after 1969 show new-brain functioning. The new brain can tolerate extremes of dissonance or discord. In a perceptual process that would otherwise be harmonious, disruptive, and inappropriate stimuli are processed without the individual noticing the discrepancies. New-brain people have grown up with contradictions, and they can handle them. That which used to produce a split or division of consciousness, today is the norm. The "new indifference," the mental ability to unite elements that are not logically related and the failure to recognize severe logical fallacies—results in a young person meeting everything with equal indifference. Because the brain can't bring contradictory pieces of information into any kind of relationship, it treats everything with a relative uniformity of low-grade response.

Consciousness is becoming more restricted, the research claims—the brain processes more intense levels of information and less of it reaches our consciousness. The brain has always adapted to changes in its environment by changing its own organization. But now . . . our brain is not adapting. It is rebelling against the world and changing the world experienced by changing itself.

The studies show that enjoyment and aesthetic levels have dropped dramatically. Fifteen years ago people could distinguish 300,000 sounds; today many children can't go beyond 100,000 and the average is 180,000. Twenty years ago the average subject could detect 350 different shades of a particular color. Today the number is 130. The brain loses its standards and degenerates into a kind of dialectic processing of sense impressions. . . . The brain stores opposing and contradictory information without creating a synthesis.

These young people must have a steady input of high-level stimuli or else sink into sensory isolation and anxiety. Natural settings such as parks and rural areas are avoided because they don't offer sensory input intense enough to keep awareness functioning. German psychologists have speculated that a generation with such changed brains will create an environment of such intense stimuli that a normal brain might not survive.

As a means of comparison, the total sound level of a preliterate jungle society is about that of a modern refrigerator.

What "Fortunate" Children Lack[19]

In my book *Evolution's End,* I related Marcia Mikulak's research on sensory registration in children in the mid-1980s. Anthropologist Ashley Montagu and French physician Alfred Tomatis had both reported on our failure to physically nurture infants through touch, leading to increasing sensory deprivation and neural impairment. Mikulak, an independent child psychologist, employed standard Gessel tests to determine the level of a child's sensory awareness, eventually devising more extensive tests of her own. She examined young children from a wide range of cultures—from the preliterate societies of Brazil, Guatemala, and Africa, to the highly literate countries of Europe and America—and found that the children from primitive settings averaged levels of sensory sensitivity and conscious awareness of their surroundings that were 25 to 30 percent higher than those of the children of industrial-technological countries. Preliterate children were more aware of what was taking place among the people around them and what was said to them and asked of them, as well as the general sights, smells, tastes, and touches of daily life. They knew the names and characteristics of the flora and fauna in daily life, which few if any of our industrialized children or adults do. Mikulak's studies were ignored. Those of Tubingen and the German Psychological Alliance, published in 1995, have equally been ignored.

In *Evolution's End,* I also quoted from studies made in the late 1980s of the learning ability of children in so-called primitive groups such as those in Guatemala and similar countries that have severely low standards of living. When these "deprived" children were put into a learning situation equal to those provided for our well-cared-for children, the deprived children showed a three to four times higher learning capacity, rate of attention, and comprehension and retention than our "fortunate" children. Deprived of advanced electronics, these primitive children were given the most necessary things—love and nurturing—and they played continually and developed to the maximum their society afforded.

World Deterioration[20]

For thirty years I have made the unpopular proposal that our treatment of our children has made them increasingly uneducable by the time they reach school age. Mark, then, a further prophecy, made by a score of better heads than mine, that computerizing schools will bring this whole mounting chaos to its terrible, irreversible conclusion. Age-inappropriate use of electronic devices undermines the very value of those devices.

Bioculture and the Model Imperative[21]

Research published in 1998 provides a clue to our evolution and development, and perhaps to the slowly swinging cycles of civilization. This research concerns brain growth during gestation and, in addressing its subject, manages to cast a light that illuminates our current personal and social dilemmas.

If a pregnant animal is subjected to a hostile, competitive, anxiety-producing environment, she will give birth to an infant with an enlarged hindbrain, an enlarged body and musculature, and a reduced forebrain. The opposite is equally true: If the mother is in a secure, harmonious, stress-free, nurturing environment during gestation, she will produce an infant with an enlarged forebrain, reduced hindbrain, and a smaller body.

The oldest evolutionary brain in our head (and body), you recall— the reptilian or hindbrain—provides for fast physical reflexes, is geared to brute strength driven by primary survival instincts hardwired for defense, and is reflexive, not reflective and not very negotiable. The forebrain, on the other hand, gives rise to our intellectual, verbal, and creative mind, functions more slowly, is reflective, and is far more intelligent and negotiable than the defensive, hair-triggered, and reflexive hindbrain.

In her evolution, nature didn't add a forebrain with its reflective, creative intelligence until she had worked out the logistics of a protective, survival-oriented brain upon which she could build her new one. So nature's shift in uterine brain growth toward the kind of environment that a new life must deal with follows an established, adaptive common sense that would please the most ardent Darwinian. Note, however, that nature shifts from an emphasis on physical survival to an emphasis on intellectual enhancement whenever she gets the chance; that is, she moves for a bigger forebrain at each opportunity, asking in effect, at each conception, can we move for greater intelligence this time or must we protect ourselves again? This is, after all, an organic and most intelligent life process, not a rote chemical mechanism. Perhaps at times of catastrophe our general brain structure suffers a setback, but because evolution obviously moves toward higher forms of intelligence, nature can recoup quickly whenever the environment is favorable, responding even to individual cases and the internal environment of just one mother.

The Bioculture Dynamic[22]

For years Bruce Lipton and other enlightened biologists have observed that environment influences genetic coding every bit as much as conventionally recognized hereditary factors. Lipton found that from the simplest cell on up, a new life unfolds in one of two ways: it can defend itself against either a hostile environment or open, expand, and embrace its world. It can't do both at the same time, however, and environment is the final determinant in the decision.

That neural growth will shift from a defensive, combative stance to one that is reflective and intellectual—or vice versa, according to the mother's emotional state—offers us the chance to make a profound shift in our history and to take our evolution in hand. Even in the middle of pregnancy, if there is a change from negative to positive in the mother's emotional life, the direction in fetal brain growth changes accordingly.

That a mother in a safe space produces a strikingly different brain and child physiology than one who is anxious clearly illustrates nature's model imperative. The mother is the model of the eventual child on every level, and a new life must shape according to the general models life itself affords. For, as is true in all cases of nature's model imperative, the character, nature, and quality of the model determine to an indeterminable extent the character, nature, and quality of the new intelligence that manifests.

This all indicates a bio-cultural dynamic—our biology influences our culture and our culture influences our biology. A sufficient number of children born predisposed toward defensiveness and quick reflexive survival reactions will tend to change the nature of the society in which they grow up.

Culture has been our principal environment of mind for many millennia, and through the dynamic of culture and biology, humanity fell into a vicious cycle long ago, a trap from which only the prefrontal-heart dynamic can deliver us. Nature has continually offered us this escape, but, time and again, circumstances breeding fear in us have turned her down.

Culture as a Field Effect [23]

Accept for sake of discussion this definition of culture as an aggregate of ideas about survival, a taxonomy that lifts disparate notions into a coherent and powerful whole. Culture as a field effect is thus inviolable, its contents or expressions interchangeable and even incidental because culture absorbs and transforms any content into its own formative structure. Similarly, anxiety is a state of chronic, free-floating fear— fear without an object. Such a state acts as a catalyst, changing every object, every event into its target, making an event fearful whether or not it deserves to be considered so. Anxiety can become the lens through which we interpret our ongoing experience. . . . Culture, then, is a mutually shared anxiety state, a powerful catalyst of thought that converts all events to its own nature.

Once set in motion and locked into our ancient reptilian brain and its hardwired survival memories this cultural effect reproduces itself automatically and is thus passed on. . . . Our greatest fear, the late philosopher Suzanne Langer said, "is of a collapse into chaos should our ideation fail us. Culture is that ideation or set of ideas. The foundation and framework of our worldview, self-image, mind-set, faith, and belief are culturally determined. Our grounding in culture and culture's grounding in survival are so intricately a part of our mental fabric that such roots are seldom ever exposed, and even then can hardly be recognized for what they are. Culture is the mental environment to which we must adapt if we are to survive, and in our adaptation and survival we automatically sustain culture. . . . Threaten our current cultural body of knowledge and you threaten our personal identities, our core being. Such a threat can lead us to behaviors that go against survival—at least for the victims of our reaction.

Culture can become a kind of psychic entity that can possess and/or inflate a person or even an entire country and achieve its violent ends through such possession and inflation.

Enculturation and Socialization[24]

Socialization in this sense is instinctual, while culture is not. Our social impulse arises from the so-called herd instinct inherited from our mammalian ancestors. The pleasure in gathering together with our own kind, found in most mammalian and avian life, is the source of community and fosters the model imperative, extended nurturing and care; mutual sharing of aesthetics, events, dreams, hopes, ideas, and ideals; mutual appreciation of works, skills, creativity, cooperative ventures; and the sharing of the higher, broader expanses of love—love of neighbor, self, and God.

Enculturation, on the other hand, is not instinctual but instead the result of conditioning, our enforced learning and adoption of ideas about survival, including techniques believed necessary in our particular cultural environment in order to survive. Our imitative monkey-see, monkey-do compulsions actually arise from our oldest reptilian brain system, which is linked to survival and fight-or-flight injunctions of the old mammalian brain. Ironically, this combination provides the principal tools employed in enculturating our children. Enculturation is not instinctual; we must capitalize on and use our survival instinct to bring it about. With regard to enculturating our children, lacking all conviction otherwise, we move with total, passionate intensity. Convinced we must pass on this survival knowledge, we pound it into our offspring "for their own good" as it was pounded into us for our own good. Schooling is treated in a similar fashion—no matter how much pain schooling may have caused us, to save our sanity over having lost the richest, loveliest years of our life to the process, we rationalize that it must have been good for us! And we then subject our children to it in turn; they prove our point by becoming like us, confirming our world-view, joining our mass anxiety, and verifying it by coming on board. We have very little choice in the matter, but hope springs eternal that this time we will make schooling work. . . . It never has.

Our Children's Growth:
Joyful Learning of Cultural Conditioning[25]

A child's socialization, which can be characterized as learning in its most complete form, encouraging reflective thought, is instinctual and arises spontaneously on its own. Culture is something quite opposite: an intellectual, arbitrary conditioning and enhancement of automatic reflexes that must be both induced and enforced. A society—the product of socialization—is made of spontaneous nurturing and love, while culture can bring quiet hate, which can lead, sooner or later, to a child's subtle or flagrant rebellion. Such rebellions are forcibly put down through the infliction of pain, fear, guilt, and shame, or, if none of these works, then through isolation, exclusion from the group, or the labeling of the rebellious child as dysfunctional or unfit.

Many parenting books focus on how best to enculturate your child, carefully cloaking advice with the current politically correct phrasing and playing on parents' concerns over the child's education, place in society, career, fame, and fortune and the constant threat of failure to achieve these.

Without exception, these cultural techniques involve carefully masked threats that prey upon the child's rapidly learned fear of pain, harm, or deprivation, and more primal anxiety over separation or alienation from parent, caregiver, and society. No matter how we camouflage our intent both to ourselves and to our child, most parenting and education (except, perhaps, Waldorf and the best of the Montessori's) are based on "Do this or you will suffer the consequences." This threat, in fact, underlies every facet of our life, from our first potty training through university exams, doctoral candidate orals, employment papers, income tax, on and on ad infinitum down to official death certificates and burial permissions, no matter how high on the cultural totem we climb. Culture is a massive exercise in restraint, inhibition, and curtailment of joy on behalf of pseudo-safety and grim necessities. We live out our lives in the long shadows its casts. . . . Such cautious directives continually activate our instincts of defense, which enculturation plays upon so well.

The Enucleated Self: The Power of the Negative[26]

All mammalian young are genetically driven to interact with the objects and events of their environment, upon which they build their neural imprints. Any new, unfamiliar object or event powerfully signals our young to interact with it to build such a structure of knowledge. As a rule, in their initial encounters with their environment, infant animals check for their mother's okay, which she gives through a variety of subtle sensory cueing, before they interact with a new phenomenon.

In the nest or home all objects and events are safe for interaction, but in the great outdoors, caution is the rule. Our toddler points to something unknown and checks his caregiver's response. If positive, the toddler follows through with a complete sensory inventory of that phenomenon—tasting, touching, smelling, listening, and talking to it—in order to build from it a structure of knowledge. Such imprints include the name, if given, and the emotional state experienced during the exploration. Thus, the world the child constructs will be one shared with the mother.

Seldom will a young wild creature disregard a mother's cues that an object or event might be dangerous. Such warning is the primary signal on which mammalian life has depended throughout history. In our evolutionary past a child disregarding the danger signs of a caregiver was tiger's lunch and left no progeny.

Problems arise, however, when the child follows his genetic encoding and explores an unknown in the safe space of home but meets with an emphatic NO! or DON'T! from the caregiver. What was automatically safe to do seems suddenly and arbitrarily not safe—a conflict of signals.

Thus NO! becomes a powerful and terrible word to the child and is generally one of the first words he speaks as he tries to get a handle on that malevolent negative force. Countering negative with negative, like fighting fire with fire, may be our first learned survival strategy. Sooner or later survival overwhelms the most rebellious will; the toddler conforms to NO!, ceases his exploration in proper fashion, and becomes one of us.

This explanation might strike you as overstated, but the youngster, caught in a serious contradiction of terms, experiences ongoing confusion, ambiguity, and uncertainty. If the safe space is no longer safe, where do we turn? Using negatives to correct behavior is at the very heart of enculturation, however, and the logic never improves. "Thou Shalt Not" is a wellspring of law and religion, the cement holding together, the source of all legal systems, prisons, war, and our downfall.

The encultured mind is cued to respond to the negative as a point of focus, which largely screens out or ignores a quiet stable base, and, because it sharpens and maintains our alert awareness, we actually begin to look for the negative.

Toddler at the Crossroad[27]

In human development the early toddler stage is the fountainhead of cultural renewal. At stake is the activation and development of the child's sensory system and knowledge of the world, and the equally important building of his emotional-cognitive system's knowledge of what relationships with that world are like. By about the eighteenth month after birth, the child's emotional-cognitive system has formed patterns of response that will determine the nature of his relationship for life—the neural foundation of all learning. Maria Montessori claimed that "a humankind abandoned at this earliest formative period becomes the worst threat to its own survival."

Psychologist Allan Schore's research shows that we all experience abandonment of a kind, which perpetuates our culture and seriously impairs our emotional-relational system itself. Recall how the emotional state of the mother determines the actual character, nature, and shape of the infant's brain in utero. Schore shows how this relationship exists through the first two years after birth as well, further determining the growth, shape, and nature of the child's developing brain. One of the major growth spurts of the brain takes place after birth, and the fate of the new neural material introduced at this time is subject to the same model imperative as that introduced before birth. The way the brain is used, based on its model, is the way it forms and grows.

Schore's study concerns affect regulation, or our ability to modify or modulate initial impulses from our sensory or emotional system, and the role this plays in the organization of our self system, that unique sense we have of being an individual distinct from the world out there. Growth and development of the connections between the prefrontal lobes and the emotional-cognitive brain, with its direct connections to the heart, are what is at stake here.

A Caregivers Prohibition[28]

Although the sizes of the hindbrain and forebrain are determined by the mother's emotional state while a child is in utero, the growth of the prefrontals is determined by mother-infant interactions in the first eighteen or so months after birth, and, you recall, the prefrontals are critical to all higher intelligence and to transcendence itself.

Allan Schore points out that growth and development of the prefrontals is experience-dependent, which means that the actual cellular growth and functioning of the prefrontals is dependent on appropriate stimuli from the environment. For a child in the first year and a half after birth, that environment is the mother: "Interactions with the mother directly influence the growth and assembly of the brain's structural systems that perform self-regulatory functions in the child . . . and mediate the individual's inter-personal and intra-personal processes for life."[29]

Not only does the extent of cellular growth depend on environmental stimuli, but the character or nature of what does grow and develop is determined by the same model imperative. "The physical and social context of the developing [child] is . . . an essential substratum of the assembling [brain] system. . . . The tenth to eighteenth months mark the final maturation of the system in the prefrontals essential to regulation of affect [emotion or relationship] for the rest of that person's life."[30] (This observation must be qualified based on evidence that the prefrontals undergo a major growth spurt at adolescence, a discovery not commonly known when Schore was developing his theory.)

So, with the mother present to fulfill the model imperative, the toddler learns to walk, plunging with spontaneous excitement and abandon into his exploration of his new world and the interaction of his body and self with it, only to be met with an unexpected obstacle. Schore reports, "The mother of the eleven- to seventeen-month-old toddler expresses a prohibition on the average of *every nine minutes,* placing numerous demands on the infant for impulse control." (Italics are mine.)

By prohibition, Schore means the mother's NO! or DON'T—and, all too often, physical punishment—concerning some action the toddler undertakes, such as reaching for an object in the grocery store. The impulse control demanded by the mother is selective and arbitrary, determining what is permissible to be learned through exploration and what isn't. While there are times when a mother is genuinely and legitimately concerned for a child's safety and well-being, above all she is concerned that the child learn to mind her and obey her commands as a matter of principle more than practicality. A good child is one who obeys, and a good mother is one who has a good child. Both judgments are levied by culture.

In turn, the process of breaking down a child's resistance to these restrictions, which is equivalent to breaking his will, constitutes what is conventionally called socializing a child. Of course, as covered in our last chapter, this is not at all socialization, but enculturation.

And here Schore goes into great detail explaining, "Shame is the essential effect that mediates the socializing function." The authorities Schore quotes assume axiomatically that this "socializing" must be enforced; that prohibiting self-generated impulse actions is absolutely necessary; and that instilling a sense of shame is absolutely essential to such impulse control, leading to proper socialization.

In the final analysis, parental prohibitions extend to virtually all forms of tactile interaction. The untouched child is met with the command DON'T TOUCH! more than any other—and we adults are met with the same words regarding children.

Threatening the Bond[31]

The mother can accuse and shame a child simply through her look. An accusatory or scolding look becomes a substitute for verbal command and warns the child that his action could break his bond with the mother and bring isolation. This shuts down the child's positive emotional state on which exploration and learning depend, leading to his withdrawal from that exploration out of fear of further threat to the bond with the mother. Schore puts it this way: "The mother utilizes facially expressed stress-inducing shame transactions, which engender a psychobiological misattunement."[32]

Schore describes over many pages how each prohibiting NO! or shaming look brings the shock of threat, interrupts the will to explore and learn, and produces a cascade of negative hormonal-neural reactions in the child. Schore then describes at length the child's depressive state brought about as a result of these episodes of shame stress.

Passing on the Shame[33]

Most of this shaming isn't so much from parents' concern for their child, as rationalized by all of us, but from the parents' own enculturation and serious concern that their own social image might be tarnished by their child's behavior. This personal concern of parents can far outweigh concern for the child's welfare. If their child doesn't conform to cultural expectations, they, the parents, will be criticized, by neighbors, other parents, grandparents, in-laws, the psychiatrist, maybe even the law! This personal fear cloaked by an overtly displayed concern for the child is a major way by which culture perpetuates itself.

Shore points out that "shame is internalized and becomes the eye of the self looking inward. . . . The other person [the caregiver who originally induced the shame] is then not needed. . . . Shame becomes an imprint, a mental image of a 'misattuned' mother face." Such misattunement between child and caregiver "engenders a rapid brake of arousal and the onset of an inhibitory state." Inhibition is a form of depression; the same hormones are involved. "'Signal shame's results, an internal mentation alerts the child that [an] external event might be a painful affect." That is, the child develops awareness that an action he is about to take could bring painful emotional reactions.

What occurs as a result of this entire mechanism is that nature's imperative to explore the world at large is overwhelmed by the greater imperative to avoid the pain of a broken relationship with the life-giving caregiver. What will be developed in the child is a capacity for deception as he tries to maintain some vestige of integrity while outwardly appearing to conform. Living a lie to survive a lying culture, the child forgets the truth of who he really is.

The Work of Shame[34]

Shame breaks into this natural process and the premature awareness that results is a split between self and body, an inner rejection of body rather than an acceptance of self as the whole being nature intended. From this will grow our rejection of the larger body of man and a rejection of the living earth demonstrated in the rape and desecration of our planet.

From citing Darwin, Schore moves onto citing heavyweight Sigmund Freud, who states that the shift occurring at the end of the toddler period moves the child from the pleasure principle to the reality principle. And this shift takes place through shame. Note that the toddler is being extricated from the darkness of the pleasure principle and moved to the light of a "reality principle" through the "enlightening" principle of shame! Freud's logic sets "reality" against pleasure in an either-or opposition typical of the dark cultural and religious inhibitions of life. Herein looms the lifelong cultural verdict driving both East and West: Pleasure is bad! Pain is good for you!

Jean Piaget spoke of a major characteristic of childhood being an unquestioned acceptance of the given. To the young child everything is as it is—wonderful, exciting, inviting, and entrancing—and all of it draws him into an intimate rapport and total involvement and interaction with the world. Once shame is imprinted, however, there will never again be "unquestioned acceptance of the given. Instead there will be a faltering hesitancy as doubt intrudes and clouds his knowledge of self and world.

The work of shame does not stop with doubt, however. Shame stress brings the same overload of cortisol and depression and withdrawal found in children who experience psychological abandonment or separation anxiety.

"Increased cortico-steroid levels are also found in twelve-month-old infants undergoing separation stress from the mother," Schore notes, and, "[t]his condition results in avoidance of mutual facial gazing." Mutual face-gazing is the foundation of all audiovisual communication and is primary in all brain development. In some autistic and many depressed children, eye contact, so critical to development in these earliest months, was not available when required and, when offered later, too often indicates hostility. As a result, eye contact is regarded by such children as threatening and is avoided. . . . Schore's words should be writ large; they articulate the fall of the human from grace into culture.

The Great Neural Pruning[35]

This brings us to the most critical of all Schore's observations from his twelve years of work and 2,300 research citations: the negative aspects of our biology. But first a reminder, the prefrontal lobes are experience-dependent; the environment must furnish the appropriate stimuli if full growth is to take place.

Yet, shortly after that major preparatory growth spurt in the prefrontal-limbic connection, nature deconstructs those very neural structures—and thus the very orbito-frontal loop that she has just established! Recall that the prefrontals are nature's latest neural creation, and this orbito-frontal connection is the fourth brain's link with the ancient emotional-cognitive brain and, through it, with our heart.

Schore relates that the emotional shaming experience the toddler undergoes brings about a "degeneration and disorganization of earlier imprinted limbic circuit patterns . . . [and] produces a wiring of orbito-frontal columns." He then details not only how the actual neural growth of structure and hormonal balance in the child are impeded by shame, but also how shame actually brings about the deactivation, severance, and pruning of those very superabundant connections that have just been established between limbic and prefrontal systems. In Schore's words, "a period of maximum synaptic excision occurs within the human prefrontal cortex at the end of the first year and thereafter declines. . . . Such alterations are known to be related to functional use-disuse."

The worst is yet to come, however. Far more devastating than this pruning is that nature then brings about a corresponding increase of the connecting links of the emotional circuits in this cingulate gyrus with the lower survival fight-or-flight structures of the amygdale, that neural module linked directly with our ancient defense and survival system in the reptilian brain. In this way, a sharp curtailment of connections with the higher, transcendent frequencies of mind and heart is brought about in order to shift growth toward the lower, protective survival systems.

This is, again, just what we observed happening to the brain of the infant in utero when the mother is subjected to anxiety. Nature has again provided an excessive amount of neural material for a movement toward higher intelligence, and again has had to retreat on behalf of survival. This will happen again and again, particularly in the parallel adolescent period when corresponding growth spurts once more take place between the emotional brain and prefrontal lobes. (Occurring at adolescence is an advanced form of maturing analogous to that of the early toddler stage, when emotional connections are again uppermost in importance.)

There is a precise devolutionary process occurring here. At this most critical time, when the toddler begins exploring the world, the prefrontals lose the very synaptic connections they have just made with the limbic system and, through it, with the heart, the connections prepared for during the in-arms period and throughout the general nurturing period of that first year. When all the rest of the brain is growing at its greatest rate and enormous world exploration is supposed to take place, the prefrontal-emotional connection is cut back, withdrawn. Which area of the brain is instead receiving that energy, attention, and stimulus for growth? Of course, it is the hindbrain and its emotional loop, busily building defenses against a world that betrays and can't be trusted.

This loss of prefrontal material is brought about because as the caregiver becomes the "socializing" parent, emotional deprivation takes the place of nurturing in that second year—and the excited, exuberant child is turned into a "terrible two." More is involved here than use it or lose it—we witness a major shift from higher levels of intelligence to lower levels of defensive instinct, a natural survival reaction of the child's system must make to a harsh emotional environment. And we applaud this as successful "socialization" of a child.

Why Bother and Who Cares? Bonding and Domination[36]

A major argument of this book has been that transcendence, the ability to rise and go beyond limitation and restraint, is our biological birthright, built into us genetically and blocked by enculturation. Were we to conceive, deliver, and bring up our young within the bonds of love, where our young would feel unconditionally wanted and accepted and were never betrayed by their matrix world, our full human nature might unfold with no more struggle than any other aspect of our growth. We do not have to struggle mightily to encourage or force those molars to break through at age six and twelve, or wisdom teeth at eighteen. The word *God* might never have been coined were we free-flowing expressions of God's creation, much as the word *healthy* would never have been invented were we never unhealthy. "Man is born like a garden fully planted and sown," Blake claimed. This world is too poor to produce one seed." But we as individuals and our world as a whole must nurture and protect the seed we bring.

This is why Jesus made his aforementioned comment that to "cause one of these little ones to stumble" was a major, nearly irreparable crime. And it is one reason at least that Jesus didn't refer to spiritual paths but to a way of being that opens only in this moment, for which there is no preparation, and that has no conclusion. Today is the day, and this is the hour—moment by moment.

Jesus's way, then, is its own goal and leads nowhere; it only exists as created anew, moment-by-moment. Thus his way offers no place to lay our head, no final goal or stopping point, only a journey into God. . . . But we, strangely, can't let his way be in that simplistic state. We insist on creating an unending, ever-new supply of macho and tough spiritual paths with mountainous obstacles, urging each other to be brave, carry on, and not stop halfway up. We rig up graded systems of spiritual success in which to measure each other, determining how high up the ladder we ourselves are, forming hierarchies of the superior professional athletes of the obstacle course, and hiring them to travel the ever-burgeoning lecture circuit. We seem oddly offended that transcendence should be our nature rather than our reward for overcoming nature.

All his way asks of us is that we invest our life, not hoard it; risk ourselves rather than waste our energy defending against the stochastic nature of this venture. The timid recluse afraid to invest his talent loses it. Apprehensive and fearful of the evils of life, the brooding contemplative retreats into his safe mental cave of reflections. Afraid to risk relationship, the armored person further arms himself in celibacy for "spiritual reasons." Worried about losing his soul, he bargains with God, fate, or destiny, trading the juice of life for a supposed safe space on cloud nine or a reservation in that house of many mansions. Such a timid, protective person isn't much a partner in a creator-created dynamic. To worship in spirit and truth is to throw our life without reserve into that force that through the green fuse drives the flower.

Death and Resurrection[37]

The objective of this book is not to try to define or describe a transcendent state, but rather to present the biological truth of transcendence, which, I claim, was the central theme of Jesus's good news. As have all of history's great beings, Jesus tried to wean us from the limitations of our fear-based mind-set. The miracles of mind over matter were part of his ploy, his attempts to shake us out of our sleep, which is how miracles have been used by teachers in the East.

Our first task is to stop projecting onto romantic myths and assume responsibility for our part in the creative dynamic, starting with ourselves and our infants and children. With our present knowledge of brain-heart interaction, conception, pregnancy, childbirth, and child development we could bring about the most immediate and dramatic revolution of our history. Before we can accomplish this, however, we must get out of the defensive postures that keep us in servitude to our hindbrain.

Perhaps our bodily immortality is not what we should be after, but rather we should be addressing our premature morbidity and serious under development because of a foreshortened life.

Numerous studies show that eradicating anxiety and stress and their accompanying cortisol would, in itself, greatly increase longevity and decrease illness.

Above all, stress and anxiety might be largely alleviated if we realized that Jesus's good news was the truth. If we could accept that we are children of a good and loving creator, like sons and daughters apprenticed to their fathers and mothers, that we are what we, in our heart, believe ourselves to be; and that greater gifts of spirit than those displayed by Jesus are available to us, we could live in spirit and truth. We would abandon ourselves to our heart and allow our intellect to serve that intelligence. Were we bonded to our heart from our beginning and given models for its development, we would grow in perfection. As Blake and the Sufi claimed, what lay before us might then be limited only by our capacity to imagine.

I would like to suggest that the notion of an immortal self, mind or soul existing beyond death, may have occurred to the earliest true human on the emergence of the prefrontals. Through millennia of ancestral longing for immortality we may have posited that possibility within the creator-created dynamic, similar to the notion of atoms being posited by the Greeks and brought to realization by modern science. This longing to survive death may have had no historical precedents before the greater prefrontals formed because without the prefrontals we would not be capable of imagining beyond our limits of body and brain. The possibility, once injected into the creator-created dynamic, may well have become a field effect, a projection that our creative mind fed into the hopper of creation, so to speak, like Hamilton and his quaternions and requiring long periods of gestation and growth. Jesus, in owning the Hebraic projection of God and realizing it is a God of love, may also have owned the long-simmering projection of resurrection and given it some sort of close approximation. Until his time, the Jews had no concept of an afterlife.

Like the fire walker who models in impossible action others can then emulate, Jesus's feat should have broken the stranglehold death has on the human psyche. Fear of death locks our mind into survival strategies that counter our discovery of possibilities other than death. The biological cosmology of transformed cells proposed by Aurobindo and the Mother may have been echoes of this very feat of Jesus. The Mother and Aurobindo, and their disciple Sat Prem, felt that one person breaking through into the new modality would open the way for all, that shedding the conviction that death is inevitable would break the hold of that notion and its inevitable results. The history of Jesus as a model of this greater life shows, however, that a one-man shot can't easily dislodge the cultural stranglehold.

Bodies within Bodies[38]

After my first wife died, at age thirty-five, she made several dramatic returns to us, always in relation to and in the presence of her fifth and last child, who was about a year old when my wife died. Up to her last moment, my wife was passionately intent on healing that infant, a victim of severe cerebral palsy. While the first events are far too involved to explain in full, suffice it to say that a few days after her death, she let her presence be known in two remarkable paranormal occurrences involving the infant. These were followed by a visit that was very powerful, as objects were moved around and the body of the infant was manipulated. All of these visits paved the way for what followed.

She then came to us in two manifestations that were altogether visible—she appeared in quite solid fashion. She first appeared at about ten in the evening and stood over the infant's crib for a surprisingly long time. In the second, my wife appeared, looked intently at the child, and then looked long and steadily at the child's grandmother, her mother, who planned to take the infant home with her and care for her while I took care of our four other children. In both these manifestations, my wife appeared as she was when she was about twenty-two, dressed in her favorite pink suit she was married in and that she had carefully kept. Perhaps the form she assumed was a combination of her self-image, her mother's most lasting image, and my fondest memory of her. Each appearance lasted for what seemed a long while.

A third such manifestation occurred in New England a month or so later, where my wife's mother had taken the child. This time my wife came late in the night, standing between the infant's crib and the grandmother's bed. This immediate proximity drained all of my mother-in-law's body heat. She awakened nearly frozen and terror-stricken and later recounted to me how, after sensing her daughter's immediate presence again, she began to pray to her daughter fervently and silently to move away from so close a position. At this point my wife moved to the other side of the crib and her mother's body heat slowly returned. My mother-in-law called me on the phone as soon as she was able, at an ungodly late hour, and was seriously upset over the body heat business. She said I was the only person she dared tell because I was the only one who might believe her rather than send for the men in white coats. Actually, I was not too surprised, having read of such ghostly accounts in esoteric literature (and even in *Reader's Digest*).

At any rate, although these manifestations took place within a few weeks of her death and were not repeated after the last one at her mother's, I had experienced in quite a tactile and sensory fashion events that are not correct to talk about in our sane society and would surely be dismissed in scientific circles.

The Power of Passion and Compassion[39]

I bring up this story of my wife's return to make a simple observation: If a present-day mother, driven by her extraordinary concern and passion for her damaged child, could break through the barrier of death and manifest in the way that she did, why should history's great model, driven by his passion for the whole of our species, not have done the same? The fact that such manifestations are products of our own visual system, as is the swinging sun at Medjagorge, is simply an example of Humberto Maturana and Francisco Varela's observation that the eyes see what the brain is doing even as the brain does according to what the eyes see. The creator-created dynamic is a function without boundaries, and at times we are graced with a breakthrough of our personal ones.

And so I say to all the modern theologians who apologize away the resurrection and the miracles and to the noise of literal fundamentalists who go to the opposite extreme beyond all common sense and so miss the point: it's not just that most of the reported miracles of Jesus can be found duplicated somewhere even today, in random, scattered fashion, but that they are actual examples of the human potential that we all possess. Deny them in Jesus and you surely deny them for us all. We quickly seal any cracks in our cosmic egg lest the unknown assail us, even when that unknown is an expression of our highest nature and what is known is killing us. To maintain our position of fear and victimization requires enormous expenditures of energy that could be employed otherwise.

Jesus and the intelligence of life did what they could to heal our fractured minds and hearts, and culture did what it had to do to squelch his magnificent gesture and make a religion of it, "a homeopathic remedy for his viral threat" to culture. Projected onto that mystical Christ floating in the heavens, we can dismiss the reality of Jesus and his cross and the unconflicted nature of his faith. The whole operation can be moved into the ethereal realm of marshmallow make-believe, and culture will remain supreme. There, I suppose, we can at least all believe and go down together, no doubt as a good, praying congregation begging mercy from that tyrannical "moral governor of the universe" and his "only begotten son," that equally victimized moral whip and judge of a victimized, fated species.

Or we can pick up that cross and reclaim our birthright; rescue Jesus from the Christians, bring him down from cloud nine, and find him reflected in our mirror; see him in each and every face on the street as Whitman did, find him even in the least of these our brethren behind bars. We too can risk ourselves, throw ourselves to the winds as he did, drop our fearful defenses, judgments, self-justification, shame, and guilt and embrace that life of greater gifts that he displayed, performing, as he promised, even greater works than his, and so rise and go beyond.

The Resurrection of Eve[40]

Morris Berman, in his sobering and prophetic work, *The Twilight of American Culture,* recounts that with the collapse of the Roman Empire at the hands of the Visigoth barbarians, who overran and sacked what passed for civilization, monks in monasteries began collecting all artistic, philosophical, or religious treatises they could lay hands on in order to hide them for safekeeping. Thus the literary treasures of Greek and Roman culture were preserved in the coming Dark Ages, to be discovered anew centuries later, sparking the so-called Enlightenment of the Renaissance in Europe. Today, Berman argues, we need the same—a new monastic order that will harbor the elements of culture as we sink into that twilight that he and many others foresee.

Saving our cultural heritage may be a mixed bag at best; it would be the collections of a monastic order saved according to male notions of what is important. Perhaps, along with salvaging what artifacts we can from our existing culture, we would carry over the virus infecting it. We might, to better advantage, try saving our biological heritage, a well-worked-out package billions of years old that has behind it the intelligence of life and not just the intellect of a patriarchal fiasco. With our biological apparatus intact, we could create cultures at will, even benevolent ones, and let the past and its miserable bloodlust fade away.

Around the mid-twentieth century, some two hundred male medical students at Harvard University were interviewed to determine the extent or lack of parental nurturing they experienced in infancy and childhood. The subjects were grouped into positive and negative categories accordingly, those nurtured and those not. Forty years later the surviving men were given physical examinations. Of those who rated their parents supportive and nurturing, 25 percent had illnesses related to age. Of those rating their parents unsupportive, 89 percent had age-related illnesses.

Gary Schwartz and Linda Russek, of the University of Arizona, made a further test of a representative group of these men in this manner (my summary of that study is markedly abridged but essentially accurate). Each subject was wired for EEG (brain) and ECG (heart) frequencies and was seated three feet from the interviewer (Russek), who was herself wired in the same manner. Within a short time the averaged EEG (brain-wave) patterns of those subjects having positive childhoods synchronized or entrained with the averaged ECG (heart-frequency) patterns of the interviewer. The EEG patterns of the subjects with negative childhoods showed a much slower-forming and weaker correspondence to the interviewer, if any at all. Recalling that the immune and emotional systems are of the same order, the implication here is that emotional derivation in infancy and childhood predisposes an individual to a lifetime of essential loneliness or isolation, as well as to the attending susceptibility to disease. We learn to love by first being loved, and love seems the best armor against illness.

So the first order in lifeboat building is to recognize for whom the boat must be built—in this case, obviously, the child. A child's lifeboat, however, is made up of that child's creator and caregiving parent and/or parents. She who creates and brings the child into the world also models for him, educates him, and leads him forth into knowledge. She, then, must be one with the knowledge of that greatest and most priceless good news of who we are: one with our creator and a principal part of the dynamic of creation, not a victim of it.

Surely fathers are indispensable for this sea change, but we must start with mothers and women at large. Males, it seems, have lost their moorings, leaving Plato's words truer today than ever: "Give me a new mother," he said, "and I'll give you a new world."

Laying the foundations of a new mind and new world has been her task from the beginning, and substitutes just haven't worked. Patriarchy has failed us. Recall the marvelous fairy tale of the noble king who falls into error, sinking down into his basest self to find himself locked in a beast's body from which he cannot extricate himself. Another tale relates how the handsome prince finds his erring ways have trapped him in the body of the lowly frog. From human to old mammalian to reptilian—to where now, when the only lower step is death itself? The resolution comes, our tales tells us, not from knights in shining armor and mighty exploits of strength and courage, or even the wisdom of sages and seers, but through the gentle gesture of the eternal She, whose nurturing kiss alone can save him from himself.

The reptilian foundation on which human life is built is lifted into ever-greater orders of functioning. Again and again the higher incorporates the lower into its service, changing the nature of the lower into that of the higher, until that which was lowest is lifted to the highest, wherein we have risen and gone beyond all limitation and constraint: the resurrected human. . . . Forget the many ways in which patriarchy inverted this magnificent tale of our beginnings— from that ridiculous Adam's rib nonsense down to the sentencing of Eve to great pain and turmoil in childbirth as punishment for her erring ways (a myth that took strong hold in our Judaic-Christian psyches and so proved to be the case, as can happen easily with negative imprints).

Fathers are the bridge between nest and world at large and they are as important and subject to the same model imperative as are mothers in pregnancy, a child's infancy, and a child's first three years. (For those interested in a stunning model for fathers, I would heartily recommend David Albert's remarkable book, *And the Skylark Sings with Me,* which is an account of his experience helping to bring up and homeschool his precocious daughter.)

Children thrive under the protective umbrella of both mother and father, rare though this is becoming. But the American-style nuclear family was an accidental expedient perpetuated by corporate manipulation and state, religious, and political opportunists. Consider that in the 1890s roughly 94 percent of all Americans lived on farms where the extended family was the rule because it was economically expedient. One hundred years later, 96 percent of all Americans live in cities and towns, which is most expedient for corporate, political, or state-religious concerns, but is unviable and disruptive to the nuclear family. In these environments the nuclear family has been short-lived and rightly so. Obstetrician and childbirth specialist Michel Odent points out that the nuclear family by itself is an unnatural and nonviable relationship but when the nuclear family is the nucleus of the extended family, and the extended family of society, the system works beautifully. If you strip away the extended family, however, as we have largely done, the nucleus implodes. Most of our legal nuclear couplings collapse, and too many of those that hold us are of men and women "living lives of quiet desperation," as Thoreau would put it, enduring their lot for a raft of culturally imposed sanctions that rest on guilt, shame, and fear.

[*Note:* Joe often described how each successive volume was an opportunity to deepen, expand, or correct the previous, resulting in some duplication of themes expressed differently. Often we find, embedded in the current book, a foreshadowing of the next. The following from *The Biology of Transcendence* is just such a preview of things to come in *Death of Religion and Rebirth of Spirit*.]

Creating the Mythical Story of Jesus[41]
The word *evangelist* means "one who spreads good news." The problem for the original evangelist was that the good news of Jesus was at a

radical discontinuity with the mind-set of the culture of that time, just as it automatically is to ours today. The early evangelists didn't hesitate to correct this shortcoming in the gospel by changing the radical nature of Jesus's message itself in order that it might be heard and accepted, thereby becoming the new culture. In interpreting the gospel so that it might be heard by the old mind-set, they put the new wine in the old wineskin and no one was the wiser, as we shall see. That which was thought to be a new mind-set had become the old in new form, with all the old murderous issues still intact.

Among many techniques used for translation, the evangelists adopted a series of mythological overlays for Jesus and the events of his time on earth, a myth that gave new life to the ancient practice of a father sacrificing his first-born son to appease the various gods and goddesses of the ancient Middle East.

The Christian movement didn't really gain momentum until the archetype of father-son sacrifice was wedded with the invention of the Second Coming, or imminent return from the heavens of Jesus as the Christ. This hypothetical end, always just around the corner, even today, justified whatever means could be found to alert the populace to prepare for that soon-to-come demise of the whole world.

Twenty centuries of this intriguing theology of sin, guilt, and damnation, with the hope of possible redemption if we jump through all the hoops just right, served to create within humans a deep sense of the validity of that very sin, guilt, and hovering damnation. It is the one injected archetype from which we haven't recovered, even in this age of science, just as some of us have not recovered from the shame induced in infancy, which we carry throughout our lives and which colors every event.

Old God in New Vestments[42]

In addition to the revitalized (if inverted and reinterpreted) sacrificial myth, the evangelists, following Paul's lead, established a relationship between Moses and Jesus—between law and love. They paired the ancient Hebraic testimonial of God and human with the newest, in order to make their product acceptable and desirable to the old temple customers. Thus the crack in the cultural egg, here represented by the cross, sealed quickly and became a cultural support, strengthening culture's protective shell.

Paul's Intellect as Cultural Backlash [43]

It was primarily through Paul that Jesus's way was converted into the cultural effect from which Jesus sought to free us. Paul represents the roaring return of intellect to replace Jesus's intelligence of the heart, and he did this with a thoroughness that is astonishing. He was one of those brilliant intellects and systems builders who must tinker with every issue or event and erect great edifices of thought and invention around it, often obscuring the thought or event itself. Thus Christianity became the lengthened shadow of Paul, not Jesus.

Having revived Old Testament notions of justice, the plot thickens with Paul's pontification on judgment. Consider carefully this excerpt from 1 Corinthians 6, announced to his new fellowship of believers: "You are judges within the fellowship. Root out the evildoers from your community. . . ." This call for exorcism is followed by his far more generic and universal proclamation that will ring down through the ages: "It is God's people who are to judge the world." (This is a chillingly dangerous viewpoint and suggestion that foreshadows such logic as that of the Holocaust and other ethnic cleansing, particularly when it is held as the verbatim word of God.)

Paul writes this concerning his Roman recruits who take too seriously Jesus's injunction that love is above law: "Every person must submit to the supreme authorities. . . . There is no authority but by an act of God, and the existing authorities are instituted by him; consequently, anyone who rebels against authority is resisting a divine institution. . . ." Paul tells us that cultural authority is authorized by God, a concept compatible with Moses, perhaps, but the complete antithesis of Jesus's way.

Standing at the Gate[44]

At any rate, Paul couldn't see what Jesus saw—that there was no difference between Roman law and temple law. . . . Jesus was, of course, speaking of temple law standing at the gate to the kingdom of heaven within us, which translates as intellect blocking the intelligence of heart.

Women figured prominently on Jesus's scene and in his consideration of them he stood squarely—dangerously—opposite the cultural practices of his time. We have only to note his forgiveness of the woman at the well; his intercession on behalf of the adulteress about to be legally stoned by the mob; his defense of women against the gross injustices of the divorce laws of his time; and his willingness to eat and consort with women of ill repute—all subversive acts in that cultural climate. Some Gnostic gospels give women a very high place in Jesus's hierarchy, even considering the "beloved disciple" of John's Gospel—that quiet presence at virtually every scene with Jesus, to have been Mary Magdalene. James Carse picked up on this in that strange, surrealistic little gem of his, *The Gospel of the Beloved Disciple*. . . . But Paul put women back in their place, and quickly reinstated patriarchy and the authority of a new temple priesthood.

Paul's Christianity adopted the accusation of sin and the selling of its antidote as the principal ways of spreading the word—a word based on guilt, shame, and punishment. Already in the Acts of the Apostles cultural intellect in regaining control, making its inroads into the guidance of spirit. Already the direction toward which the cross pointed is being reversed until the way that it offers, the crack in the egg, is eventually sealed shut.

The Waning of the Paraclete[45]

The early church identified the Paraclete as the Holy Spirit. The presence of the Holy Spirit is to claim rebirth of prophecy, direct communion with Spirit.

Even more critical than other reversals of Paul was the dissolution of the Paraclete, which should have evolved into the most powerful field effect in our life. Paul's judgments replaced in one blow our opening to, direct contact with, and sole dependence on that wisdom of the heart Jesus brought about, the intelligence that is our ever-present friend, companion, helper, and inner guide.

It is easy to see how, in those early years of Christianity, the foundations of authority shift from the Paraclete and individual—our own heart and mind—to Paul, and from Paul to the long parade of elders, deacons, bishops, and popes. Finally, adorned in its robes, occupying high places, seated at the heads of tables and then nations, this supreme—if not quite divine—authority is backed by mighty armies, makes the decisions and choices, and shapes the opinions of its followers, guiding them like lost sheep. With this, we are back to zero. The gospel is dead. Long live the Church, Creed, and King, Caesar, Pope, Emperor, right down to the holy global economy. The Christian culture is born.

Monuments over the Murdered[46]

Gil Bailie and Rene Girard wrote brilliantly on culture surviving through murder. War is, after all, organized and religiously sanctioned murder, as is the death penalty. Indeed, imprisonment is a macabre, government-sanctioned form of slow execution spread out over years.

Our definition of a *prophet* is a person who threatens culture's power structure by holding up a mirror to its folly and showing where such folly leads. Jesus observed that culture kills such a prophet, and, having killed the prophet to be rid of his threat, that culture then builds a "monument over the prophet's grave." These monuments are the constructed mythologies through which prophets, once they are safely dead, can be converted from cultural critics into cultural supports and made objects of saintly hero worship to serve culture.

American culture killed Martin Luther King, Jr., and then, once he was safely out of the way, built a monument over his grave as well, making a saint of him, naming streets, boulevards, schools, and institutions after him, at the same time allowing the condition of his people to steadily deteriorate under new words covering the same old cultural travesties. Political correctness, while seeming to promote racial sensitivity, is an agreed-upon form of social lying in which the most biased and prejudiced among us can unctuously say the proper words and thereby cloak our continuing destructive patterns.

Not only was Jesus the target of just such a cultural power struggle, but also the people caught in that struggle ultimately became the target for the new religion woven around him. It is plain to see, then, how it is that the Jewish people rejected Christianity. The same cultural cycle of murder and glorification of the murdered simply turned again. In the hands of the literal-minded evangelists, however, the lofty heights of Old Testament thought became a travesty through which the Jewish people, along with mankind as a whole, lost the best of both worlds: the Jewish people the light of their greatest prophet, the Christians the light of the Old Testament.

The Church as Mediator[47]

Christianity turned Jesus from our evolutionary model into the greatest tool of culture. Converted into the Christ, Jesus became the Great Mediator. No longer the model of higher development, the one who draws us toward him through lifting us up, Jesus as the Christ became a go-between, mediating between the wrath of that same old tyrant Jehovah and the same old sinful, victimized, and helpless human.

This additional mythical creation, the Great Mediator, was itself mediated by the church that invented the idea. The church became the mediator between an individual and his or her own spirit—a double mediation or double indemnity or a double cross. With this new and powerful role, an extraordinarily efficient means of cultural and social control was instituted.

"By Their Fruits You Shall Know Them"[48]

The most powerful criterion for behavior ever conceived is found in the simple statement "By their fruits you shall know them." There is no judgment implied in this admonishment by Jesus, but it is the one criterion that none of us, and surely no institution, can tolerate. Know us by our public relationships, slogans, statements of policy, mission statements, lofty ideals, creeds and beliefs, confessions of faith, brochures, proposals, and public apologies—but not by our fruits, results, actions. Even if an action were to be suspect, the institution as a whole is never held at fault—it's just some bad characters in the ranks, human nature, you know, rotten apple in every barrel!

We have scant modeling or instructions for transcendence in our day. Culture feeds the ancient survival modes of our brain and keeps us locked into them. The gospel countered these cultural chains until the church created its own gospel based on its accusation of sin—and we couldn't hear the gospel of love for the noise of the Doomsday trumpets.

Even in its guise as advertisement, textbook, and school, state-religion continues its accusations, suggesting that we are guilty of incompleteness, lack, separation, not belonging, and/or of being cut off from God. From conception, enculturation is an automatic, cellular implanting of this conviction of sin, and one that is self-fulfilling.

Whether or not we have any kind of religious affiliation or religious belief makes no difference. The Christian accusation of sin is part of the very fabric of our culture, and the more subtle its presence, the more powerful its effect. It underlies our whole legal and legislative fabric and convinces us that without law and its justice, society would run amok just as it convinces us that without harsh prohibitions, our children would do the same.

To suggest that we are not guilty of anything, that our children are perfect as they are, that we would not turn to murder and mayhem were the long arm of the law not omnipresent, or that all our needs would be met by a benevolent nature, as seems to have been Jesus's position, can be a major cultural heresy today, as in Jesus's time. To reject the accusation of sin undermines the foundation of culture and its church and schooling. So to call culture's great belief—that without enculturation humankind would be beastly, primitive, and dangerous—nothing more than a lie is a major heresy of our or any age.

"By their fruits you shall know them" is the one no power system can tolerate, above all the institution of Christianity. One burned heretic or drowned crone shoots down the house of cards, whether the house be Catholic or Protestant. And where in history can we find the equal of that arch misogynist John Calvin? Parading from village to village with his small well-armed army of Protestant inquisitors, Calvin's search for witches outdid that of the Catholics, and for crude, barbarous vulgarity is unmatched anywhere. Calvin overwhelmed the peasant farmers with their pitchforks as they tried to protect their women, and forced the women to disrobe so that he might find any trace of the infamous "witch's tit." (It seems that beneath the Puritan fanatic there existed the puerile voyeur.) Drowning and burning women, sometimes en masse, he went about preaching his gospel of predestination, sin, and death. (And we revere him today as the founder of the Presbyterian Church—the businessman's church back in my childhood, perhaps because it offered sanction for wealth predestined by God.)

Martin Luther, having declared every man his own priest, turned on the peasants with his own army when the peasants revolted against their oppressive landholders and crushed the ensuing chaos with a bloodbath of no small order. And that Bible-bearing, gun-toting, purifier of culture Oliver Cromwell tried to eradicate not only all forms of art (which, said Blake, is the first act of Satan, followed by the removal of pleasure, and leaving only grim necessity), but also all signs of heresy, such as, ironically, Catholicism, whose followers were prime heretics in his book. The march of Cromwell's stoic, hymn-singing Roundheads left as horrible a wake of murder and pillage in Ireland as can be found in history, hardly eliciting a love of the English in that torn land.

Bitter Fruit[49]

I recall the newsreels when I was a child, showing the pope blessing the Italian army on its way to bomb, gas, and machine-gun the spear-wielding Ethiopians (whose country, ironically, was home to the earliest Coptic congregations by the end of the first century, and was the first Christian "nation"). The pope had a long precedence for such benevolence. The eleventh-century Pope Urban the Second cried: "God wants it! God wants it!" as he blessed the knights on their way to kill the Moslems in the Holy Land and, at the same time, set a precedent for future mass murders. And we too had our own Cardinal Spellman, who blessed the troops on their way to "Christ's Holy War" in Vietnam.

Just as marriage—a cultural institution—is generally a disaster for all but the strongest and most enduring relationships, religion—another cultural institution—has been a disaster for humankind's relationship with God. Surely both deserved something better. The cross was the attempt to bring new life to that relationship and Christianity was culture's means to nullify that attempt, culture's "homeopathic remedy for the viral threat of Jesus."

We don't need church under any brand name, with its accusation of sin and selling of redemption, its huge bank accounts and real estate, lawyers and lobbyists, political games and public relations, radio and television stations. We do need that steady stream of selfless people, particularly women, the church has given us, in spite of itself. People like Peace Pilgrim* simply materialize to exemplify the gospel. They crop up continually, if always on the fringe, always suspect by the authorities and respectable church people. Little Second Comings occur all over the globe.

There are no mediators between our heart and mind, just the blocks of our defenses, fears, and doubts, as Peace Pilgrim clearly displayed. So we might as well take the chance, quietly and without fanfare, not for public display but in our private place of heart. We might as well take the leap and drop defenses, judgments, the fearful passion for prediction and control, the dreadful need for self-justification, with no thought of tomorrow. This is that simple, private move the gospel offers us—picking up our cross. Rumor has it the burden is light.

---

*[Peace Pilgrim, née Mildred Lisette Norman (1908–1981), was a spiritual leader and peace activist and the first woman to walk the entire length of the Appalachian Trail in one season. She gave up all her earthly possessions and spent her life walking for peace. —Ed.]

6

---◆---

The Death of Religion and the Rebirth of Spirit (2007)

A Return to the Intelligence of the Heart

THE BACKSTORY FROM JOE

Both our current religions, scientific and ecclesiastic, may well be offended at my contention here that they are destructive to life and civilization and that they are not nurturing but are, in fact, devolutionary. Yet recognition of this devolutionary effect is necessary if we are to clear the decks and open ourselves again to the evolutionary force of love and altruism that seems to lie behind our life and cosmos. These higher intelligences, giving rise to us, are our true spirituality and would be served by a true science.

In trying to cope with the hydra-headed assaults on humanity and nature wrought by both religion and technological science, we lose all trace of the origin of these assaults; we become so caught up in dealing with their harmful effects that we can't see their causes. Cultural anthropologist Leslie White observed that a culture self-destructs when the problems it produces outstrip its capacity for solution. When every move we make seems flawed by hidden error and every correction of an error creates two more errors in its wake—as seems the case today, no matter how sophisticated and scientific our apologetic terminology or how lofty and pompous our religious moral protest—the ground beneath us simply crumbles.

EXCERPTS FROM *THE DEATH OF RELIGION AND THE REBIRTH OF SPIRIT*

Introduction[1]

Cultures have risen and fallen throughout history, and when they fall, it has always been by their own hand. Whether or not by our own hand, our culture is rapidly waning as a widespread anxiety waxes. Philosopher Susanne Langer claimed that our greatest fear is a "collapse into chaos should our ideation fail," and culture is a major plank in our ideation. Threaten our fabric of beliefs, practices, and perspectives that make up the system of our cultural ideation and our very sense of self is threatened.

As culture is a major plank in our ideation, religion is a major plank in our culture, and it, too, is on the wane, which has given rise to fundamentalism as a political-cultural force. Arising from the adherents to all religious systems, old and new, fundamentalists fuel the fire of the very cultural collapse we fear.

At the same time, our current scientific technologies, which have become an even more powerful plank in our culture's ideation, damage us on every hand—physically, mentally, and morally—and because their work is indirect and subtle, it goes unrecognized. As we used to turn to religion as our hope and solace, we now turn to science, a religion with its own brand of protective fundamentalism. Both of these religions, scientific and ecclesiastic, are equally destructive to spirit, mind, and nature and equally give rise to violence and civility's decline.

While we do have a culture, our actions are hardly civil, and in spite of our many religions, a spiritual void seems epidemic. The mounting ride of violence toward self, earth, and others intensifies, while sporadic movements toward a spiritual renewal fragment in uncertainty. The impending death of religion, however, could bring—or at least allow—the rebirth of spirit.

In his book *Darwin's Lost Theory*, David Loye describes how Darwin, in the latter part of his life, went beyond the accepted thought of his time to explore biology's relevance not only to a theory of evolution but also to what we know today as the fields of psychology, anthropology, brain science, and moral philosophy. *The Descent of Man*, Darwin's final work (which I will hereafter refer to as Darwin 2), is distinct from, yet complementary to, his earlier and widely accepted study, *The Origin of Species* (which I will refer to hereafter as Darwin 1).

Both are works of brilliance and insight, though Darwin 2 had a markedly different reception than did Darwin 1. Loye examines the strange fact that the last work of Darwin has been ignored, while his first has long been an accepted part of modern academic and scientific thought. In this contrast lies not just the evolutionary history of humankind but also an explanation for why we tremble at the gates of disaster today.

In Darwin 1, Darwin clearly describes how ages of mutation, selectivity, and survival of the fittest gave rise to mammalian life in general. On this foundation, as Darwin 2 shows, evolution then employed markedly different forces—"higher agencies," as Darwin called them—to bring about the far more advanced human species.

Using copious quotes from Darwin, Loye shows that these "higher agencies" translate as love of both self and other. Certainly, terms such as *love* and *altruism* are hardly in keeping with current academic and scientific (neo-Darwinian) acceptance as critical forces in evolution. Yet if love and altruism were developed they would be the basis for not just our survival but also our recovery of an ongoing evolutionary momentum we have lost.

The catch lies in the word *developed*. If we look at contemporary societies worldwide and our historical record in general, we find a marked failure to develop love and altruism, even though remarkable forces apparently gave rise to us. I propose here that the higher force of love of self and other is both our true nature and the substantive foundation of our genetic system as described in Darwin 1. Further, I suggest that this higher force moves as powerfully as ever in us today, for our stake in evolution is evolution's stake in us, a typical strange loop phenomenon.

The higher agencies are a combination of an instinctual base of love expanded upon by—and functioning through—nurturing. Nurturing goes far beyond simply nursing infants, as our simian ancestors did. According to Darwin 2, benevolent instincts of nurturing and care were the evolutionary springboard for our appearance, which may have been more recent than we have considered up to now.

During many decades as head of the National Institutes of Health's Department of Brain Evolution and Behavior, neuroscientist Paul MacLean mapped out the evolutionary nature and structure of our brain. He clearly showed that in our head lies the Darwin 1 foundation of an ancient reptilian or hindbrain, which served as the basis for a forebrain consisting of an old and new mammalian brain. Upon these three evolved structure, the fourth human brain could be added with little of the slow, trial-and-error processes of the evolution leading up to it. This Darwin 2 phenomenon of a human brain operating from the higher agencies of love and altruism apparently brought us about as recently as forty to fifty thousand years ago, merely yesterday on the evolutionary timeline. Standing squarely on the shoulders of eons of Darwin 1 process, we with our fourth brain are apparently quite new on the neural scene.

Now, as our history and present circumstances indicate, and as this book will explain, our newest brain is continually being dominated and overruled by those very ancient systems on which it rests—systems that function largely through instinct rather than intelligence. Despite what we would expect from evolution's design, our history illustrates a constant struggle between, rather than synchrony of, the old and new neural systems in our head. A severe imbalance between defensive, old-brain instincts and intellectual new-brain systems is evidenced in our continual outbursts of violence and destruction.

This periodic seduction of the new by the old is in opposition to an overall evolutionary drift and totally counter to the higher agencies that brought us about. This continual usurping of the capacities of the new brain by the old has resulted in the fact that our new, fourth brain is largely undeveloped. Driving us to predict and control a nature and world we then can't trust, these upheavals either indicate a breakdown in evolution's biological plan or show that the plan is not yet complete and nature is still working out the glitches, searching for some design in which evolution can continue instead of self-destructing.

We assume evolution produced our advanced intelligence to predict and control earlier and inferior forces. Yet this neatly linear progression is a deceptive half-truth, for it overlooks and betrays the principle part of the creative process that underlies evolution itself and gave rise to us.

Consider turning upside down this notion of moving from inferior to ever more superior forms, for this conventional, commonsense notion puts the horse before the cart and its driver whereas with us humans, the driver came before the horse. The more advanced an evolutionary neural system, the more fragile it is. Our Darwin 2 brain, with its much higher form of intelligence, is radically dependent on these earlier neural systems for its own functioning, so the most logical and perhaps only feasible method of progression would have been for this higher Darwin 2 intelligence first to work out, through the slow and careful Darwin 1 selective process, what the higher had to have as its foundation in order to be.

Here, then, is an example of a strange loop phenomenon: a new potential, sensed within an evolutionary process moving infinitely in all directions, brought about the appearance of what seems to be an older system required by the newer one. This strange loop is a major factor in creation and evolution found throughout the world and probably the cosmos. Our failure to recognize this strange loop constitutes a lapse in our current knowledge and understanding, although such an interdependence has been recognized by other cultures and civilizations before ours. Neo-Darwinism, a limited and fragmented scientific view of Darwin 1, has vainly sought to prove that a "mode of being" gave rise to Being itself, which is patent nonsense.

Both our current religions, scientific and ecclesiastic, may well be offended at my contention here that they are destructive to life and civilization; that they are not nurturing but are, in fact, devolutionary. Yet recognition of this devolutionary effect is necessary if we are to clear the decks and open ourselves again to the evolutionary force of love and altruism that seems to lie behind our life and cosmos. These higher intelligences, giving rise to us, are our true spirituality and would be served by a true science.

In science and technology, we have created a self-propelling machine we can't turn off, however, and like the sorcerer's apprentice, we are overwhelmed by forces unleashed through our arrogance and ignorance. Every brilliant solution our technology and science have thus far presented has set up a counter-wave of quite subtle, slow, and patient destruction, just as religions rapidly give rise to noisy and turbulent violence.

Over a half century ago philosopher Susanne Langer made the observation that we would do well to reconsider our unquestioned belief that modern science is a blessing to humanity.

Suzanne Langer's mentor, mathematician-philosopher Alfred North Whitehead, once proposed that science and technology could have arisen only in a Christian culture, though their roots are even more ancient. Examine only one thread in the rich sequence behind such a notion: Following the Greek influence on the inventive creations of Paul the Apostle's Christology, Christianity had demonized body on behalf of soul, declared a state of war between spirit and flesh, and pronounced nature the archenemy to be vanquished, brought to her knees, and made to yield her secrets and do our bidding. As a result of this conquest, a scientific priesthood arose that overshadowed its waning ecclesiastic parentage. Ultimately, in richest irony, the priests of each faith, old religion and new science, have played mock battle before the hapless humankind that has lost out all the way around.

Years ago, David Bohm, Einstein's protégé and physicist at the University of London's Birbeck College, wrote of the substrate of reality being an "implicate order" of energy that is consciousness itself. . . . By an implicate order David Bohm meant a single underlying energy that has implied within it all potential, all possible fields of energy.

We will explore both culture as a major implicate force shaping our explicate life and field effect as a shaping force in culture. . . . The mirroring relationships or strange loops of cause and effect, field and mind, question and answer, discovery and creation, in which each seems to give rise to the other and the very existence of each relies on the other.

Culture and Darkness of Mind[2]

Culture as a habitual mental process has grown out of attempts to control nature and predict its events—even as culture is, by default, a factor in the nature we examine and attempt to control. In fact, our own human nature, with its wild assortment of behaviors, is the principle target of control. But we are culture itself, and we attempt to control our actions through the abstract force of a culture we create through such actions and are, in turn, subject to—a strange loop indeed.

Charles Darwin proposed that any activity repeated long enough will become a habit, and any habit repeated long enough can become instinctual, operating automatically below reason or the limen of our awareness. Culture is actually a collection of habits repeated over millennia, and many of these habits have become so instinctual as to function automatically, beneath our awareness. These are imprints that form our own consciousness, to varying extent, and that are passed on to our children both deliberately and unconsciously.

Passing Cultural Patterns to the Next Generation[3]

A new discovery in neuroscience concerns *mirror neurons,* large groupings of cells scattered throughout our brain that, beneath our awareness, automatically mirror or imprint various aspects of the world around us, locking them into our memory and cognitive process. Patricia Greenfield, neuroscientist at UCLA, claims: "Mirror neurons provide a powerful biological foundation for the evolution of culture." Previously, she observes, scholars have treated culture as fundamentally separate from biology, "But now we see that mirror neurons absorb culture directly, with each generation teaching the next by social sharing, imitation, and observation."

"Social emotions like guilt, shame, pride, embarrassment, disgust, and lust are based on a uniquely human mirror neuron system found in a part of the brain called the insula," reports Christian Keysers, who studies the neural basis of empathy at the University of Groningen in the Netherlands. While mirror neurons aren't exclusively human but are also found in many higher mammals, they play a major role in how we humans pass cultural patterns to the next generation without being aware of it.

Somewhere in our past, these cultural patterns became not just imitative but enforced behavioral modifications based on fear of both the natural world and our mentors and models who insisted we conform. These models were likewise culturally formed as infants, as were those who came before them for millennia. Eventually, group safety became associated with predictable actions of individual members, giving rise to a rich fabric of taboo, law, prohibitions, and conventions, along with punishments and reprisals for failure to conform.

Today, culture has become a primary formative force, a major organizing field of energy distinct from nature, which works to isolate us from what was, is, and might be natural. We might look on culture as a surrogate parent acting somewhat in the manner of our real mother, nature, but on behalf of an arbitrary system foreign to and against our real heritage. We are like children kidnapped by a foreign power and brought up to serve nefarious schemes.

We have been separated from our original humanity by culture, which has itself become an automatic reflex, a near-unconscious, animal instinct. In fact, to think or act outside cultural dictates, once imprinted, has become almost impossible. This cultural effect has expanded to such power that it has become the very fabric of our conscious awareness—an awareness that results from being conceived, born, and brought up in it. Taking over and shaping our brain-minds accordingly, culture shapes even our attempts to examine or become objectively aware of its very force.

Violence, as the French historian Rene Girard and his protégé Gil Bailie point out, is inherent within culture. In fact, the two—culture and violence—bring each other into being. What's more, a "global mind" already exists, to our detriment, in the form of the very substrate of culture that shapes our lives and now floods the planet with a uniform field of electronic media, with its integral structure of violence. . . . It is this force that accounts for an overall mass conformity of mind beneath the various surface colorations.

Only an individual mind can pick up on the evolutionary drive of life itself and create independent of the artificial overlays and restrictions culture imposes. We humans were made for and long for that lost individuality.

The Force of Spirit as Life and the Force of Cultural as Violence[4]

Admittedly, I have somewhat personified or made an object of culture, which is actually a psychological or mental field effect, a sphere of influence or force like gravity, intangible except for the disastrous fallout it produces. Culture as a field effect can contain within it a multitude of subcultures, which, in their energy, novelty, and markedly different textures, colors, and languages, are constantly in conflict with each other. With violence and religion as both the products and producers of culture, the resulting tangled web often obscures the presence of culture itself.

How does culture engender violence? It is brought on by the constant pressure of restrictions, prohibitions, and ceaseless demands for conformity to its abstractions. These constraints block our longing for life, which, ironically, intensifies accordingly. Of incidental consequence is that individual or group toward which cultural violence is directed. We always seem to find or create a target for our violence, whether internal or external. Should our internal violence leading to illness and neuroses fail to fill the bill, ideological clashes between subcultures are always with us, providing obvious external targets.

Interestingly, the United States has not only the largest collection of atomic bombs, the ultimate symbol of cultural hatred, but also the largest prison population of any nation. More subtle imprisonment can be found in our continued subjugation of women, which, though less overt than stoning them to death, as is still sanctioned beneath the auspices of the Muslim religion, nonetheless is ill treatment that serves our corporate-economic machine and harms all of us, males included.

And the violence extends to self: In myriad subtle but effective ways, we drive our children to internal or self-violence, resulting in one of the largest populations of unhealthy children in the world and the highest level of child suicide of any nation. Directly or indirectly, we sell those children the guns to slaughter each other in the more dramatic and publicized external forms of youthful rage.

The Role of Law in Culture[5]

While a principal characteristic of culture is religion and its ever-waxing violence, a second, far more pervasive, and ever-expanding element is law. Law, made necessary by violence, is itself a cause and a form of violence.

We keep our prisons filled with the indigent and poor who can't afford lawyers or who are assigned indifferent ones while the rich create their own laws that make them wealthier and protect their fortunes. This admired thievery has a long historical precedence in the millennia of tyrants, emperors, princes and kings, dictators, popes, and presidents who have fed on the social body while culture holds them up in the history books as models for our children.

Virtually every breath in our enculturated life is monitored by law, either blatantly or subtly. We live in a web of legal constraint and limitation accepted and adhered to unconsciously and unconditionally. From ancient commandments learned in Sunday school to the stately volumes of philosophies learned in higher education, we find an underlying strata of that cultural dictum: "Do this or else!" As a result, we live in the shadow of angst lest we fail somehow and "they" find us guilty of some infringement of law—perhaps of one that we were not aware even existed. Taxes, speed limits, bills, enculturation of our children from birth, schooling, and college—all are part and parcel of the ever-expanding web of limitation and constraint that makes up life in culture to which we must adhere or else!

Culture and War[6]

War is a direct cultural effect. Why do we engage in it again and again, generation after generation, millennia after millennia? We do so because war is absolutely necessary to culture, as Gil Bailie and Rene Girard claim, and we are blindly autonomous servants of the cultural effect, having been born and raised within it.

Culture as a field effect functions much like language acquisition: it results in a spontaneous, imitative learning below the limen of our awareness.

We killed some one hundred million of ourselves in the twentieth century through the wonders and efficiency of those most jealous cultural gods, science and technology, and because of their efficiency, we probably have but few wars left before we are altogether eliminated—humanity destroyed by its own cultural petard.

Slaughterhouse Five[7]

At seventy-six years of age, when the Twin Towers came down in gory 9/11 flame and everlasting fame, I glanced briefly at the televised footage of that spectacle and assiduously avoided looking at it again. Having no television in my house, I was to some extent spared direct exposure to the vast negative field that was building through our benevolent government's manipulations.

A more powerful resonant memory overlay it all, and I saw not so much the Twin Towers flaming but my long-ago inner image of the bombing of Dresden, Germany, in World War II. Played against the backdrop of that now-aging and near-forgotten war, 9/11 brought a single phrase to my mind, one that wouldn't stop repeating: "As you sow, so shall you reap."

The German high command packed an estimated four hundred thousand women and children into Dresden, thinking that in all of Germany it was the one unlikely target for revenge.

The allied high command, however, hearing of this massive refugee center, decided to destroy Dresden in order to break the spirit of the German people and thus supposedly shorten the war. Winston Churchill made the final decision, an act of cold hatred and culturally righteous revenge that was carried out by the British Royal Air Force. An estimated one hundred thousand women and children were cremated that first night, while those not blown to smithereens at the outset were torched by the firebombs. Death lingered long and hard behind those ancient walls.

Some ten years after that war, by chance my next-door neighbor was a young woman who had lived through the Dresden holocaust. She gave graphic descriptions of climbing down into the sewers of the city where she and thousands of others spent four days in pitch darkness, linked arm in arm, to form long human chains in order to hold each other against the tide of fetid water that flowed through, waiting for the flames and heat to subside. Invariably, someone would lose their grip and let go, with the chain regrouping to hold. I learned that what I thought a myth might well be true: people's hair can turn white overnight. . . . Dresden, however, had been but a dress rehearsal for the sons of liberty and justice.

The radio announcements of the atomic annihilation of Hiroshima and, shortly after, Nagasaki, where we incinerated unknown tens of thousands of Japanese women and children—admittedly, as their air-men would have incinerated us—came through quickly. The second bomb was loosed it was later reported, to see what difference in effect there would be between a direct ground contact explosion of this new wonder of science and one exploded in the air. (Little was made of the fact that it was dropped on Nagasaki before the Japanese government had a chance to recover from the shock of Hiroshima and surrender.)

So to me, with World War II and its more than thirty million dead standing as a major milestone in my youth and seeming only yester-day, the Twin Towers episode, which killed three thousand people, was almost incidental.

Shock and Aftershock [8]

Periods of shock are times of great opportunity. The mind—even the mind of a nation—stops briefly at such times, and with the right leadership during that post-9/11 period we could have changed the course of history, for, because of the media, the shock resonated world-wide. We could have broken the ancient cycle of reciprocity, justice-seeking, revenge, and retaliation locked into the cultural mind-set, the fuss that have ignited every war and change the very shape and nature of a violence-prone species.

We could have initiated a transformative shift in the very mental apparatus that drives us to our self-destruction again and again. We had the opportunity, obscure as it now seems, to break the cycle of cultural enslavement, thereby freeing humanity from culture and dealing a death blow to that darkest and most powerful of all the principalities and powers to arise in our sad history. Many people were primed and ready for a radical shift, but we had no leaders at all who could envision this course of action—only a more lowly group of schemers than usual who in a base, despicable, and even demonic way used every event, calamity, and disaster to further their own greed and lust for power, all the while hiding behind the cross for camouflage, justification, and public support.

Culture as a Field Effect[9]

An enculturated mind *is* culture, and the force of culture is directly dependent on our mind responding according to our own enculturation. In implicating culture as our hubris and nemesis, we implicate ourselves, an uncomfortable and threatening direction to pursue, one that immediately puts us on guard, for we automatically deflect any direct negative reference to our own personal sense of being. In this we seek to preserve our own integrity, a reasonable survival instinct, and effective defense maneuver that operates largely beneath our awareness and often drives us to perpetual or periodic war.

We want to change the effects of culture, but because we are identified by it, loss of culture is synonymous in our minds with death. It is our identity, making the cause of culture and its effect simultaneous, each giving rise to the other.

Paradoxically, our attempt to change culture and its negative effects on us actually preserves culture. . . . In fact, nothing furthers the cultural effect as strongly as this compulsion of ours to change it. In our attempts we project our internal disease onto external causes, thus masking our real dilemma. In our projection we see that our problems, angst, and frustrations are brought about by phenomena or events of our neighbor or the world out there. We are driven by our defensive survival system itself to bring about the needed change in our neighbor or world as we simultaneously hold to our ideation lest we collapse into chaos—and that ideation is culture.

We cloak our compulsion to change culture under a multitude of disguises, nearly always virtuous: we want to make the world a better place for our children, build a better tomorrow, create the kingdom of God on earth, shape our future through stalwart effort and responsibility, win our wings on the social scene or in the marketplace, be somebody, work for the happy marriage of religion and science, be a real mover and shaker, prove our merit, justify our existence—the list goes on ad infinitum. . . . So, while the content of culture changes continually, through our constant drive to escape it and make life better, culture as a malevolent formative field effect never changes.

Consider again that mythical cultural lie concerning hypothetical human nature: without the constraints of culture, we would be demonic, brutal beasts. . . . What results is periodic warfare brought about by the cumulative buildup of social rage and frustration, which is brought about in turn by the limitations and constraints we enforce on each other and our children for their own or the social good. . . . We pass off this crippling of spirit as the failings of human nature and look on religion as the culturally acceptable solution.

Mind and Intuitive Perception[10]

In 2004, discoveries at the Institute of HeartMath, a heart-brain research center in the Santa Cruz Mountains of California, revealed that we have within us a clear intuitive sense. Our heart, researchers there found, senses the nature of particular events ahead of time, before these events actually occur. The heart clearly signals the brain if an event about to manifest is negative in nature or is one to which the individual will react negatively. This newest discovery falls outside our current parameters of accepted possibility and even those determined by the Institute of HeartMath up to now. Besides revealing an intuitive intelligence within us, it implies a distinction between brain and mind.

The HeartMath experiments were originally set up to further investigate various well-known aspects of sensory perception. The predictive capacities displayed by the heart were an unexpected peripheral effect that opened up a new branch of research. The Institute of HeartMath ran 2,400 trials before they released their first paper on this intuitive capacity, and they have since continued with their research.

What is most significant here is that the wired viewer is unaware of his or her heart's four-to-seven second anticipatory activity or predictive function, and is only aware of the actual appearance of the image on the screen. Therefore, it seems, there is a heart-brain awareness in us that oddly precedes our mind awareness.

Original Wisdom[11]

More than fifty years ago I came across an account from a naturalist concerning intuition in wild animals. His most vivid story was of his daily observations on the progress of a mother fox and her kits, secure in a deep den several feet up the bank of a rushing mountain stream. The kits were finally beginning to appear for short stretches when mama fox would bring mice and moles to them. One balmy, clear day, when a high breeze was blowing, that mother fox did something the naturalist had never seen before and that briefly baffled him: the vixen suddenly emerged from her den, scrambled some fifteen feet up the bank, well above her home, and, with dirt flying, began furiously to dig another den. In a short time she had disappeared into the new hole, still digging away, and finally, reappearing, she ran down to the original den and laboriously carried each little kit to their new home, where she safely deposited them.

Within minutes after completing this unusual feat, a flash flood tore down the steep mountain valley, creating a wall of water that carried masses of debris. The former den flooded and remained submerged for quite some time until the jammed water subsided. It seems a massive cloudburst had loosed several miles upstream, unbeknownst to the naturalist on that balmy day but not to the vixen.

Following the great Asian tsunami of 2004, caretakers of several of the wild animal reservations in the island countries of Sri Lanka, Malaysia, and the rest of the area reported that some ten minute before the great wave struck, the animals in their reserve all stampeded away from the shore and to the highest ground. A similar account concerned a group of elephants kept by a luxury tourist hotel on a Malaysian beach and trained to carry visitors on a sightseeing tour through the jungle and along the shore. The beasts were secured near the hotel, each with one leg tethered by a chain linked to the post driven deep in the ground, not so much to keep them from wandering but to reassure the tourists who clustered around to feed them and gawk. Several minutes before the tsunami struck, the elephant that was then on his trek and near the beach suddenly turned and rushed back to the tethered group, trumpeting loudly, much to his driver's and passenger's alarm. The maverick then began helping each elephant pull its tether out of the ground, after which they all rushed noisily to the highest point of ground in the area. Many from the native population rushed after them in alarm just as the great wave struck.

The Conflict of Biology and Culture [12]

Human females are born with somewhere between four and seven million eggs on their ovaries. . . . Each egg potential is a particular folding of DNA, no two of which are identical. DNA is sensitive to a wide variety of signals from mother, family, society, and world.

Our male children, on the other hand, are born with no active reproductive functions or suitors yet to come. Such creative work will not even begin until that period of puberty, just about the time those lovely ladies are preparing for their monthly offering. Once that male production line begins, however, it is an ongoing, nonstop, twenty-four-hour-a-day operation. By this delayed and then constant production method, each male sperm is automatically updated moment-by-moment by that male's environment and his own experience. Theoretically, by maturity, he can contribute enough of those aggressive little creatures in a single encounter to fertilize every fertile female on earth who might be ready for fertilization at that particular time.

As biologist-anthropologist Ashley Montagu pointed out, the female, as the stable biological base of life, is the stronger of the two needed to create life, while the male variable is more fragile. Note that in reproduction a single egg awaits while hundreds of millions of variable males run to meet this one. Being a male is precarious; a sperm is more difficult to produce and keep alive and, sadly, is expendable after contributing his small part.

In the several natural spontaneous abortion periods of fetal life (such as around the tenth week and the fifth and seventh months) 80 percent of the aborted embryos or fetal infants would have been male had they not been aborted—and odds are strong that they would have been dysfunctional if they had been carried to term. Of all dysfunctional children born—those who are deaf, blind, missing various body parts, deformed, and so forth—a majority are males. Of all autistic children, a majority, again, are males. Adult females outnumber males, generally live far longer than males, and can live without males altogether far more successfully than males can live without females. Sigh! (As an aside, it is interesting to note that Ashley Montagu's milestone work *The Natural Superiority of Women* was written long before the women's movement began.)

Strangely, in Western societies male infants, though more fragile, are given less care than females; they are "toughened up" according to our current mythos, apparently to deal with a hypothetical saber-tooth later on. Meanwhile, we overprotect our little girls. In peaceful, preliterate societies, however, male infants are breast-fed far longer than females and are generally treated as more fragile. It seems our mythos betrays us, however. Nature gave humans our higher brain structures that we might outwit saber-tooth, but she did not give us larger, tougher bodies to outwrestle him. We have seriously misread the signals. Without nurturing, our males grow up aggressive and angry, do not make stable families, and are prone to violence against spouses, offspring, and each other.

In their respective works on brain and development, James H. Austin and Allen Schore both point out that our survival today depends on producing males who are nurturing, benevolent, compassionate, and caring, which, in turn, requires just such treatment of males from birth and particularly at the toddler and adolescent periods. This notion, however, is so diametrically opposite current neo-Darwinian capitalistic cultures, with their emphasis on competition and survival of the fittest, that the chances of such a radical turnabout seem slim—as indeed our general survival itself does—but we might at least give it a try.

So life and its creation is stochastic, with random chance a factor, but an obvious purpose lies behind this randomness and the nature of the selectivity reveals an intelligence of profound depths. In fact, the whole scope of creation reveals a strange loop design of incalculable brilliance, as Walt Whitman pointed out in looking at a simple blade of grass.

Nature's Biological Plan[13]

The scale on which nature unfolds is infinitely huge when viewed through scientific technologies such as telescopes, magnetic imaging, electron microscopes, and so forth. The immensities found in both directions, within and without, seem to reduce us as individuals to utter insignificance, as is so often implied by scientism. The Greeks, by contrast, looked at the nameless stars and wrote their names all over them, and all was well.

But our implied insignificance can be tempered by two simple observations. First, we are as big to the smallest as we are small to the biggest. Modes of being are relative. Our body, for instance, is made of upward of thirty-trillion cells, each a creature functioning semi-independently and intelligently, though by and large in harmony with its neighbors. If we look inside the inner cosmos of which we are made, we find it to be as bewilderingly immense as when we look out at Hubble's cosmos. Both directions require the same general type of scientific technology to observe, and though we could live here happily without either observation, we are curious by nature—nosy, inquisitive, attracted by anything new. Chimpanzees or bonobos, for instance, stay in the same locale, by and large, but apparently humans, from their beginning, wondered what might lie over that next hill, whether literally or figuratively, physically or mentally.

Discovering the cell was on the same order as discovering the moons of Jupiter and made for excitement and adventure for those interested in such discoveries. In time, our awareness of the cell's complexity increased with the complexity of microscopes used to travel there. The electron microscope revealed a whole world within each cell. In simplest terms, a cell is a body cradling a nucleus of DNA that folds and unfolds within it. The substance around that DNA contains tiny creatures called mitochondria, who busily convert energy into food and vice versa. All this is in a filling or substance called *tubulin,* which makes up much of the cell's interior. Tubulin, in turn, is made of microtubules that are oscillations of frequencies, a force that turns off and on untold times per second. When on, the microtubules are there, when off, they aren't. This seeming on-off whimsy gives a solid basis for cellular structures, but if followed, undermines the one absolute eternal law of physics that has been writ into the stars and heavens: energy can be neither created nor destroyed. But the final, ultimate truth is the fiction of a stuff called *energy.* If energy "turns off," and at that point is not present, where is it? It is no more here than when it is "turned on." The oscillations of the microtubules are the very genesis of the strange loop phenomenon that gives rise to matter and the universe it can manifest. As author Robert Sardello explains, energy is a proposal of early science that has never really held water but was invented as a semantic screen for an unknowable force beyond our conceptual frame. Thus, those ghostly, oscillating effects such as the neutrino and microtubules are labeled for convenience by science to screen out a category of being that would simply unhinge scientific tautologies if brought to light.

A sperm is a very tiny cell consisting of a body that is not much more than a folding of DNA and a tail or flagellum by which it propels itself toward the egg. That tail is made of nine microtubules arranged in a circle and supposedly powered by mitochondria. On admission to the egg, the tail falls off, as they say, but in actuality the mitochondria simply stop powering the microtubules, at which point they aren't—because they are not needed any more so tubulin, made of countless microtubules and making up much of a cell and thus our body, is of the same order of magnitude in reverse as that cosmos out there (which we assume is made of more tangible stuff—though such stuff is still an assumption we need lest our mind-set truly fall into chaos.

The second observation tempering our insignificance is that when you own the mint, as nature does, you don't have to pinch pennies. Said differently, nature's profligate and endless redundancy and massive apparent wastefulness of so much to achieve so little can't be overstated. But why not operate this way? Create one particle or wave of energy, if only as an illusion or play of mind, and relate it to another—such as nine microtubules combined to make a perfectly serviceable tail—and the process is put in motion to create anything and everything forever.

This cycle movement has no need ever to stop because in the strange loop effect found everywhere in nature, creation doesn't begin anyway—at least not in any logical or linear way according to our sensibility. Creation simply *is* an ever-present origin that hinges on the relationship of things that were themselves created out of waves, vibrations, or frequencies.

The early child, in its play, creates an interior imaginary world. He then projects this on the exterior world of his senses, which are assembled, and by that same imaging brain-mind he plays in what developmental psychologist Lev Vygotsky called the "modulated reality" of his own "let's pretend," but such play can never be other than actions of that very same brain-mind. This amounts to a true and functional tautology—a tautology that can work! All the child wants to do is play in this state, a kind of divine play in which he has dominion over his created world. He is actually playing God. Stop the child's play and you kill both his rising dominion and natural divinity.

No effort is actually involved in creation. With no effort, the child at play creates worlds to inhabit. Creation is free. Only when we arrive at higher, mature forms of life, such as adult humans, do we see that this free ticket is lost and charges for everything start accruing. We then tend to make effort of everything, perhaps as a means of establishing self-importance or giving meaning. This peculiar human compulsion taking the form of a search for meaning or the desire to be important arises from a notion that we are unworthy of such a grand event at this life, a peculiar pathology that seized us somewhere along the line of ancient history and wrecked our play. We even act as though we're not supposed to be here at all and must somehow justify our existence or buy our way with blood, sweat, and tears. Because of our enculturation, we can't grasp the idea that as the end product of this stochastic trick of creation, we are, by default at least, co-owners of that process that brings us about. No matter at what remove, we are heirs to both the mint and the process of making mints, yet we seem to prefer to squander our lives in scrabbling, cheating, lying, stealing, murdering, and warring—over pennies.

Bonding Nature's Imperative: Relationship and the Heart[14]

Our heart maintains relationship between and within our cells, organs, brain, and body and the world of others. Appropriate relationship is intelligent action, and within the heart lies a neural complex or "brain" that plays a principle role in this ability to relate to our environment and each other in ways that lend to well-being and pleasure. This body, brain-mind, and heart dynamic determine the kind of world experience we have, which in turn feeds back into that dynamic. The heart is the common center in this play of relationship and mind is the reciprocating recipient.

The heart is neutrally connected with every facet of the body and brain but has no neural complex for making judgments. The ability to qualify experience and judge the value of an event is assigned to the heart's servant—the brain in our head. As a result, the overarching intelligence of the heart rains equally on the just and unjust, leaving out of its domain our tangled fabric of judgment. To begin with, the heart doesn't register such information as content; apparently, it registers only an event's emotional nature.

Wisdom results when the judgmental capacity of brain is in synchrony with the heart's intelligence, resulting in discrimination, discretion, and logical common sense as passed down through generations. Judgment, on the other hand, is wisdom run amok, the brain functioning without the heart, leading to culture and its constraints.

Universal heart and individual mind are mutually dependent, each necessary to the other. Judgment of a person disrupts relationship, an unintelligent error the heart is apparently incapable of making, but which the brain-mind seems fatally subject to making unless it is bonded with that heart. Out of the reciprocal mirroring of heart and brain our universe arises, with our individual self as its center.

Unity and Communion Must Occur through the Heart[15]

The dynamic of the heart-brain-mind relationship in a dialogue of balance is the foundation, not the goal, of the great journey of relationship. . . . The goal of full heart-brain-mind dialogue is simply reestablishing our basic natural integration before enculturation splits our system. This does not imply a kind of Luddite, back-to-the-jungle time, but it may be that only by getting us back to some hypothetical point zero of our natural state can a movement into full relationship and development take place.

The fulfillment of the heart's relationship occurs through one heart relating with another heart. Because there is only one heart, however, it can relate to itself only as itself in another person. It is through this that the proposal that heart as both universal and individual takes on cosmic significance. In taking on the colorations and characteristic of that self or person in whom it is lodged, the heart has simultaneously both unique individual expression and universal ground. Two hearts, each experienced as an individual self in its unique variation, can experience ecstatic relations with each other through their individual selves, fusing into the universal aspect within each. Two hearts beating as one in their physical overlapping necessarily include a corresponding overlapping of their individual electromagnetic fields radiating out at the same time that the universal within is fusing. It is telling to note that we and bonobos are the only mammals who make love face-to-face, thus heart-to-heart.

To function, the individual heart and mind must be separate and unique on one level, but on another level their unity, the ground from which their uniqueness springs, never changes. Only through their uniqueness can relationship take place, and only through relationship can reality be created and experienced. On this rests the whole riddle of existence, though it leaves hang the primal paradox around which our life circles. As Sören Kierkegaard said in his great prayer, "Even the fall of a sparrow moves Thee, but nothing changes Thee, O Thou Unchanging."

From conception, our enculturation separates us from that heart-self within (which Robert Sardello calls the "soul of the world") and prevents us from, through our head, getting back in sync with that universal within us.

The claim that pleasure and joy are the whole purpose of life is hotly contested by our entire cultural ideation, our very mind-set, and, above all, religious belief. We are here to serve culture under its myriad guises: worshiping god, serving humankind through self-sacrifice, suffering and working for the welfare of those out there, and so on. This world of cultural counterfeits clamors for our attention and drains our lives. Sooner or later, we find each counterfeit an empty delusion, a virtual reality that leaves us with nothing but our un-assuaged longing heart. . . . Intent outweighs all other factors, and the intent of the mind united with the heart unifies all culture's fragmentations. As Kierkegaard said, "Purity of heart is to will one thing."

The Role of DNA in Mirroring[16]

To be initiated and enveloped, each infant-child's potential ability, even those genetically inherent in us, must be given direct contact with an example of that particular potential in its developed, functional form. Only if given resonant signal information from a model can the DNA within the infant-child build its own fair copy because this building involves mirror neurons and resonance between the DNA of child and model. We are born mimics. Through imitation new life and creativity arises.

In this we find why, as mentioned by those investigating mirror neurons, virtual realities betray the developing child. Resonance between entities, Paul MacLean proposed, is the way all relationship and events unfold; the way the brain communicates its many relationships; indeed, the way the whole neural system of body-brain works. Resonance is relationship, and relationship, again, is all there is. If you pluck a string on an instrument, a faint humming occurs in all strings resonant with the one plucked; they vibrate through the waves set up by that primary string. The whole physical basis of harmonics rests on this relationship, and when we walk into a room and note that the "vibes" feel good we are simply experiencing resonance. Virtual realities involve frequencies that can stimulate certain audiovisual and positive-negative emotional reactions but offer no resonance, nothing synchronous with the heart's feeling-sense, nothing similar to the resonance we pick up in wordless communication with others, the feelings that can nurture, comfort, and strengthen us. Feeling and sensory stimulus are hardly identical.

DNA is acutely sensitive to signals from its environment, particularly those "molecules of emotion." The emotional centers that control the immune system are extremely sensitive to these molecules broadcast from every direction.

A 1998 study shows a similar phenomenon. Briefly, it states that a pregnant mother's emotional state critically influences the brain growth of the infant in her womb. If the mother feels secure, loved, calm, and cared for, or—of paramount importance—if she can establish such a state within her regardless of environment, she will give birth to an infant with an enlarged forebrain (the source of higher intelligences) and a smaller hindbrain (the ancient reptilian survival system). If a mother is depressed, fearful, or anxiety-ridden, she will give birth to an infant with a heavier musculature, enlarged hindbrain, and reduced forebrain, a common-sense move of nature's, though a devolutionary one.

If DNA were not sensitive to information signals from its environment, evolution could never have taken place and our remarkable adaptability would not exist—and the higher in evolution we go, the more critical this DNA-emotional factor is. At every conception in our species, then, nature asks, in effect: "Will we be able to move into the higher realms of intelligence this time, or must we defend ourselves again?"—an evolutionary question answered by the molecules of emotion in our mother.

The Heart as a Brain[17]

The heart is a major endocrine gland of our body, producing a whole family of hormones that affect the functions of every organ and, above all, the brain. Which hormone is released when to influence what is determined largely by information sent to the heart from the emotional-cognitive or old mammalian brain in our head, as well as from our body as a whole. The heart has a complex neural structure or "brain" that connects with the brain in our head and every organ in our body. Thus the heart literally orchestrates the whole complex of body-brain-mind.

Rudolf Steiner predicted that the greatest discovery of late-twentieth-century science would be that the heart is not merely a pump but also a major source of intelligence and that our greatest challenge would be to allow the heart to teach us a new way to think, which, it seems, would open us to higher worlds. Steiner pointed out that the heart picks up and responds to both the inner senses of our body and the outer senses of the world. . . . Dropping our ideation and assumptions thus can reconnect us with the heart, a first step to ever-deeper and more conscious connections with our life.

In our enculturated blindness, however, we screen out this present moment on behalf of a constant replay of past knowing, like a religion bending our present back onto a dead past or implanting a dead past into the present.

The Death of Play and the Birth of Religion[18]

In 1975, while working on my third book, *Magical Child,* a schoolteacher asked how he was supposed to teach children anything and prepare them to face the hard reality of life when all they wanted to do was play. I realized that all I had wanted to do as a child was play or be told stories (a form of play), and all my own children had wanted was to play or be told stories.

I knew this teacher's "hard reality" was a fiction made real by eliminating play. (I remembered too well when I was six years old and being sent to what I thought was a nightmare world (school) splitting me from the real world of play.)

Play is life living itself, nature celebrating herself, with no explanation or need for justification. We are born to play. . . . From the moment of conception, life expands through bonds of belonging, pleasure, and joy. Relating with each other and the earth is play. The more complex the organism, the higher its intelligence and the more complex its play of relationships, with the highest of all being the ever-unfolding expressions of love. Play expresses life's love of itself, the highest moral imperative.

The Importance of Play in Relationships and Learning[19]

Early on, the infant plays with the nipple, plays peek-a-boo with that benign face up there—indeed, with great delight it plays at everything, knowing of nothing but play (until we set about to adjust it to reality and teach it to take life seriously). In play, every action is a learning, our brain free to imprint without censure or pressure. Under any such pressure, energy shifts back to the hindbrain, making difficult forebrain actions such as learning.

Primary mother-infant bonding assures affectionate-sexual love in the adolescent and adult. Loving, playful relationship that extends to society, the living earth, and creation itself is our natural state.

Through the ongoing mirroring of relationship within ever-widening matrices, children discover and define who they are and what their place in the world and, ultimately, the universe might be. Through the nature and quality of the mirrored relationship between individual and parent and then between individual and society is determined what is learned, which capacities are developed, and even what is remembered. As Michael Mendizza explains, what is actually learned at any time is the state in which the learning takes place—playful and joyful or grim and threatening.

Joy and pleasure are the bricks and mortar of physical, psychological, social, and spiritual development; and the developing brain must experience joy and pleasure if the complex integration of sensations is to take place. In those first three years or so (when the amygdala locks in its repertoire) an infant-child denied joy and pleasure, touching, caressing, and movement develops a brain that is "neurodissociative," as James Prescott explains, one that fragments rather than integrates experience. The same critically holds true at puberty and adolescence. Eliminate the safe space of pleasure and joy, acceptance and nurturing, and this expansive, integrated exploration of the world is curtailed and impeded. As a result, the adolescent regresses or dissolves into self-defensiveness, with its implicit violence that will finally surface as domination of others or be internalized as neurosis, illness, or suicide. The emotionally malnourished child may also experience an intensified sexuality at adolescence to compensate for an impoverished sensory-emotional system, but this sexuality is devoid of affection or love, is often violent and destructive, and is hardly conducive to family and nurturing of offspring, should any ever come to be.

The Origins of Religion[20]

A fundamentalist Christian, a seemingly bright woman with a Ph.D., explained to me at length that it was our duty as adults to break the will of infant-children, teaching them to obey in order that they, having then no will of their own, could be open to God's will and be obedient to him. If we fail to do this, she said seriously, and leave the child willful, both the child's soul and the adults' souls are imperiled and we face the risk of hell. So much for a loving god. Books urging corporal punishment from at least the fifteenth month on have been and still are bestsellers. "Spare the rod and spoil the child" has a long lineage, but we might change the phrase to "Spare the rod and spoil the corporate world that relies on such 'broken' children for laborers and our Pentagon that needs them as their fodder for wars." Without that rod, an actual individual might appear—a danger to culture itself.

A university professor I knew, a preacher in his early years before awakening to the travesty of his belief, wrote a brilliantly researched book on what he considered a major error of history: monotheism. (I remember our sixth grade teacher explaining to us that monotheism was the greatest realization our species ever had.) My friend's history showed that as long as any social group or individual could freely discover God within themselves and their world and work out whatever relationship seemed to flow, peace reigned. But when the notion of one God came along—a jealous, violent male God to boot—it wrecked everything, resulting in "Your god and mine can't both be the true one, so one of us has to go!" Thus the battle begins.

How many centuries have Muslims and Jews been at each other's throats, playing eye-for-eye, with both sides blind as bats as a result? And they may well yet bring the world down, leaving us with the one true god: the god of absolute destruction.

A recent historian wrote that the language Jesus must have spoken was Aramaic, not Hebraic. The Greek translations of the Hebraic translations of the supposed Aramaic sayings of Jesus coming down to us in our gospels were made by the blatantly male chauvinist followers of Paul the Apostle—and in every case of Jesus's reported use of the word for creator or creative process, these Greek translations use the word *father*. The actual Aramaic word used can in some cases be interpreted as gender-free but is generally feminine. Throughout history, that which brings about life, growth, harvest, that which gives birth of any sort is feminine, as is logical according to experience. Mother Nature is acknowledged worldwide, while Father Nature is apparently a Christian novelty.

The Demonizing of Sexuality[21]

Religion as a foundation of culture plays its trump card by reversing our natural reward-threat systems with a demonic twist so that pain and suffering become virtues and physical-emotional pleasures become sins. Religion levies this brooding accusation and guilt against us all by, among many devious ruses, connecting this inversion to sexuality. Through this cultural ploy the human spirit diminishes while the religious pathology of guilt, sin, and hoped-for salvation (that is, being bailed out of an impasse from which we can't ourselves escape) becomes the fountain not just of culture but of our conscious mind itself.

In violation of evolution and countless millennia of social-biological heritage, the integrative nature of joy and pleasure (rewards) and the dissociative nature of pain (punishment) have been reversed to further control and modify behavior in ways opposite nature's imperative. Through fear and pain, outright physical punishment or the even greater pain of abandonment and being cast out, religion wields its deadly sword.

Religious belief creates gender inequalities that strain the bonds of male-female dynamics on which family life and society depend whether Hebraic, Christian, Islamic, Buddhist, or Hindu, religion represents the creator-creative process in the paradoxical, irrational, and destructive image of a male God (the only male in history to give birth, however, metaphorically) who instills in us the intensely powerful energy of sexual drive only to then promise to punish us severely or even eternally if we give in to this drive in any way except through tightly controlled cultural channels of restraining. Checkmate!

Religion's deadly finger of guilt is levied on females as the originators of this sin of sexuality (turning on us males-as-victims with every movement). But it also touches male children as well, making sex or even bodily functions "dirty." Particularly in the Catholic tradition, any deviance from these cultural constraints concerning sex is considered especially sinful if we should enjoy the act. (If you must engage in such acts, however, better to marry than burn, as Paul the misogynist put it.)

How renunciation of sex became a religious issue isn't difficult to trace. In this we find the most efficient stranglehold on humanity ever achieved by culture: religions teach that renunciation of body and its pleasures on behalf of spirit is the quickest route to salvation, which means deliverance from hell invented by a God of justice who was in turn invented by rage-filled humankind.

In *The Biology of Transcendence,* I claimed that sexuality can be a key to transcendence, an opening of the higher worlds, and a premonition of union with our Ground of Being, which can be a truly mystical journey between a spiritually bonded pair. . . . Thus, of all our joyful expressions, sexuality is the one that must be curbed and crippled by culture, lest culture's bondage be cast aside. Culture brings endless ways of rejecting the body, leading to emotional and touch deprivation in infancy and childhood, particularly in the form of the inability or refusal to breastfeed infants. Breastfeeding is designed by nature to be a richly rewarding sensual experience for the infant-child and an equally rewarding sexual-sensual experience for the mother. As many mothers privately confess, orgasm is a frequent companion to nursing and a definite part of nature's plan.

The joys and pleasures of relationship are obviously the glue that bonds and makes possible a true civilized society, while the virtual reality of electronics and medical prosthetics offer synthetic counterfeits that only further isolate and substitute for those needs they block and replace. Pleasure and joy are not only moral but are also morally necessary to develop a truly nonviolent, intelligent society. Pleasure and joy are literally the purpose of and prime impetus in the evolution of our cosmos, planet, species, and life itself.

Religion, however, in all its forms throughout all cultural history, has renounced the devil and all the desires or pleasures of flesh. Whatever the religion, body is bad, and soul is good.

The Rebirth of Spirit and the Resumption of Evolution: The Faith of the Fire Walker—Our Growing Fields of Influence[22]

We assume that technology and science are the highpoints of evolution. But evolution has been involved with the development of greater neural structures of the brain and the subsequent human capacity to move beyond the limitations and constraints of the lower animals. It has nothing to do with the objective, physical devices brains create for altering their environment. A rocket to the moon does not represent an evolutionary expansion. Reaching Steiner's higher worlds, Sardello's exploration-expansion of soul, a discovery of humans' immunity to fire and cold, or our freedom from having to eat food—are clear cases of evolutionary expansion. Our move beyond violence, war, and hatred would be a high-water mark of human evolution.

Meanwhile, every modern device we have invented is slowly (or with dizzying speed) changing the brain that is involved in the invention process itself. We are changing ourselves and destroying nature by the virtual reality we create. As both biologist Gregory Bateson and theologian James Carse as well as cellular biologists Williamson and Pearse have determined, mind and nature are a necessary unity; what we do is what nature is doing, and what we do to nature, we do to ourselves. It goes without saying, then, that just as we are an integral part of nature, nature is part of evolution, for evolution is a self-contained process accountable to nothing. Like space, it apparently goes on forever.

Through a tenacious and open-minded interaction over a number of years, Dutch psychologist Robert Wolff found a wondrous world occupied by the Senoi people who lived nearly invisibly in the Malaysian rain forest. Not only did these people exist in a world closed to our five senses, but they also experienced an unbroken state of peace, love, and harmony with their world and each other. They had, as Wolff explained, no sign of the tension, anger, or depression that we take as a matter of course as part of our human nature, and they possessed and needed virtually no objects of any kind. Each day unfolded a new adventure in discovering an ever-changing world of delight.

They had an edge on the Australian Aborigines in that the Senoi could tune into and comprehend something of the ways and wiles of the white man who had invaded them. They certainly could tune into Wolff, who had to some extent tuned into them. Western thought was destroying the Senoi as a people by systematically destroying their rain forest to build rubber plantations. But the Senoi considered the trees sacred and communed with them. It was symbolic that they and their astonishing reality as reported by Wolff were dying off with their trees.

After several years of association with the Senoi, Wolff was casually and wordlessly initiated into their cosmology, their structures of knowledge, and he was thus able to discover at least something of the astonishing world the Senoi inhabited. This turned out to be the most profound experience of his life and an event that changed the country of his mind. He became aware of the profound setback in evolutionary development that Western humans and our Eastern counterparts have undergone. His conclusion and lament: we have no idea what we have lost.

We have no idea what states of being other civilizations—even those disappearing today—might have brought about or what they might have offered us. All we can seek, grasp, or understand is the difference of physical products, the tangible objects and artifacts, the man-made stuff that different societies and cultures have left and how these compare to what our technology produces. We consider any society that has no technology as our evolutionary inferior.

Should we as a species become tone-deaf—that is, lose our capacity for total discrimination—we would be unable to perceive music as a sensory phenomenon or even comprehend the word *music*. It would be impossible for us to grasp that we had lost something if we had no neural system for experiencing that which was lost. We might at some point read of an ancient society that had once all but worshipped a phenomenon they called *music,* but we couldn't explain this phenomenon outside of its own parameters of sensation because it has no metaphoric equivalents. We can't say music is like anything. *Tone,* for instance, is what it is, not what it is like. And, for a tone-deaf species, *music* would be a useless, meaningless word without referent. If we follow this analogy, we might understand Robert Wolff's deep frustration at trying to get across to us what the Senoi had opened him to. Indeed we have no idea of what we have lost.

From age two or three to age six or so, the child develops internal imaging, which can then be projected onto external objects. At this stage, a matchbox might become a boat, a spool of thread, a car, and so on, with the child playing for hours in a world of his own making—divine play in its preliminary form. From around age six or seven to eleven or twelve, the child builds on this earlier play by developing concrete operational thinking, or the ability to take those internal images and actually change corresponding external objects in the world accordingly—that is, operate on an object with his abstract notions of what it might be and thus change that actual object. This is divine play on a higher level.

At around age twelve or so, the child enters the stage of formal operational thinking, in which he stands outside his brain itself and operates on the very possibilities of thinking and imagination, thereby moving into states of consciousness beyond concreteness. This higher level is itself only a preliminary exercise for the formal operation of creativity, which does not re-create in any way but instead originates states of consciousness outside the boundaries of matter entirely. We have no idea where this process of evolutionary development could lead because the entire evolutionary ladder by which we might grasp this potential has been truncated.

The Australian Aborigines developed these formal operations to an astonishing extent, encompassing capacities that we can in no way comprehend or duplicate (not even with drugs or with our virtual reality). They intuitively knew where all members of their tribe were at any time, though they might be separated by vast miles, and where in those desert wastes the underground water lay. They could detect a rainfall fifty miles away and move to intercept it, and they lived in perfect harmony and balance with that harsh land for near fifty thousand years. While the Aborigines were able to make some of the most sophisticated physical objects through concrete operations (such as the boomerang, which is a double hydrofoil wing assembly that can travel three hundred yards without varying up or down and, if it missed its target or prey, would return to the exact spot from which it was thrown), they kept their objects of possession to a bare minimum, emphasizing instead the state of mind that was their true treasure and mark of maturity. As a cultural practice, the Aborigines left no trace of themselves in their walkabouts, which, because they were hunter-gatherers, were constant and ongoing, believing the earth was sacred and should be disturbed as little as possible. Indeed, physical artifacts were rarely used because they were deemed a hindrance or encumbrance to their state of dreamtime in which they communed together and which they considered the real world.

Since we Westerners could not perceive the states of consciousness the Aborigines inhabited and saw these people instead as only naked savages, we considered them the lowest form of human life. In fact, we justified, they were too stupid even to build houses or make clothing. Dreamtime, which apparently was far more rewarding than objects such as houses or clothing, was outside our perspective and world.

As developed, science is an expression of formal operational thinking limited to that which can be expressed physically, which means through concrete operational process. In scientific practice, then, the next higher rung of the evolutionary ladder, formal operations, finds expression through a form of concrete operations, a lower evolutionary ability. While this lifts the lower into the nature of the higher, as evolution is designed to do, the higher becomes entangled with the lower, as evidenced in our fascination with all manner of novelty products, which leads to the net devolutionary decline that is today destroying our earth. As a people stripped of all interior worlds, we have rapidly become dependent on the virtual reality we've created. Riveted on such a reality and its constant changes, we are changing with it. Science as an abstract application of concrete operations becomes a religion and a self-destructing process.

Life's Strange Loops of Mind and Nature[23]
When I, a layman, consider DNA, I genuflect in awe. DNA and life seem to be a unity—a paired, reciprocal dynamic as in mind and nature, or creator and created. "Lift up the stone and I am there, break the stick and I am there"—wherever there is life there seems to be some form of DNA saying everywhere "I am here." Where does this double helix come from? It comes from life, just as life comes from DNA. Life is found deep in the ocean under incredible pressures, where an environment made by boiling thermal fissures provides for great slithery creatures, some as much as six feet long, that live and die like the rest of us. In gross polar extremity, life is also found in the form of algae locked in Antarctic ice.

A Different Kind of Sight[24]
DNA produces photons, little bits of light, on a regular periodic basis, although that double helix is itself too narrow to be registered by a light wave (it is less than ten atoms across and is thus invisible to anything but an electron microscope, which, in turn, makes it visible to us). If each of the more than thirty-eight trillion cells in our body nurturing DNA produces a periodic photon, then a light body dwells within us.

"If your eye be single, your whole body is filled with light," Jesus said. The DNA strand in each cell, though only ten atoms across, is about six feet in length. If you stretched out, end to end, all the DNA in one single body, that strand would stretch around the earth and to the moon and back several billion times. Looking within, we find the same eternity as that which stretches out.

Our inner vision, which comes from the heart, can overlay our outer seeing of the world and give creative insight. To be chained to outer vision is to be sense-bound and constrained at every hand. It splits our vision from the unity of the heart, which prevents us from rising and going beyond limitation and constraint and closes us off from the possibilities of divine imagination.

The Importance of Positive Coherency [25]

While our body as a whole radiates varying forms of coherent positive energy, which is life-supporting, as we have learned, negative incoherent waves go no further than their immediate surrounding because they can't cohere with anything. The Neoplatonic philosopher Plotinus proposed that creation is the expression of love searching for its own reflection and fulfillment. If this is the case, to be sustained within our universe of coherent frequencies we call love, our world must radiate back out into that universe those very coherent frequencies.

Interestingly, a reciprocal energy exchange between earth and the cosmos may be undergoing alteration in our day because of the proliferation of electronics worldwide and the related flooding of the earth with the virtual reality of media. All forms of media, computers, televisions, and now cell phones (some equipped with televised visual stimuli) are everywhere in the world today. Media focuses on negative (at times violent) content, which, as it activates our startle-alert survival instincts below our awareness, grabs and holds our attention. Locked on to such potentially dangerous signals, our old sensory-motor brain is loath to turn away from them, even though our mind, the last to be informed, might hate what we are watching. The overall effect of this worldwide negative energy nurtures culture even as we and our living world slowly succumb to depression. Meanwhile, the Vastness of the whole doesn't know that anything is wrong because it is a positive radiation outside all incoherent frequencies. Coherency and incoherency can't cohere.

Cosmic Chaos, Cosmic Order[26]

A recent satellite image of the earth's magnetic activity shows a remarkable mish-mash of chaotic pulses forming a deep web of confused circuitry on the surface of our earth. The image also shows that our earth still radiates those orderly torus fields of electromagnetic energy as found around the sun in its vast multiplicity and in simpler form around our heart. If we look closely at this recent image, however, we can find no trace of any coherency in such a messy bag of electrical worms covering the surface of the planet.

Our evolutionary neural system was born from and geared for coherent electromagnetic fields in orderly harmony. Each of the myriad electromagnetic torus-like fields of the sun is, within itself, coherent and orderly, as are those large-scale fields of earth holding our planet's relation with the whole solar system. But the jumble of chaotic surface activity revealed by this satellite image is where we live and breathe, and our earth's protective belts can't protect us from our own man-made harmful radiations. Meanwhile, a strange planet-wide feeling of unease is slowly spreading, and the overall effect of this created chaos remains to be seen.

Our cosmos is geared for coherency within itself, and our life and brain-mind arose through harmonious relations within an orderly world. We are not built for chaos or disorder, but for lifting chaos into order. Coming into sync with our heart, which maintains within it the coherency of the cosmos, can lift us up and out of our predicament if we will take the time to tune in.

Laughing Together, Weeping Alone[27]

As we "think" in our heart—coherently or not—so we are, and it may be getting more and more difficult to think positively in the heart.

Despite our serious intent on a positive focus, energy tends to be drawn to defensive procedures below our awareness. If the way to get in touch with a higher power is through positive frequencies, which our depressed state lacks, we are, as we have seen, in an apparent double bind. While to him who has more and more is given, from him who hasn't more is taken away—even that little he has, our great model observed two millennia ago. This is true of individuals, nations, worlds.

This brings us back to the issue concerning the temporary state of worldwide shock following 9/11. As the world's most powerful nation and with the eyes of all trained on us more intently than ever, with the appropriate leadership we could have—for the first time in recorded history—changed the course of human events through forgiveness and reconciliation rather than retaliation and war. Our leaders, however, fed on that state of shock to loose a long-schemed web of insidious machinations for domination, while doing their dirty work by not only hiding behind the facade of waving flags, as is common for political tricksters, but also using the infinitely more noxious ploy of hiding behind the cross—the very cross on which was born into our world forgiveness as a way of deliverance from ages of strife and sorrow.

Brain Change[28]
How do we escape the trap of culture's religious and rediscover the intelligence of heart and a life of spirit? To prescribe a remedy for our ailments, we must first have an accurate estimate of just what the ailment is.

The Shutting Down of the Brain[29]
Neuroscientist Marian Diamond said our higher functions of brain will continue to shine brightly as long as they are challenged and used, but the higher newest brain in our system is the "laziest muscle in the body" and wants to go on the shelf early. Our ancient instinctive brains require far less energy and maintenance than the later evolutionary systems.

My physician friend Keith Buzzell pointed out that just as we build our brain from the earliest reptilian on up, adding the newer additions like layers on a cake, we sadly and too often die from the top down. Societies and cultures can undergo profound changes in overall brain development through changes in usage and application of those brain systems and can also die from the top down through disuse or misuse of them.

As we explored earlier, the emotional state of a pregnant mother affects the nature, structure, size, and function of the infant brain forming in her womb. Consider the ramifications if her own awareness and emotional state are equally affected by her culture.

Our brain evolved in a low-intensity sensory environment, but today at birth and in the early years it is overwhelmed by our new electronic, high-density virtual reality overloads.

Rather than some glorious evolving toward the stars or higher states, research shows specific devolutionary deterioration in brain growth and mental function from these changes. Those in charge of the study at Tubingen, for instance, observed that these young people tended to create an environment of high-density stimuli because, without it, they were subject to boredom bordering on anxiety. Their sensory gate screened so rigorously that ordinary or natural stimuli made little impression. The young people suffered a form of sensory isolation and anxiety when in quiet, non-technological setting.

The nature of movies, computer games, popular music, and media in general grows in intensity to compensate for the growing insensitivity of the populace as a result of the higher gating of the RAS, which, in an ongoing cultural loop, is itself brought about by that high-intensive sensory level.

Recent studies in the United States have stated that the average six-month-old infant spends two hours a day in front of a television screen. . . . This television exposure results in the primary sensory patterns of our reptilian brain locking into a danger-alert mode in reaction to the underlying flicker of the screen and the rapidly shifting imagery that create such sensory confusion that they indicate possible threat. This old-brain startle effect keeps the high brain alert for emergency and entrained with the lower brain as the child stares at the screen. Of course, the resulting immobility makes the infant-child "safe" so parents can neglect him.

All of these developmental guideposts previously observed have been challenged recently, however, which means nature's orderly plan for development itself may be breaking down or shifting and the old norms are becoming outmoded. We need only consider the remarkable change in the onset of puberty—down from an average age of fourteen or fifteen to eleven or twelve in less than a half century.

Virtual reality gives counterfeit substitutes that work against development. It creates artificial environments much as the culturing of an organism in a test tube does. Entire societies or segments of them are undergoing serious changes as a result, and the norms by which we can look objectively at our own situation may themselves be so altered that the old abnormal will become the new norm.

Voices in the Wilderness [30]

If we tally up the studies of James Prescott, Alice Miller, Lloyd deMause, and Riane Eisler, to mention only a few, we might see how evolution's higher organizing forces bringing about humanity move to strengthen and renew the fragile hold love and altruism have in history. In this stochastic creation, the human has sunk to subhuman levels time and again, but those higher forces that formed us continually move for our well-being, in effect staging slow evolutionary comebacks at each of our backslides.

Maria Montessori's sobering comment that a humankind abandoned in its earlier formative period becomes the greatest threat to its own survival was made years before Alice Miller's study showing how the Nazi Holocaust in Europe may well have arisen from just such lack of nurturing in childhood.

This book has had as its target what Rudolf Steiner referred to as the "mystery of Golgotha," for I have long sensed that in that event lay a key to the way out of our mirrored madness. So entangled are we in survival issues that we can't be fully aware of the part we play in them, though we might see the play of forces in projected form. Safely long-gone and mythological overlaid, Golgotha, as symbolic of the struggle between culture's darkness and creation's light, might break through to us unawares, slip in under our protective radar, and show us how the major portion of the human condition and of our current dilemma is nothing new but instead has played out again and again.

The Field Effect That Produced Jesus[31]

Jesus was a product of his culture yet did not fit its pattern. Otherwise, he could not have been open to that which was radically other than that culture itself. As a product of his culture, he brought to completion a major aspect of that culture's field of longing, which was centuries in the making, just as Mozart or Bach were products of the rich field of music inherent in their day, or Gordon Gould was a product of the field of physics in his. The lightning bolt that Jesus experienced generated out of not only the long quest of those Semites but also the general quest of that historic period as a whole. The great beings who have cropped up in various areas and times throughout history have focused on serious ontological issues, not on local politics.

Over time, then, these Hebrews, perhaps inadvertently, had produced the right circumstances that led the way to the evolutionary breakthrough that tried to take place in the events culminating on that lonely "hill of the skull." The word *tried* is key for we must remember this is a stochastic creator-created world, which is to say Golgotha failed in any direct effect, though it has not yet failed completely in a long-range one. The wheels of evolution can grind slowly.

Mythologizing Great Beings[32]

Only genuine movers and shakers, whether or not we care for the nature of their moves or shakes, capture the imagination and qualify as targets for such historic movements of mind.

Once the process of mythological overlay begins, that original figure is fair game for the plays of mind made by anyone attracted to or resonating with that figure, even if the attraction is negative. Through this attraction, whether positive or negative, an individual adds to this mythologized figure his or her own bit of interpretive or imaginative insight. It is this very interpretive overlay and the compulsion that engendered it that can become the real value of the original figure.

Through mythical overlay, the kernel or seed or origin of such figures grows like the layers an oyster grows over an irritating grain of sand. And these mythical figures, however varied their linguistic cloaks, were probably real cultural irritants in their day. Nevertheless, most of them finally emerged as genuine pearls of great price—a price that all too often each personally paid. Over time, these legendary figures with their accumulated layers of belief, theories, and passions are bartered, bought, sold, lied about, and warred over until the original person underlying them may be long forgotten.

If we delve into such mythical beginnings, we generally find a fictionally reconstructed childhood and romantic history by which we can anchor that figure in our own emotional memory and time-space. . . .

The question thus arises: Will the real Buddha please stand up? This can be a futile question, however, even if the answer could conceivably be unearthed, for the original figure might be quite insignificant—even of little worth—once stripped of the finery added over the centuries.

Unless our great beings of history can somehow remain fairly unbound by tradition, they too lose their effectiveness—and we serve a dead tradition. . . .

The word *tradition* comes from the Latin *traducare,* "to traduce," "to betray," to trade in or barter away. Tradition is a snare, locking the present into a replication of the past, a dynamic similar to the one that led to the fate of Sanskrit, with its vitality diminished and its fresh content immobilized in formal overlay until it had gone stale and was spoiled and of no use—except to those diehards upholding the tradition, those whose identities are locked into it, whose egos are invested in it, or whose fortunes depend on it. Tradition and religion go hand-in-hand—two cultural supports tying us to replications of the past and blocking the unfolding of our future in the present.

As a result of mythological overlay, asking the real Jesus to stand up is futile, though he might stand quite tall in the divine imagination of those of us caught in his overall drama of soul, which is where the true power lies anyway. In my own case, at several pivotal crisis points in my adult life, this mythical image of Jesus formed within me since birth (as I mirrored my parents, who themselves mirrored theirs), concretized in my childhood, and was rejected in adolescence. But when I was around age thirty, Jesus made a dramatic resurgence in my mind's eye, which clearly shifted me into a less chaotic mode of mind and even, on occasion, indicated a particular decision I should make or actual direction I should take. Further, this mythical figure seemed to fill me with the strength to carry out these decisions. Regardless of which part of my psyche was talking to which, my experience showed me that Julian Jayne's bicameral mind is always with us in some Laski Eureka! fashion—and that things aren't quite as simple as we might prefer.

Socrates and Jesus[33]

The intelligence of the heart, that Darwin 2 higher force of benevolence and love, had risen to the occasion through this sacrificial figure who manifested that intelligence—possibly for the first time in history as we know it—only to get strung up for his trouble. This heart solution presented by Jesus would have brought about the complete dissolution of that age-long accumulation of field effect we have referred to as dominator culture—and culture as a self-surviving psychic entity was not about to let this happen . . . not then as not now.

So Jesus arose at the height of the chaotic axial period, and, as happens again and again with those great beings who are "lifted up," when all was said and done, he was not so much a victim of the Romans and that cross as he was of his chief chronicler and mythologizer, Paul. Jesus in fact disappeared in the concoctions of Paul, who, once on the scene, turned to his own advantage (as in the way of many followers) all the patched-up scrapbooks that gave Jesus some background—despite the fact that though Paul's ego needed this, the event at Golgotha did not.

As is so often the case, this extraordinary and giant character Paul himself became the nucleus of extensive mythological overlay that was destined to eventually overshadow the original figure he exploited. As *The Biology of Transcendence* discusses at length, if we look closely at this Pauline phenomenon, we can see some of the roots of the mess we are in today and why we have faced trouble for two millennia, instead of living in the peace and harmony of life that that prince of the heart tried, and is still trying, to bring.

Eureka! Moments and Cracks [34]

Cracks in the cosmic egg are generally sealed almost immediately by the egg itself, a point I brought out in my first book, *Crack in the Cosmic Egg*, a half century ago. The crack that was Jesus's experience and the subsequent translation, concretizing for all to see, could have given us not only a new face of God but of ourselves and a new understanding of the way this wondrous world works. This crack should have been a light bursting into culture's cave of mind, but this would have erased that cultural effect and thus was countered in short order.

The Sealing of the Crack [35]

In the same way that Gould's Eureka! (laser discovery) lifted the field of optical physics, Jesus's Eureka! should have lifted the field from which it arose (ancient Israel) into a new order of functioning that, sooner or later, would have spread worldwide. This lifting up, however, though attempted again and again throughout our history, has never yet been fully achieved. Instead, we find repeated the devolutionary breakdown of evolution's loop. If we consider the long centuries involved in the transition from the bicameral mind to an individual mind, the translation of Jesus's Eureka!, which involved this very transition, almost surely would have taken generations to complete, had it been allowed. It was Paul's intervention, however, that broke the loop, and humanity reverted back to a previous state of mind without knowing anything had been lost.

Thus Paul's Christology usurped Jesus's God in the heart and reinstated old Jehovah himself, resurrected out of the Hebrew Scriptures.

The God toward which Jesus pointed is found only in the heart, that creative force that rains on just and unjust equally, without judgment. Paul, however, presented Jehovah in new garb, a God who claimed to be the epitome of love, but who raved away as always about laws, demands for sacrifice, foment of wars of retribution, and revenge without end. In effect, the summation of Hebraic history through Jesus and his heart was canceled by Paul and his Christ, and history's failings were reinstated pretty much intact.

It was Paul the Apostle, then, the most quoted authority in Christendom and its loudest voice, who sealed the crack that Jesus created in the cosmic egg.

Upstaging Jesus[36]

Thus arose Paul's Christology in which Jesus disappeared and a vaporous heavenly figure formed as the archetypal image of an ethereal otherworld. Toward this image and the afterlife of this otherworld all attention began to center. Like Moses in Jewish antiquity, Paul's Christ was also backed by the Law—the very Paul had opposed yet had become a chief exponent of in new dress. Paul's Law of love supposedly made obsolete all other laws (much as we fight wars that are to end wars). Law itself, however, is, like culture and its wars, a primal error regardless of dress, setting in motion endless tangles of sorrow and conflict.

Religion, so focused on God and cloud nine and afterlife, tends to ignore life as a gift given in this moment, which, to be accepted, must be lived fully in this moment. Even more, culture tells us that first we must get our cow out of the ditch, bury our father, tend to this and that—all backed by that grim "Or else!" should we do otherwise. Culture tells the child he can't live in the joyful world of play but must instead spend those magical, precious years in grim preparation for that which never arrives. Treating this miraculous gift of life as only preparatory to some cloud nine fantasy is culture and religion's great seduction. But our life isn't a dress rehearsal for some vapid, abstract eternity. It is the big show itself, and our living earth is the place and our body our means.

7

◆

The Heart-Mind Matrix (2012)

How the Heart Can Teach the Mind
New Ways to Think

(Originally published in 2010 as *Strange Loops*
and Gestures of Creation)

THE BACKSTORY FROM JOE

In defense, I began writing my first book, *The Crack in the Cosmic Egg,* in the late fifties. The book itself was a protest having been called "mad" by my colleagues. It was a protest against the prevailing academic, consensus view, which narrows our perceptions and limits us to grim necessity, as William Blake would say, to the death of spirit. The series of paranormal events I described challenged the foundations of classical thought. These events took place with abundant objective witnesses. Over time, however, I watched how these witnesses screened out or blurred-over their own perceptions, and I realized this was a necessary move to keep intact their established consensus of what was real. This selective tendency of the brain-mind to screen out what does not fit is part of a general maintenance system, which keeps our collective world experience stable and seems to function below awareness, healing little rifts in the fabric of the known.

Since these paranormal events were my direct experience, not just witnessed, I questioned their meaning, which opened a whole new realm of possibilities, and I wondered how much of our potential this automatic survival-system filters out? Through studying child development, I saw how our cultural self-worldview was formed by our social models; and how this view is locked into the very neural structures of our brains, not as opinion but as a world-forming, perceptual-conceptual process. When writing my third book, *Magical Child,* I started giving workshops and seminars to get feedback on my ideas. By the time I completed the book this feedback had enlarged my original focus to embrace the much larger field I now describe as our astonishing capacities and self-inflicted limitations, to draw our attention to these undeveloped capacities and the limitations we impose on ourselves and on our children.

We have to clarify our use of the term *culture.* We're not bothered about the positive aspects of our culture but by the negative. In regard to either one, to say we create that culture is not the case, nor is it the case to say that we're simply bystanders of a self-creating culture. Culture and the individual involved, rise to each other. There is no culture without the people making it up. There are no people making up a culture without the culture. It's a reciprocal interchange that is found in all aspects of reality. There is not one tiny particle that's not the result of this mirror-to-mirror process. The process underlies everything. People often say we create our reality or I create my reality. That is an illusion by which a negative culture maintains its stranglehold on us. We don't create that negative culture. We enter in through the process of its creation as an integral part of it. We participate in it by just living within it, but we're not creating the culture, nor is the culture creating us.

In my last couple of books, I talked about creator and creation giving rise to each other. You can't have creation without a creator. You can't have a creator without creation. They give rise to each other. If you don't like the word *creation* you can substitute something else, but we're talking about the same thing. And that is the way the whole process functions; evolution being the same thing.

I started off part of my last book disturbed by what's happening in the educational field with the attempt to throw out evolution because of creationism, creationism being, of course, a belief in a creator outside the creative process, which is simply extending the same error. So I'm trying in this book to show the futility of that. There is no creation without a creator—creator giving rise to creation which in turn gives rise to creator. It's simply one of the many ways by which we can look at the way things happen.

You find here again that reciprocal interaction, which was recognized a thousand years ago, between heart and brain. That without brain, heart is nothing. Without heart, brain is nothing. And the great tragedy of the human race in the building what Riane Eisler would call a demonic culture. Once it's arisen and established—this interaction on its own demonic dark level—how are you going to change it? We're talking about the interaction of the whole creative process and once it goes sour, you've got some real problems on your hands.

You see, here is the whole issue. All of us intellects are going to get together and map out our future. We're going to grab the tiller of the world and run it right, and the new spirit opens up and the new spirit being the realm of what—in the last analysis? Not the realm of spirit, but the realm of intellect, intellect at its highest evolutionary point, which then would do what? It would run the show with this incredibly intelligent process in the brain. We've gotten into some real difficulties with that. Culture as a function is not demonic or anything else, it's simply the gathering together of humans because they can do so much more as a group.

Anything in the world of the intellect is going to be a reflection of the past. It's impossible to not be. Even the use of language, each word that the great Meister Eckhart talks will be an image. Every word is an image, and it's an image of the past replicating itself. So we can never escape our past, and all of our human endeavor is to escape the dreadful mess we've made in our past, me and my childhood, me as a parent, and so forth. We have committed all these dreadful errors, but it can change if we can just get to the point where we can open to that which is new. But if we get there, what will we do? We find that we're opening it in order to preserve our agenda lest we should fall into chaos. So every knight in shining armor who rushes down to clean up the mess in Washington, in a short time will simply become part of the mess. Why? Because that agenda carries within it the whole history of this kind of activity: political and so forth.

Nothing can ever happen other than it replicating itself. It will repeat. And now life is exactly the same thing. So the intellect makes just the slightest shift, this infinitesimal shift of your intent behind it and you have got something that's a red-hot sore on the new age scheme, and you'll get some big famous television star backing it up with her money and so forth and so on and you're big time. That's a real reward but this is what I will call a cultural counterfeit. And that is what has kept this demonic culture in force, according to social scientist Riane Eisler, for at least 6,000 years.

The counterfeit is something that culture creates. It's a representation of something, and the more real you can make it the more powerful it is. One of the greatest issues we face today— and here I'll really get into another huge issue, but one that is doing us in and will be the final destruction of the species—is virtual reality. Virtual reality is a counterfeit of what is real.

Today we find that virtual reality represents about 90 percent of a young person's entire experience on a sensory motor level in this world. The average six-month-old infant spends two hours a day in front of a backlit screen, not found in nature, only on the computers and televisions because the child is held on their parent's lap. They will not take their eyes off the screen and will not move. The average five-year-old child has spent 6,000 hours of television viewing, which has supplanted and taken the place of the construction of what has been called "a structure of knowledge of the world." We're talking about straight biology. We're talking about hardcore neural connections in our brain. Today the vast majority of that construction of reality is virtual, not of the real world out there but a representative created within culture itself. And in that we find this sharp deterioration of brain as we have known it.

What has taken place is that our extraordinarily erratic and psychotic species has finally come up with a way to anesthetize their own destruction because the brain that goes through all of this virtual conditioning is anesthetized against any actual occurrences in the real world out there.

I believe it was a couple of books ago I mentioned a university in Germany where they did that work and found profound changes taking place in the actual neural organization of our brain over the past fifty years brought about by virtual reality. And those studies from Japan, on the remarkable changes in the neural organization of the hand and the brain through these little handheld games the children play, and they all play them now. That's how they spend all their time with these little handheld games. Virtual reality bypasses all the structures of the brain involved in relationship, so we find that schools are social disasters because our children have a very low flashpoint in anger control. They go into rage easily and it's uncontrollable. We find these pronounced changes in the neural structure of children brought about by the kind of games children are involved in, which has completely replaced authentic play. Play has been almost totally eliminated in the child in the Western world by virtual reality. Only a very few, exceptional children escape this.

We find that the entire culture is armored, in every sense of the word, against opening up, really identifying with what it means to be human and how the whole structure works. And the whole structure is biological, the incredible, awesome, logic of the life process itself. A book by Douglas Hoffstater, a physicist from Indiana University, was titled *The Strange Loops*. Hoffstater describes how these reciprocal strange loops exist and how science won't pay any attention to them. It's threatening to the scientific community. Why? Because the scientific community's involved in the strange loop process and can't admit it, and the same is true for each of us.

The last chapter of this little book I've just written is about giving up even hope— embracing the state of absolute hopelessness. I remember my friend George Jaydar, saying, "Hope is our greatest enemy." It took me a while to understand it. When I did, it took my breath away. Well of course. Hope is our greatest enemy and the way by which negative culture always wins. The only way out is a total embracing of radical despair where no hope exists at all. Then you let go. And in that letting go, that emptiness of ego and intellect, something completely new emerges. To let go in this way requires the highest degree of nurturing and boding. Without that, the survival-defense system locks us back into fear—the very fear that feeds and sustains culture. Check mate.

EXCERPTS FROM *THE HEART-MIND MATRIX*

The Fall of Man[1]

> *A humankind abandoned in its earliest formative stage,*
> *becomes its own greatest threat to its survival."*
>
> MARIA MONTESSORI, M.D.

Holding in mind the well-known and well-worn issue of Charles Darwin's first opus, *The Origin of Species,* based on genetic mutation, selectivity, and survival of the fittest of those mutations, we will skim over his equally great second, ignored, and almost unknown work, *The Descent of Man.* In this second work, representing the later and more mature half of Darwin's life, he shows how humankind arose through the "higher agencies" of love and altruism. Selectivity and survival, being foundational, are retained, but in service of this higher and more complex life form.

To say the least, Darwin's second work (referred to here as Darwin 2) was not just ignored but virtually buried. In earlier climes the book (and perhaps its author) may well have been the subject of some public bonfires, except it received even less public attention than that. A most powerful tool of materialistic science is simply ignoring, if not ridiculing, alternatives to its mental straightjacket, and accepting love and altruism as our genesis rather than survival of the fittest was beyond the pale of virtually all of contemporary thought.

The issue of this higher evolutionary cycle found in Darwin 2 lies with *nurturing,* which instinct gives rise to, fosters, and allows love and altruism. Nurturing proves to be not only the way by which this human species arose (out of its animal ancestry), it proves to be the only way by which we evolved creatures can then be fully *developed,* from conception to maturity. Nurturing is the staff and stuff of human life, the one indispensable necessity for life (yet it has become so rare).

Those evolutionists aware only of Darwin 1 were and are far too heavily invested in the interwoven fabric of "Neo-Darwinism" to heed any arguments concerning Darwin 2. Neo-Darwinism, an extreme materialist notion arising in the late nineteenth century, has been the genesis of a wide swath of twentieth-century science, in all its branches, and influencing nearly every facet of contemporary culture.

The issue in what follows here centers on this unsung factor of *nurturing,* or the lack of it. That *nurturing* is automatically overlooked by the cultural mind-set of our times is necessary *to* that mind-set, however, that which could not hold *as* a mind-set were the importance and function of nurturing understood and accepted, since culture as we know it would be transformed were nurturing re-instated.

Our most ancient origins, as found in Darwin 1, can be graphically traced in the parade of skulls preceding us, as put together by Ashley Montagu. We were announced quite visibly, so to speak, some brief forty to fifty thousand years ago by the appearance of a braincase with an abnormally large area right above the orbit of the eyes, in the frontal-most part of our skull. (There is a striking difference of profiles of Neanderthal and Cro-Magnon, assumed to be the first fully human creature.) This bulging forehead houses a *prefrontal cortex* found, but scantily at best, in our immediate predecessors and setting us off quite markedly from all our forebears. This particular prefrontal neural grouping constitutes the high point of evolution to date, a large addition to the three-fold structure found in the heads of our nearest evolutionary kin, such as the Neanderthals, and Darwin 2 attributes this addition to the nurturing of love and altruism.

Nurturing gave rise to and is the combined effect of both love and altruism in typical strange loop form. Whatever its roots, nurturing sustained us for millennia and what should have been human life thereafter, with the sky as the limit to what such a system could do.

Paradise Lost[2]

Somewhere along the way, however, nurturing was compromised, diluted, adulterated to the point of being sidetracked, insignificant to the point it finally lost out to survival concerns to varying extent and in different climes and times. (The history of this loss is complex and hypothetical at best while its reality is all too evident.) Today, nurturing, as needed by our species and the earth, has all but disappeared. Pockets of nurturing remained, even into mid-twentieth century, in a few remote and isolated human groups (see Liedloff's *The Continuum Concept,* Wolff's *Original Wisdom,* Colin Turnbull's *The Forest People,* and a few others), offering us critically needed models to study and examples to emulate, if we are to recoup our loss of this major evolutionary tool as nurturing proves to be.

Mirror-to-Mirror—Which Reflection Comes First?[3]

The reason such an evolutionary setback as loss of nurturing became near permanent wherever it occurred, is simple, ironic, and can happen rapidly, within one generation (see Jane Goodall's account of a rogue ape resulting from failure of nurturing). This un-nurtured humankind that resulted and, even with its vastly superior brain, was almost immediately caught up in a deluge of self-inflicted *disasters of every description,* multiplying at every level that followed on the heels of this nurturing failure. In fact, the intensity of the crisis arising can be attributed to that "vastly superior brain." It takes some extraordinary brilliance and creativity to make the incredible mess we have made. Precisely as Maria Montessori warns, we were so immediately absorbed in surviving the results of our own reactive patterns, brought on by failure of nurturing, we had no time, energy, or interest to reflect on how or what happened or was happening to us. This is our condition today, where such loss and projection of the causes of such loss have been replicated age by age, our survival concerns greatly expanded and changing with the times since the sharper this new intellect of ours, the deeper our crisis. (And we are getting smarter all the time and less intelligent.)

The Cultural Counterfeits[4]

To grind on this a bit, failure to nurture expresses in such a myriad of constantly branching critical problems that all objectivity to a possible cause is long since lost. (I spelled this out in the chapter "Time-Bomb in the Delivery Room" in my 1977 book, *Magical Child*. My effort did nothing to counter the effects of that delivery room or bomb or prevent the ongoing production of the two unabated, culture being the power it is.)

Could the importance of nurturing and significance of its loss be realized, we might strive a bit more vigorously to reinstate it, as a *survival response,* while all we have in its place is a mass of cultural *counterfeits* of nurturing. These counterfeits absorb us and constantly betray us even as we are seduced by them. Caught up in trying to make these counterfeits *work,* such attempts *sustain and increase* the counterfeit incentives. And those counterfeits, products of our new and sharper intellect, can border on genius itself, spinning our web of error ever tighter.

If analyzed and brought to light, disasters from our cultural embeddedment are immediately countered by a cultural *counterfeit* of the analysis as the obvious solution for us, thus nullifying any threat of change to the culture itself. Thus culture is a self-sustaining field-effect, and our rationale is at its service.

Consider a species that had no capacity for tonal discrimination. Such creatures could not comprehend the phenomenon of music, could not recognize it if it were played for them, couldn't grasp the fact that to a hearing species they were deprived in auditory sensory experience. How could we be consciously deprived of something we have never known or experienced, nor even heard about since any words describing it would have no meaning since it had no physical referents?

In just this way we have never regained that benevolence-driven mind-set, which was and is the most fundamental feature of humanity, simply because we are now, as a rule, neurally insufficient to the task, just plain lacking the smarts needed. Plenty of smarts, just not the right ones. Our razor-sharp intellect can create and build atom bombs and destroy the very atmosphere of our earth, but the basic intelligence needed to grasp this fundamental problem of loss of nurturing is *gained only by brain-heart development itself.* And brain-heart development is a major thrust of the nurturing function itself, which is, in turn, dependent on brain-heart development. They are a Strange Loop giving rise to each other.

And this is what is lost in enculturation and its counterfeits. The cultural practice creates a condition wherein the cause of our ongoing breakdown can't be perceived. It will always be deflected or projected by an enculturated mind, a typical Catch-22 double bind.

Nurturing should have opened ever-new evolutionary pathways—and still could. Instead, we have locked into a survival mode, which is now considered to be not just the norm, but the "human condition" and/or "human nature." outside of which our mental machinery simply doesn't extend. Around our automatic survival response we have invented an incredibly complex and non-viable environment that we must attend with our whole being to *maintain,* in order to survive that very self-created environment itself—trapping ourselves at every turn and on every level, as Montessori warned decades ago.

The failure to nurture results in serious brain-mind alterations such that any moral-ethical persuasions concerning nurturing are useless. We have had love preached to us for at least two thousand years with virtually no appreciable decrease in violence or increase in love. An approach that might work (and one I have long promoted) is a straight biological-neurological one that, in turn, arises from a Darwin 2 position. The issue lies within the fourfold nature of our "evolutionary" brain.

History of Our Internal Civil War[5]

One of our earliest neuro-scientists (over a half century ago) to realize that this complex brain structure of ours had evolved out of and from earlier creatures was Paul MacLean (whose work more than ever needs to be kept on the front burner). MacLean paved the way for our discovery that we have within our skull not one but four distinct and essentially separate, interactive neural systems, developed over four distinct evolutionary periods. Through the appropriate integration (possible only through nurturing), these four neural systems cooperate as an integrated function in alignment with the heart. Should this fourfold integration fail, we are not only a seriously split-system, but brain's intimate connection with heart is seriously compromised, resulting in what we historically term the "human condition."

Split between these basic evolutionary drives, and largely isolated from the intelligence of the heart, we do indeed end at war with ourselves, individually and socially, each of us with Self split between the intelligence of the heart and a fragmented brain-mind. Self as Mind locks into its most primary survival systems, with culture and its violence reigning supreme, our morbidity breathing down our neck like a specter haunting our days, with fear dominating at all levels.

The Four Evolutionary Stages[6]

In briefest brief, these four evolutionary neural systems in our head and their historical periods of origin are, in their respective evolutionary order: first the so-called reptilian, or "hind," brain, most powerful biologically since the oldest and most firmly entrenched through usage. Karl Pribram described this as the "world-brain," the capacity to sense our physical world and the ability to respond to that world intelligently enough to survive in it.

The next evolutionary step up the ladder was the "old mammalian" brain built on "top-of" and thus outside our sensory-motor foundation. Through this network humankind could be aware of, "witness," and interpret the nature of *relations* between us, sensing creatures and the objects or events encountered and interpreted by our "world-brain" as out-there, rather than just react to such events to avoid or devour them, as would the older reptilian "hind" brain.

This old-mammalian capacity to relate gave rise to ever more sophisticated forms of relating. (For, as pointed out, all creation is relational. Nothing stands alone. Everything *is* only through relationship with something other-to-it, whether selves, souls, minds, worlds, universes, even Creators and their Creations, on and on.)

So the reptilian brain gave content to which the mammalian system could relate, and out of such relationship evolved an emotional (relational) structure giving rise to relations with *meaning* and *significance* and group interactions. In turn, out of groupings of relational meanings or concepts, Nature developed a new neural structure that could project beyond the sensory brain entirely. This *"new* mammalian" brain gave the rudiments of thought and speech through which we could reflect on an event in an abstract way; that is, extract out of direct sensory contact a mental and objective viewpoint *of* such relations and even their possible outcomes.

This "new mammalian" system could be guided both by heart-intelligence and constantly updated concepts or generalized thought-collections concerning events rather than just instinctive sensory awareness of and reaction to an event as itself. This new capacity, in turn, called for, made necessary, and gave the foundation for a fourth "governing," or coordinating, brain to organize into a unit or single system of these three independent foundational systems (reptilian sensory-motor, mammalian-emotional, and rudimentary thinking brain).

This fourth coordinating and governing body of neurons (called the *prefrontal cortex*) emerged when conditions were right—sufficient maturity of the three preceding brains, reptilian, old and new mammalian, and the appropriate nurturing. Critical as well were the appropriate environmental conditions; namely, a warm enough climate that all effort did not have to be devoted to bare survival, making possible the sufficient *nurturing* critical to this new system and its marked superiority. Once established, this new "governing" fourth brain could bring about adaptation to extremes of climate and physical conditions, which means overcome the limitations and constraints that might arise. Evolution was taking wings (and a major step was taken in overcoming our species constant awareness of its mortality and attempt to move beyond it).

Creation and the Prefrontals[7]

Through this fourth, newest, large, and superior brain, the *prefrontal cortex,* nature could organize all capacities inherent within the first three systems and bring them into a coherent, focused attention and response. Above all, this fourth brain was (is) capable of creation in a literal sense: first creating internal images not present in the outer world (creative imaginations), then concretizing, making real, such inner images *in* the "outer" sensory-world shared with others ("concrete operational thinking," to use Jean Piaget's term).

This, in turn, prepared for and brought about the possibility of Formal Operations of mind, as Piaget called them, wherein we can think and imagine outside all concrete, material realms, and, in effect, operate on our very own brain structure from which mind and such operations emerge. Nobelist Roger Sperry referred to this as mind *emerging* from its matrix—brain—this emergent system can then bend back on, analyze, and change that very matrix giving rise to it. (A wild analogy might be of an automobile coming out of a complex assembly line and turning around to rearrange the complex of assemblies giving rise to itself.)

Transcendence, Incorporation, and Integration[8]

So we humans evolved through a series of new neural-physical structures, each developed to go beyond the limitations and constraints of those coming before and giving rise to it (which is the meaning of *transcendence*). Yet each new system is critically dependent on the older one as its foundation. Though we transcend this older system we must utilize it to function at all. And, in the process of utilizing any previous system (a sensory-motor system is handy after all), the earlier system is *itself transformed* by the higher, with which it must be integrated, in order for the lower to *serve* that higher system. Which is surely both a Strange Loop and the last word in tautologies, but it also allows us to say the "reptilian" or sensory-motor brain in our head is light-years beyond essentially the same component parts in the brain of the black snake in my woodpile. A sparkplug that fires the Model T Ford is of the same general construction as that plug sparking a 16-cylinder Deusenberg.

By this incorporation-integration, the older function becomes compatible *with* the newer and then can serve that newer system into which it has been integrated. Then the older serves the newer with those older functions, which the newer doesn't have, except *through* such incorporation of the older. (Recall the wondrous symbiosis of mitochondria and the cellular systems it serves. Nature established this Strange Loop as the basis of her creative system.)

This system of incorporation-integration carries right on up to that frontal and prefrontal cortex, our highest evolutionary brains. The transformation the new brain brings about in its older brain *maintains, enhances, and completes* those earlier foundational *capacities as needed by the newer system to complete its own structure.* Again a classic Strange Loop foundational to evolution-creation.

(This is a procedure truly worth a bit of study because here we will find why a dysfunctional culture replicates itself in spite of all efforts to escape its very dysfunctions. Rather a case of serious misapplication of right and left hands not knowing what the other is doing. Culture is a split-system that splits everything within it from every angle.)

In sum, the higher brain function enhances the lower with capacities, which complete the lower, and enable it to work cooperatively *with* the higher. The higher brain must have those capacities the lower brain developed, but are unavailable within the higher brain by itself. Recall Rudolph Steiner's claim that the new way of thinking the intelligence of heart could bring about in the intellect and thinking of the brain, was the means through which the heart itself finds its new level of evolution. (Or, again, Meister Eckhart says that "without me God is helpless" while at the same time he, Eckhart, is himself transformed in that service of "helping God.")

[*Note:* There is a rough similarity or resonance in all this to Mitochondria's universal role in cell development and evolution. Symbiosis is an aspect of the strange loop that underlies just about everything.]

This incorporation-integration process plays a profound role in child development and could lead us into a rediscovery of our true nature (as co-creators in our life). Above all, here we find why abandonment of the infant-child in its earliest formative stage is such an *ongoing* disaster.

Strange Loops Looping[9]

This series of interacting loops between these evolutionary brain parts—moving forward, doubling back—to pick up elements or capacities needed but unavailable *until such movement forward and doubling back* takes place, is critical. Follow this loop: The newer brain system incorporates the older into its service, giving the foundation on which the newer is built, which incorporation transforms the nature of the older into *enough resonance with* the newer to function synchronously in coherence with that newer, while enhancing the original capacities of that older system. All of which reciprocal interaction is then integrated into the newer and its supportive older system for a more advanced dual function, a new situation impacting the entire brain system to that point.

A great being said, "If I be lifted up I draw all mankind toward me," a statement that is an ontological truth far transcending the petty religious applications that have so misconstrued most of that great beings observations. As this "mythical He" draws all mankind toward him he is himself transformed anew in typical symbiosis, and can thus quite truthfully state, "I am ever becoming what you have need of me to be," through just this continual growth-expansion of both "sides" of the loop. By the generational love and recognition of that mythical figure he is, himself, continually "lifted up"—giving the imagery greater power to attract and lift up, round and round.

We are a peak of evolution's strange loop wave. Bear this above scenario in mind when considering that extraordinary myth of Abraham's "many-breasted" god saying, "Move!" And Abraham moving—which move brings about the direction and destination of such a move. Abraham did not whine about "where" he should move *to* since there was no such "where" *until the movement forward was made*—such movement creates the *where* the total movement leads. The only way Abraham could know where his movement would lead would be if that "where" were a replication or duplication of a past event. In which case God is left out of the equation and not needed, since we are then thoroughly ensconced in our familiar cultural cul-de-sac.

This transformation of an older, primary brain system into a newly emerging one, which new one is, in turn, dependent *on* the older for its own development and transformation, is not only an example of the Strange Loop phenomenon, but is a major key to our evolution. For this ongoing, continual evolutionary process moves to go beyond the limitations and constraints of any current state, as such limitations arise, and which transcendent action itself gives rise to new states and evolutionary possibilities not necessarily even *extant* before, while eventually seeking out the limitations and constraints even then becoming apparent, and kicking off another round of evolution. (Neurologist Frank Wilson wrote a brilliant analysis of the evolutionary implications of the human hand and brain as a perfect symbiosis, each bringing more and more potential ability into and out of the other. The same is true of mind and heart.)

Herein the transformation of mind itself unfolds, and we see evolution as not only an ongoing, endless process, but always a win-win situation—or at least to the extent it is *allowed* to be, since designed to be so if *allowed* (and it is up to us to allow or impede).

This highly condensed and abstract survey ignores, for now, among many issues, the intriguing aspect of *selectivity* out of a randomly produced profusion. Such selectivity out of random profusion is another hallmark of our open-ended evolutionary system. And, our reviewing of this in a continual doubling-back on-and-of this basic material, will put this material into a continually wider, more inclusive basis relating it with other aspects of evolution. Every time we double back to pick up some new aspect of some previous discussion or possibility, that doubling-back can lift both previous and current issues into a higher order.

Integration and Its Failure in Development[10]

Large and critical overlaps take place between the appearance and full-scale development of each of these four neural systems, as we unfold from conception. For instance, rudimentary aspects of the emotional system begin to function long before the sensory-motor system is complete. For the opening period of each stage (reptilian, old-mammalian, new mammalian, and prefrontal cortex) brings in a burst of new skills and potentials demanding maximum energy-attention to get established. We have only to consider Howard Gardner's inherent categories of intelligence lying dormant until conditions are right for awakening. (The toddler and adolescent are prime examples of this factor of explosive energy to explore new domains; the source of such skills and potentials lying dormant will become apparent.) Once a new learning is established enough to *spare* the attention-energy the next stage will need, that next stage can make its initiatory opening successfully.

So development of the first, the reptilian brain system, continues at a more relaxed pace, long after development of the next, old-mammalian brain, begins *its* development. This overlap brings a period of integration of the two systems, each supporting and influencing the other in typical strange loop reciprocal fashion.

That is why failure or compromise of development in one stage can damage or compromise subsequent development of both predecessor and successor stages. This "sharing of the energy attention needed" depends on the new development getting *established* and functional enough *to share* its overall pool of energy-attention in this manner. If the second stage is compromised or damaged, the new capacities within it will not only be incomplete and dysfunctional to some degree, but will fail to provide the means for the first stage to complete its *own* development by transcending *its* own limitations and constraints through integration into the second, while also failing to provide the appropriate foundation for the next, third stage, on and on, thus losing on all fronts. (Note carefully the reciprocal interaction this involves, an example of how the strange loop functioning is quite logical in its interweaving if one carefully follows it.) Again, such integration of a newly developing function into a higher, developed or developing one, can only take place after the higher neural system's own function is *stable* enough *to allow this* integration by sharing, (or sparing) the attention-energy needed by the upcoming one.

In sum, the first neural system, dependent on integration into the second for its own completion, will be faulty if the second is faulty, and, being the foundation on which the second is critically dependent, the two "go down together" so to speak, another and sobering aspect of the strange loop. Failure within either system means both lose to some extent, the equivalent of a strange loop being prevented from completing its loop.

Now we can grasp the full insight within Maria Montessori's statement about abandonment in the earliest development period.

An infant born and not nurtured, particularly in that most critical first year, will remain largely "locked" into his primary defensive sensory-motor brain since events in his environment can't be fully integrated but bring further retreats into his defensive system. He is "armored" against his world from the beginning and development will be slow and faltering. Rather than relating to the events of his world, the only way brain-mind can develop, he defends against them, increasing his isolation.

Sketching in This Fall of Man[11]

And though many underlying factors are involved, a single major cause lies behind the mishap. Our undeveloped emotional system remains embedded in and compromised by the survival system on which the emotional system depends for its own development. This survival system is still trying to establish its genetically determined functions, which it can only do through a developed emotional system, which itself can only be completed by a functional survival system—a typical double bind. Even after the second neural system, the old mammalian or emotional, opens for its development, most of the infant energy-attention defends *against* such openness. Instead of transforming that reptilian survival instinct into a preliminary form of emotional intelligence, the higher (the intended emotional intelligence) will be incorporated into the lower and become, in effect, a part of that lower defense system. With a compromised or damaged reptilian *and* old mammalian system, the third evolutionary system, the new mammalian brain, on its opening for development, will face an obvious double—or triple jeopardy.

We can follow such a stage-by-stage compromise breakdown, as it has indeed taken place historically and within us individually, until we finally get to the point where the highest, fourth brain is incorporated in whole or in part into the first, sensory-survival mode, the whole evolutionary movement thereby inverted, turned upside down, with humankind the greatest danger to humankind.

This fourth and latest brain, the prefrontal cortex is, as stated, designed to be the "governor" of the whole system and organize the whole array into concentrations of attention-force that can carry an experience of self beyond its limitations and constraints, and move on into new evolutionary levels. But, should these ongoing and progressive *compromises* of nature's plan (which is the general case) the "human condition" becomes this compromised and crippled system, the "governor deposed" riff-raff in charge, wherein our highest evolutionary potential is bent back into the service of the lowest in a de-evolutionary setback—which well describes our current massive pileup of global-social chaos.

The Breakdown of Reason [12]

Once this reversal happens we, still locked into our survival system, automatically employ the logical reasoning capacities of our highest brain to rationalize the violent behaviors continually erupting out of our incomplete and un-integrated survival brain. We generally defend, with all logic available to us, such destructive actions on our part as *critically necessary,* and such necessity is surely the mother of our demonic inventions.

Thus, as our history shows, there is nothing more dangerous and destructive than a brilliant, genius-level reptile, of which we seem to breed quite a number, from heads of state and industry on down the social scale to the all-too-similar but unsuccessful criminal behind bars. (That is, our successful criminals are behind the corporate, political, social-scheming desks ruling our world.) But herein they can justify any atrocity as deemed necessary to our survival—individually or nationally. (The reason we must batten on our brother's blood, imprison more and more of our fellows each year, build more bombs, go to war on and on, is perfectly clear and logical—over and over, bloodbath after bloodbath ad infinitum and nauseam. Necessity and pragmatic common sense *demand* it!)

Modern Man, Reptilian Hybrid[13]

Which brings us to our present self-destructing and non-viable devolutionary state. As inheritors of the highest brain that evolution has produced, this lofty point is generally incorporated, unbeknownst, into the service of our lowest, sensory-motor survival system as detailed above. We then function as the highest in service of the lowest, instead of *being* the highest served by the lowest as nature intended. Further, we then *identify with* these lower functions by default, and compulsively rationalize the irrational and destructive actions of these primal base reactions of ours, in an attempt to justify and maintain our mind-set or "worldview," identity, and self-esteem, thereby assuming some quasi-coherence in a most incoherent mental turmoil. The "fall of man" becomes instinctual, repetitive, circular—a demonic tautology. Or, as Walt Whitman put it, the murder comes back most often to the murderer.

Death and the Evolution of Mind[14]

Following Darwin's second and greatest work, *The Descent of Man* (850 pages of fine print, on which Darwin spent the latter part of his life), we find that evolution indeed moves to go beyond even the "ulti-mate" limitation and unyielding barrier—death, and our fear of it. We can, further, plot out the nature of that barrier of fear and the kind of mutation-selectivity involved in moving beyond it—an extension of the evolutionary process that took a bit of groundwork.

"Darwin 2" explains how those forces of mutation, selectivity, and survival of the fittest, which can account for the myriad variations of species on our earth, cannot alone account for the appearance of the human species. According to Darwin's second offering, we were brought about by the "higher agencies of love and altruism," rather than simply being the fittest and surviving our predecessors.

David Loye brought this ignored aspect of Darwin to our attention in his excellent little book, *Darwin's Lost Theory of Love*. Consider as well such random items as Darwin's essays on "Selectivity in Relation to Sex," "Expressions of the Emotions in Man and Animals," and other writings and essays that reflect his involvement with the thoughts of Ernest Haeckel, Jean-Baptiste Lamarck, Goethe, and other biologists and minds of his time.

Consider these most telling items to which Darwin refers in his last work: "aiding the weak to survive . . . the instinct of sympathy the noblest part of our Nature. . . ." Where in these words can we find justification for the tooth-and-claw, Neo-Darwinian jungle mentality that swept the academic-scientific scene in the late nineteenth century and is still ram-pant today, if in ever-new cloaks or disguises? These guises justify the ever-mounting travesties and demonic actions we witness daily, sanctified, in effect, through the growth and power of materialistic-technological sci-ence, capitalism, colonialism, and the ongoing domination and destruc-tion of culture after culture. Here in this Neo-Darwinism is the very dark mind-set that paves the way for the mounting wars, death, and destruc-tion dominating the twentieth century and poisoning the earth today.

Humankind, through millennia of the Darwinian function of "higher agencies," with its "noblest instinct of sympathy," developed an awareness beyond that of any animal, a self-awareness leading to an intelligence lying at a light-year disconnect from anything that had come before. In turn, this self-aware intelligence led to a new function that is not physical, and thus not directly accountable to physical constraints such as death.

In this way, evolution, as revealed by Darwin, has struggled to bring about our ever-evolving human mind. Emerging out of evolution's matrix of body-heart-brain, we are continually being led to a higher evolutionary capacity, one that is able to go beyond ever-greater limitations and constraints, opening to ever-new matrices or sources and capacities. Mind (and here "mind" and "soul" are a tangled knot) is designed by evolution to move beyond ever-greater stages, just as the infant rises to toddler, to child, to adolescent, and so on, simply by living life to its fullest. No wonder the cultural forces of darkness recognized by Rudolf Steiner now mount in even greater opposition to our true nature bestowed millennia ago.

Mind Emergent [15]

Mind as an emergent process has risen along with a field-effect, which mind automatically attracts to itself by its new capacities and passions, and to which mind is attracted by such passionate pursuits and quests. Such related fields will be drawn through "resonant" attraction—like attracting like. Mind thus brings about or gathers to itself fields of possibility that serve as matrix for that ever-expanding mind to draw on in reciprocal fashion, as it does with body-brain and heart. These new, nonphysical matrices are fields of potential that lie—or can lead—beyond strictly physical process. In like order, physical life both belongs to and brings about a continual supply of new materials, new fields, and new transcendent minds in strange loop, mirroring fashion.

Bohm, Sheldrake, and the Field Phenomenon [16]

To further explore the nature of fields and how they participate in the evolution of mind, consider the "field perspectives" of physicist David Bohm and biologist Rupert Sheldrake, whose conversations in the 1980s were often facilitated by the philosopher Renee Weber.

Bohm brought to these conversations his concept of active information. This view holds that information passes back and forth between an electron and its environment-field, in a mind-like interplay that impacts both the activity of the electron and the form of the field it operates within—an ongoing dance that clearly echoes the strange loop phenomenon. Furthermore, Bohm's view assumed that in some fundamental sense the electron only appeared to be separate from its field; in actuality, the electron was a pulse arising from the field itself. Bohm proposed that this field-electron dynamic was applicable at many levels of reality, including the human being and the fields of influence the human being generates. Similarly, physicist Fritjof Capra noted that in quantum physics we never end with things, or the safe round solid objects sought by the materialists, but only connections, influences, forces. Or, as I have insisted in my previous books, all there is, is relationship.

Sheldrake's scheme consists of the twin concepts of morphogenetic fields and morphic resonance. A morphogenetic field is an information structure that lies outside of space and time but acts within these to give form and structure to three-dimensional phenomena. The embryogenesis of a horse, for example, is understood to be informed by a morphogenetic field specific to that type of horse. In some sense all horses of that type—past, present, and future—are connected by this field. Morphic resonance is the means by which a particular horse and its corresponding field "communicate," and is responsible for the ongoing continuity of that type of horse, as well as novel alterations and further creative development.

For our current purposes, note that both the concept of a non-local field of information-meaning and the notion of formal resonance (in which similarity of form or vibration enables communication between apparently disparate elements) contribute to our use of the term *mind field*.

Mind Fields: Resonating and Mirroring[17]

Mind fields, as we shall use the term, are aggregations taking place through resonance between events—events of a like enough order tend to aggregate as a "field" of that order. Resonance is a form of relationship, in some cases indicating some shared origin or destination of two events of some like order. Neuroscientist Paul MacLean points out that the brain's hundred billion cells function by resonance, not by the matching and sorting of facts like a super encyclopedia. "Mental" fields, being non-local and non-temporal-spatial potentials, lie outside any substantive, concrete referent (and for that reason have long been dismissed by materialists). While "field" in this sense is a handy term for various actions or states of mind, such a field has no localization. *Field-effect* is, like gravity, a verb, not a noun; a process or procedure, not a product; an aggregate of potential as in a storage battery; a hypothetical grouping of related actions and/or possibilities for action.

The focus of our concern lies with this non-physical field-effect, which is both necessary to and brought about by our emerging-evolving mind. Common logic would suggest that the evolution of mind (evolution being, again, the urge to move beyond limitation and constraint) is brought about and then spurred on by the mirroring of that mind's own evolutionary growth with its increasing awareness of its mortality. Mortality is always looming as a kind of super-constraint and limitation— bringing an ongoing "spiraling gyre," as creative evolution proves to be.

Some traditions consider such a "non-physical matrix-field-effect," as needed by such expanding-evolving mind, to be pre-existent, coming before mind, or even evolution, as in a "Cloud Nine" fancy. From this perspective, such field, suitable to be mind-or-soul's-matrix when its body goes, is generally considered to have been created by "superior forces" of some metaphysical nature, laid out for us to discover and occupy if we pursue it arduously enough and deserve it sufficiently. For our purposes, however, mind and the "matrix-field" to which mind must relate to sustain itself are a mirroring phenomenon, each giving rise to the other as a response to evolutionary pressures to move beyond limitation and constraint. While such a Darwinian viewpoint as outlined here does not rule out superior forces pulling strings behind the scene, it makes such hypothetical add-ons simply unnecessary.

All of this is to suggest that generations of this growing awareness of death, and the continual longing by our species to move beyond it, set up, and feed into such a "field" of possibility. The field itself thus grows through a continual reciprocal action between mind and its longing to realize—make real—its imagery for moving beyond its own boundaries.

> *Anything capable of being believed is an image of truth . . .*
> WILLIAM BLAKE

Marghanita Laski, in her book *Ecstasy in Secular and Religious Experience,* investigated the phenomenon referred to as the Eureka! experience, occurring liberally in the physical sciences, the arts, and religious-philosophical pursuits. The Eureka! experience suggests that if mind centers on some "image of truth" with sufficiently passionate longing, attention, and perseverance, the mirroring effect of creation can and may bring the empty category imaged into a manifestation or concretizing of that image, contributing to the "content" of such field of potential itself. This, as in all evolutionary processes, is subject to the stochastic-selective element underlying all emerging process.

Laski documents Sir William Hamilton's 1843 discovery of his famous quaternion theory, a precursor of modern vector analysis, which demonstrated the mathematical argument for a fourth dimension of space (thus the term *quaternion*). Hamilton had conceived of such a possibility as a quaternion function in math and had spent years trying, with no success, to solve the particular mathematical enigma involved. His wife reported that, time and again, he would grow discouraged, vowing to pursue the matter no further, only to return to it from a new angle.

Finally, after fifteen years of roller-coaster pursuit, Hamilton seemed to have truly quit, vowing to waste no more of his life on his passion. Shortly thereafter, he asked his wife to accompany him on a walk to a meeting at the Royal Irish Academy. As they crossed a little footbridge into Dublin, Hamilton's mind no longer chewing away over the quaternion enigma and finally at peace, the answer arrived. It came as a flash of insight, the entire theory presented in highly symbolic fashion in a split-second, "out of mind"—whereupon he carved the preliminary formula into the very stone of the bridge upon which he and his wife were walking. Hamilton reported that he knew in that moment of "absent mindedness" the complexity of the insight given him was such that another fifteen years might be needed to translate that initial symbolic web into fully rationalized mathematical terms.

August Kekulé, the famous Belgian chemist, had worked at great length on the problem of chemical structure of the benzene molecule, a problem he was determined to resolve, to no avail. One day, wearied with his efforts and frustration, he retired for a bit of nap in his easy chair by the fireplace. As he drifted into a reverie there appeared directly in front of him a clear image of a snake with its tail in its mouth, forming a peculiar circle. It flashed into view and disappeared as quickly, but Kekulé saw in this strange image the long-sought answer to his problem. A lengthy struggle was required, however, to translate this answer into the necessary chemical language. Out of this struggle emerged his famous theory of the benzene ring, the foundation of modern organic chemistry.

At a reception given in his honor by the scientific community, Kekulé was questioned concerning how such a complex, esoteric, and uniquely original discovery had occurred. "Gentlemen," he responded, "we should dream more often." Kekulé's famous response has brought many a challenge from hardline materialists and Neo-Darwinists who try to debunk any suggestion of a "psychic-spiritual" or non-substantive element involved in "true science"—as the benzene ring surely was.

Laski's Formula[18]

Laski's list of such events is long and rich, particularly when we consider the religious, philosophic, and esoteric elements she detailed at length. This Eureka! phenomenon involves creation itself, endlessly open, beyond any specific type of creative result involved. We tend to heed only those creations, which are concrete, visible, useful, and commonly shared, but the process-function involved has no boundaries, limitations, or selective requirements. In summary form, Laski's outline for this process is as follows:

- First, there is the passionate pursuit in asking the question—staking out the end-goal of some burning issue or desire that a person determines to accomplish, discover, or experience and sets out with will and determination to bring about at all costs.
- Second comes a "gathering of the materials" as assumed will be needed by the answer or conclusion, and which generally have some resonance with the nature of the topic or end-goal. Such pursuit takes place on many levels, consciously or unconsciously, and may go on for years, with an exhilarating sense of discovery along the way.
- Third comes a "plateau" period, wherein all possibilities seem exhausted, leaving a period of stagnation. The luster of the unknown dimmed and dull, most people tend to quit at this point. One may, however, suddenly think of some angle left unexplored, some possibility that might yet yield the treasure, and off we go again.
- Fourth comes the dark night itself. The seeker "bottoms out" and truly quits. At this point, the goal no longer entertained as even a possibility, the answer may arrive—or still may not, this being a stochastic realm. Idling about, thinking of nothing, the answer may arrive unbidden, filling the vacuum of thought in a single flash—an answer which may have never been seen by anyone before, since not existent until "translated" into the common domain.
- And here, in this casual mention of "translation," we find both the fifth step in Laski's formula and yet another hurdle to our common logic. Always, in a true Eureka! experience of this sort, bringing something new into our world, the answer arrives in symbolic form, which must be translated into the common domain, or the language of that discipline related to the asking of the question. It never arrives "spelled out" in laborious fashion. Nonetheless, mathematical breakthroughs come to mathematicians, since only they have the background to ask the triggering question, to rec-

ognize the significance of the symbols involved when the answer arrives, and the materials and strength of mind needed to translate those symbols so that others might share in them.

Moments of Emptied Mind[19]

The recipients of such enlightening revelations insist, however, that they were not thinking of the issue—or thinking of anything at all—when the answer arrived; all claim that the answer arrived in a single flash of insight, never "piecemeal," was highly symbolic in nature, requiring strenuous and often very lengthy translation to put it into the language of the discipline involved, and that they, the recipient, had nothing to do with the answer itself or its arrival. All attest that the answer arriving was radically different from any of their expectations and was purely gratuitous—a gift given.

In each of the cases known, this recipient's claim to a gratuitous gift given has brought a chorus of vigorous denial from the academic-scientific world right down to our day, in spite of the high-caliber minds involved, and despite the stunning greatness and novelty of the discoveries made. The receiver of the Eureka! is doubted concerning his own experience, and all but called a liar or self-deluded by the skeptics. To academic science a Eureka! could only be a discovery of a preexistent hard-core fact in the material world-out-there, if it is applicable to science and thus valid. That "mind" is involved in a creative movement over and above mind itself is just not acceptable, while ironically most major sciences themselves rest on and arise from a number of related Eureka! breakthroughs.

Equally ignored by conventional thought is the odd fact that such Eureka! answers are neither a composite nor a synthesis of all the "materials" gathered in the quest for that answer. The answer is generally at a radical discontinuity with the known materials of the discipline involved, and equally different from any of the discoveries or "facts" gathered by the recipient along the way. One wonders, that being the case, why the long search for the answer was necessary, if none of its "gatherings" had any relation to the final result. And, for that matter, how the "facts" gathered, though not part of the answer given, were nevertheless recognized as significant to the general realm of that answer, or were pointers toward it.

And in that question lies another of these valuable insights to be gained from this phenomenon: the issue of resonance—that major function by which the brain works and fields form. The brain-mind involved must have a rich, resonant field into which the answer can arrive and be tended, rather as well-tended soil for a seed given to flourish, even though all ordinary brain activities must be suspended at the point of Eureka!-arrival itself, leaving only that resonance prevailing.

Fields as Creative Process[20]

Fields of potential are not only active forces or intelligences within their own domain, they are also creative forces. Why would the mind of a Eureka! "recipient" have to be suspended or empty for its own answer to present itself? And why would the answer have to be so obscure and symbolic? It seems the mind, commonly defined as personal, was not in and of itself the cauldron of creativity forging the revelation. The recipients' insistence that they had nothing to do with the revelation or its arrival—common to all such Eureka! reports—need not be explained away or attributed to false modesty. Though this is surely true at the individual or personal level of awareness, the whole event is a cosmological-ontological function well beyond the personal, even as it embraces all minds and much more.

In each case, the personal field of mind fed into a commonly held or universal field of like order, one over and above any individual mind-brain, yet obviously in some sense the product of that individual mind, and others in the field. The very fields of mathematics (in Hamilton's case) or chemistry (in Kekulé's case) are themselves the cumulative result of the work of all mathematicians and biologists now and in the past. We create fields even as we interact with fields. We speak of going into the field of medicine or the field of architecture or the field of engineering, but "field" in this academic regard concerns shared social activities and denotes an aggregate of intelligent energy and potential.

Such a field, as experienced in Eureka! events, has no inherent localization; it localizes according to whatever mind is interacting with it. There is no field of medicine without doctors, while no doctor is that field. All is reciprocal. Field-effect is universal and personal. It is a process, a dynamic, generative aggregate of intelligent potential. Fields of knowledge such as mathematics, physics, music, and so on are in a continual flux of arrangement and rearrangement brought about by the constant input of materials from people studying and employing the fields, as well as those unconsciously interacting with them. In the case of chemistry, all those generations of students, professionals, amateurs, career scientists, and lonely thinkers, mulling over the mystery of organic chemical structure, fed into the field that led to Kekulé's Eureka! experience. There is only reciprocal action between mind, or minds, and fields.

Because of this, any field contributor might automatically be in line as a possible target for receiving some symbolic answer or Eureka! discovery brought about by and within that field. The one stipulation seems to be that an individual mind must be idle, vacant, or inactive at the precise instant of the field's creative action. Out of the ferment of a field of potential interacting with many individual minds, one of those minds may, by chance, be struck by the lightning generated in that particular field. Without a resonant mind to receive a field's creative invention of the moment, nothing could happen in either field or mind. Creativity lies in the reciprocal relation between individual and field. . . .

Questioning Creates Answering[21]

And so we come full circle, faced not only with the inevitability of personal death, but also with the looming prospect of death on a much larger scale. What we are suggesting here is that human life, confronted with the apparently insoluble problem of death early on, nevertheless, in its striving to transcend or "move beyond" even this constraint, has now brought about the necessary potentials for achieving such a goal, although hardly in a direct, miraculous wave-of-wand, but rather, indirectly through natural process. In typical strange loop form, the question—ever more pressing in light of our pan-global destructive potential—is entering into the creating of its answer, with the answer entering into and continually clarifying the nature of the passionate quest itself, mirror-to-mirror. In this way self as brain-mind has entered into the evolution of self-as-heart.

Matrix Shifts[22]

Thus we can see the preliminary outlines of an evolving shift of matrices from tangible body-brain-heart concreteness to the non-tangible "abstractions"* of a non-temporal-spatial field of mind. Bear in mind, however, that our original matrix of tangible primary survival systems, instinctual and strongly entrenched in every cell of our body, is always in this body as part of its maintenance system, and will be until death-do-us-part. This new "non-temporal-spatial state" takes time and extensive development to establish, not being an overnight quickie operation.

Generally, this development of a more advanced evolutionary system boils down to a conflict between that most primary structure of our old "reptilian" hind-brain and the open-ended potentials within our latest evolutionary brain—the prefrontal cortex. And here we arrive at a paradox: for mind-as-emergent to "escape" and move beyond these ancient survival instincts, it must fully accept and embrace the concept of death itself. Everything in our culture is designed to avoid such head-on collision through hypothetical escape hatches, by which we can maintain our illusions of bodily immortality. The issue we face is going beyond instinct (the fear of death), and then moving unknowingly into that very state of mind our instinct guards against. Such movement is

---

*Here, "abstraction" is not meant as philosophical or theoretical "flight of fancy," but rather as an actual movement into a nonphysical domain. We could equally say "extraction."

[By "abstraction" Joe means symbolic and metaphoric. There is a movement from the concrete body senses to the symbolic neocortex, as imagination and thought. But this is yet another window that opens to non-physical realms. One of the most interesting themes Joe is developing began in *Biology of Transcendence,* reaching beyond limitation and constraint. In this context, Joe is proposing that the brain's capacity to imagine, or what Bohm calls "insight," creates a nonmaterial field that transcends the physical brain-body. Where does spirit go after it leaves the body? This is Joe's proposal. —*Ed.*]

the full and non-negotiable acceptance of death, without hidden aces up the sleeve as sold by culture. To give up the notion of survival is equivalent to giving up one's life for greater life, as a wise man once put it, and such an illogical and contradictory notion proves to be a biological observation, not a religious one.

Further, as a cautionary note here, in this emergent process of mind will be found those same ironclad issues of stochastic profusion and narrow selectivity found throughout evolution. That same wise sage observed that "many are called but few are chosen," which involves far more ontological aspects of selectivity than religious aspects. This stochastic aspect centers around mind becoming fully emergent from its original matrix—a process dependent on having created a sufficient matrix to move into, as in Laski's Eureka! events, where a matrix itself forms by the nature of our question and movement toward its answer.

Only a fully developed mind can contribute to and so become, in its turn, the matrix for further evolutionary states. Emerging out of a fully emergent process itself, like an abstraction—or "extraction"—out of abstractions, mind can then move beyond any and all known physical functions and their restrictions. This of logical necessity includes the phenomenon of death, wherein further and even more complex movements extracting or abstracting out of abstractions are involved.

When poet Blake said that "anything capable of being believed is an image of truth," he did not imply that some belief is the truth as such, or even necessarily "true." But the capacity to create such images and even believe in them is the way we are "made in the image of God," even, as with any strange loop, the way we make God in our own image, both images being necessary. In such imaging, being the way by which all our vast creativity unfolds, some creative efforts indeed become true, even on a broad consensual level. Imagination—creating images of possibility—is the stuff of life and its creative evolution, and part of what our human story is all about. (Our failure, therefore, to foster imagination in children is a fatal error for humanity as a whole, threatening to undermine the very creative potentials we are exploring here.)

Evolution's Work in Progress[23]

So this species-wide development of a mind capable of recognizing personal death and then going beyond it, has taken time to establish as a possible field of potential. Mind, as self-awareness, must now further develop the capacity to imagine and project beyond its present physical "embeddedment." If the resulting imaginal state is entertained over time, it can set up a strange loop, mirroring between image and its object, beginning early on, which is in process today. The issue lies in creating a matrix stable enough for the mind to reciprocally interact with and achieve a stable-state within itself, which is rather like the stability of heart's torus—such stabilization also being an intentional-imaginal process. This stabilization is of course one particular aspect of the imaginal dynamic involved in grasping and realizing the related series of holonomic torus fields of heart fusing with earth and thus with sun. In such imaginal activity we may discover that our notions of sentiency are a bit too localized within our own personal frame of reference, opening the prospect of a more universal sentience than accepted heretofore. In this we have, as well, a near perfect example of what Rudolf Steiner claimed was our mind's role with heart, and heart's "next level of evolution."

Finally, here . . . I would again call attention to the sober fact that Nature operates by profusion and selectivity, and of necessity the selectivity grows more stringent the more complex the process involved. Constraint and limitation, like the horizon, always lie right beyond. So, that "many are called but few are chosen" is not a dictate from some hell-dealing judge or loving arbiter on Cloud Nine, but simply the way this creative cosmos is set up.

Notes

CHAPTER 1. *THE CRACK IN THE COSMIC EGG* (1971)

1. Pearce, *The Crack in the Cosmic Egg,* 1–18.
2. Pearce, *The Crack in the Cosmic Egg,* 19–48.
3. Pearce, *The Crack in the Cosmic Egg,* 49–62.
4. Pearce, *The Crack in the Cosmic Egg,* 97–103.
5. Pearce, *The Crack in the Cosmic Egg,* 110–25.
6. Pearce, *The Crack in the Cosmic Egg,* 117–25.
7. Pearce, *The Crack in the Cosmic Egg,* 162–85.
8. Pearce, *The Crack in the Cosmic Egg,* 190–95.
9. Frye, *Anatomy of Criticism: Four Essays.*

CHAPTER 2. *MAGICAL CHILD* (1977)

1. Pearce, *Magical Child,* chapter 22.
2. Pearce, *Magical Child,* preface, ix–xiii.
3. Pearce, *Magical Child,* 3–15.
4. Pearce, *Magical Child,* 16–24.
5. Pearce, *Magical Child,* 25–28.
6. Pearce, *Magical Child,* 29–33.
7. Pearce, *Magical Child,* 34–39.
8. Spitz, *The First Year of Life.*
9. LeBoyer, *Birth without Violence.*
10. Pearce, *Magical Child,* 41–50.

11. Windle, "Brain Damage by Asphyxia."

12. Pearce, *Magical Child,* 51–64.

13. Pearce, *Magical Child,* 84–90.

14. Klaus, "Maternal Attachment: Importance of the First Post-Partum Days," 286.

15. Pearce, *Magical Child,* 95–107.

16. Pearce, *Magical Child,* 127–37.

17. Pearce, *Magical Child,* 149–60.

18. Pearce, *Magical Child,* 161–70.

19. Pearce, *Magical Child,* 171–73.

20. Pearce, *Magical Child,* 194–98.

21. Pearce, *Magical Child,* 223–26.

CHAPTER 3. *THE BOND OF POWER* (1981)

1. Pearce, *The Bond of Power,* 1–13.

2. Pearce, *The Bond of Power,* 14–22.

3. Pearce, *The Bond of Power,* 23–32.

4. Pearce, *The Bond of Power,* 33–45.

5. Pearce, *The Bond of Power,* 46–62.

6. Pearce, *The Bond of Power,* 63–68.

7. Pearce, *The Bond of Power,* 86–89.

8. Pearce, *The Bond of Power,* 92–98.

9. Pearce, *The Bond of Power,* 101–11.

10. Pearce, *The Bond of Power,* 112–16.

11. Pearce, *The Bond of Power,* 121–29.

12. Pearce, *The Bond of Power,* 131–32.

13. Pearce, *The Bond of Power,* 150–61.

CHAPTER 4. *EVOLUTION'S END* (1992)

1. Pearce, *Evolution's End,* xiii–xx.

2. Pearce, *Evolution's End,* 3–14.

3. Pearce, *Evolution's End,* 16–24.

4. Pearce, *Evolution's End,* 25–37.

5. Pearce, *Evolution's End,* 38–40.

6. Pearce, *Evolution's End,* 42–51.

7. Pearce, *Evolution's End*, 55–60.

8. Pearce, *Evolution's End*, 61–69.

9. Pearce, *Evolution's End*, 71–79.

10. Pearce, *Evolution's End*, 82–88.

11. Pearce, *Evolution's End*, 103–6.

12. Pearce, *Evolution's End*, 154–63.

13. Pearce, *Evolution's End*, 164–71.

14. Pearce, *Evolution's End*, 180–87.

15. Pearce, *Evolution's End*, 217–26.

CHAPTER 5. *THE BIOLOGY OF TRANSCENDENCE* (2002)

1. Pearce, *The Biology of Transcendence*, 1–7.

2. Pearce, *The Biology of Transcendence*, 40–41.

3. Pearce, *The Biology of Transcendence*, 42.

4. Pearce, *The Biology of Transcendence*, 43–45.

5. Pearce, *The Biology of Transcendence*, 45–47.

6. Pearce, *The Biology of Transcendence*, 47–48.

7. Pearce, *The Biology of Transcendence*, 51.

8. Pearce, *The Biology of Transcendence*, 51–53.

9. Pearce, *The Biology of Transcendence*, 53–54.

10. Pearce, *The Biology of Transcendence*, 66–72.

11. Pearce, *The Biology of Transcendence*, 73.

12. Pearce, *The Biology of Transcendence*, 74–92.

13. Ho, "The Entangled Universe."

14. Ho, "The Entangled Universe."

15. Pearce, *The Biology of Transcendence*, 99.

16. Pearce, *The Biology of Transcendence*, 100–105.

17. Pearce, *The Biology of Transcendence*, 106–9.

18. Pearce, *The Biology of Transcendence*, 109–12.

19. Pearce, *The Biology of Transcendence*, 112.

20. Pearce, *The Biology of Transcendence*, 113.

21. Pearce, *The Biology of Transcendence*, 114–15.

22. Pearce, *The Biology of Transcendence*, 115–17.

23. Pearce, *The Biology of Transcendence*, 119–20.

24. Pearce, *The Biology of Transcendence*, 122–23.

25. Pearce, *The Biology of Transcendence,* 123–24.

26. Pearce, *The Biology of Transcendence,* 129–32.

27. Pearce, *The Biology of Transcendence,* 132–33.

28. Pearce, *The Biology of Transcendence,* 134–37.

29. Schore, *Affect Regulation and the Origin of Self.*

30. Schore, *Affect Regulation and the Origin of Self.*

31. Pearce, *The Biology of Transcendence,* 137–38.

32. Schore, *Affect Regulation and the Origin of Self.*

33. Pearce, *The Biology of Transcendence,* 139–41.

34. Pearce, *The Biology of Transcendence,* 141–44.

35. Pearce, *The Biology of Transcendence,* 144–46.

36. Pearce, *The Biology of Transcendence,* 225–27.

37. Pearce, *The Biology of Transcendence,* 233–36.

38. Pearce, *The Biology of Transcendence,* 240–41.

39. Pearce, *The Biology of Transcendence,* 241–42.

40. Pearce, *The Biology of Transcendence,* 242–53.

41. Pearce, *The Biology of Transcendence,* 155–58.

42. Pearce, *The Biology of Transcendence,* 158–59.

43. Pearce, *The Biology of Transcendence,* 159–62.

44. Pearce, *The Biology of Transcendence,* 162–65.

45. Pearce, *The Biology of Transcendence,* 165–67.

46. Pearce, *The Biology of Transcendence,* 167–69.

47. Pearce, *The Biology of Transcendence,* 169–70.

48. Pearce, *The Biology of Transcendence,* 170–73.

49. Pearce, *The Biology of Transcendence,* 173–76.

CHAPTER 6. *THE DEATH OF RELIGION AND THE REBIRTH OF SPIRIT* (2007)

1. Pearce, *The Death of Religion and the Rebirth of Spirit,* 2–12.

2. Pearce, *The Death of Religion and the Rebirth of Spirit,* 14–15.

3. Pearce, *The Death of Religion and the Rebirth of Spirit,* 15–19.

4. Pearce, *The Death of Religion and the Rebirth of Spirit,* 20–21.

5. Pearce, *The Death of Religion and the Rebirth of Spirit,* 22–23.

6. Pearce, *The Death of Religion and the Rebirth of Spirit,* 25–27.

7. Pearce, *The Death of Religion and the Rebirth of Spirit,* 27–28.

8. Pearce, *The Death of Religion and the Rebirth of Spirit,* 31–33.

9. Pearce, *The Death of Religion and the Rebirth of Spirit,* 33–35.

10. Pearce, *The Death of Religion and the Rebirth of Spirit,* 62–63.

11. Pearce, *The Death of Religion and the Rebirth of Spirit,* 64–65.

12. Pearce, *The Death of Religion and the Rebirth of Spirit,* 93–96.

13. Pearce, *The Death of Religion and the Rebirth of Spirit,* 98–102.

14. Pearce, *The Death of Religion and the Rebirth of Spirit,* 122–23.

15. Pearce, *The Death of Religion and the Rebirth of Spirit,* 124–26.

16. Pearce, *The Death of Religion and the Rebirth of Spirit,* 126–28.

17. Pearce, *The Death of Religion and the Rebirth of Spirit,* 128–31.

18. Pearce, *The Death of Religion and the Rebirth of Spirit,* 159–60.

19. Pearce, *The Death of Religion and the Rebirth of Spirit,* 161–62.

20. Pearce, *The Death of Religion and the Rebirth of Spirit,* 163–64.

21. Pearce, *The Death of Religion and the Rebirth of Spirit,* 164–68.

22. Pearce, *The Death of Religion and the Rebirth of Spirit,* 178–82.

23. Pearce, *The Death of Religion and the Rebirth of Spirit,* 184–85.

24. Pearce, *The Death of Religion and the Rebirth of Spirit,* 185.

25. Pearce, *The Death of Religion and the Rebirth of Spirit,* 186–87.

26. Pearce, *The Death of Religion and the Rebirth of Spirit,* 187.

27. Pearce, *The Death of Religion and the Rebirth of Spirit,* 189–90.

28. Pearce, *The Death of Religion and the Rebirth of Spirit,* 191.

29. Pearce, *The Death of Religion and the Rebirth of Spirit,* 191–95.

30. Pearce, *The Death of Religion and the Rebirth of Spirit,* 209–11.

31. Pearce, *The Death of Religion and the Rebirth of Spirit,* 219.

32. Pearce, *The Death of Religion and the Rebirth of Spirit,* 221–25.

33. Pearce, *The Death of Religion and the Rebirth of Spirit,* 227–28.

34. Pearce, *The Death of Religion and the Rebirth of Spirit,* 229–30.

35. Pearce, *The Death of Religion and the Rebirth of Spirit,* 231.

36. Pearce, *The Death of Religion and the Rebirth of Spirit,* 234–38.

CHAPTER 7. *THE HEART-MIND MATRIX* (2012)

1. Pearce, *The Heart-Mind Matrix,* 10–11.

2. Pearce, *The Heart-Mind Matrix,* 11–12.

3. Pearce, *The Heart-Mind Matrix,* 13.

4. Pearce, *The Heart-Mind Matrix,* 13–16.

5. Pearce, *The Heart-Mind Matrix,* 16.

6. Pearce, *The Heart-Mind Matrix,* 17–18.

7. Pearce, *The Heart-Mind Matrix,* 18–20.

8. Pearce, *The Heart-Mind Matrix,* 20–21.

9. Pearce, *The Heart-Mind Matrix,* 21–23.

10. Pearce, *The Heart-Mind Matrix,* 23–24.

11. Pearce, *The Heart-Mind Matrix,* 24–25.

12. Pearce, *The Heart-Mind Matrix,* 25–26.

13. Pearce, *The Heart-Mind Matrix,* 26.

14. Pearce, *The Heart-Mind Matrix,* 111–12.

15. Pearce, *The Heart-Mind Matrix,* 113.

16. Pearce, *The Heart-Mind Matrix,* 113–14.

17. Pearce, *The Heart-Mind Matrix,* 115–17.

18. Pearce, *The Heart-Mind Matrix,* 117–18.

19. Pearce, *The Heart-Mind Matrix,* 118–20.

20. Pearce, *The Heart-Mind Matrix,* 120–21.

21. Pearce, *The Heart-Mind Matrix,* 128.

22. Pearce, *The Heart-Mind Matrix,* 128–30.

23. Pearce, *The Heart-Mind Matrix,* 130–31.

Bibliography

Alexander, C. N., and E. J. Langer. *Higher Stages of Human Development: Adult Growth Beyond Formal Operations*. Oxford: Oxford University Press, 1988.

Arms, Suzanne. *Immaculate Deception: A New Look at Women and Childbirth in America*. Boston: Houghton Mifflin, 1975.

Bailie, Gil. *Violence Unveiled*. New York: Herder and Herder, 1996.

Berman, Morris. *The Twilight of American Culture*. New York: W. W. Norton, 2000.

Bohm, David. *Causality & Chance in Modern Physics*. Philadelphia: University of Pennsylvania Press, 1971.

Bridges, Katherine. *Social and Emotional Development of the Pre-School Child*. London: Kegan Paul, 1931.

Covey, Stephen. *Seven Habits of Highly Successful People: Powerful Lessons in Personal Change*. New York: Free Press, 1989.

Durant, William James, and Ariel Durant. *The Story of Civilization*. 11 vols. New York: Simon and Schuster, 1935–1975.

Eliade, Mircea. *Yoga: Immortality and Freedom*. New York: Pantheon, Bollingen Series LVI, 1958.

Frye, Northrop. *Fearful Symmetry*. Princeton, N.J.: Princeton University Press, 1947.

———. *Anatomy of Criticism: Four Essays*. Princeton, N.J.: Princeton University Press, 1957.

Girard, René. *Violence and the Sacred*. Baltimore: John Hopkins University Press, 1979.

Hall, Edward T. *The Silent Language*. New York: Anchor Books, 1959.

Ho, Mae Wan. "The Entangled Universe." *Yes! A Journal of Positive Futures*, Spring 2000.

Kierkegaard, Søren. *Purity of Heart Is to Will One Thing*, New York: Harper Brothers Publishing, 1948.

Klaus, Marshall. "Maternal Attachment: Importance of the First Post-Partum Days." *New England Journal of Medicine* 9 (1972).

Laski, Marghanita. *Ecstacy in Secular and Religious Experience*. New York: JP Tarcher, 1990.

LeBoyer, Frederick. *Birth without Violence*. Revised Edition. Rochester, Vt.: Healing Arts Press, 2002.

Liedloff, Jean. *The Continuum Concept*. Reading, Mass.: Addison Wesley Press, 1977.

Loye, David. *Darwin's Lost Theory of Love*. Berkeley: iUniverse Press, 2000.

Muktananda, Swami. *The Play of Consciousness*. South Fallsburg, N.Y.: Siddha Foundation, U.S., 1980.

———. *Siddha Meditations*. South Fallsburg, N.Y.: SYDA Foundation, U.S.: 1974.

Pearce, Joseph Chilton. *The Crack in the Cosmic Egg: New Constructs of Mind and Reality*. Rochester, Vt.: Park Street Press, 2002. Originally published under the title *The Crack in the Cosmic Egg: New Constructs of Mind and Reality*. New York: The Julian Press, 1971.

———. *Magical Child: Rediscovering Nature's Plan for Our Children*. New York: E. P. Dutton Press, 1977.

———. *Spiritual Initiation and the Breakthrough of Consciousness: The Bond of Power*. Rochester, Vt.: Park Street Press, 2003. Originally published under the title *The Bond of Power*. New York: Elsevier-Dutton Publishing Company, 1981.

———. *Evolution's End: Claiming the Potential of Our Intelligence*. New York: Harper-Collins, 1992.

———. *The Biology of Transcendence*. Rochester, Vt.: Park Street Press, 2002.

———. *The Death of Religion and the Rebirth of Spirit: A Return to the Intelligence of the Heart*. Rochester, Vt.: Park Street Press, 2010.

———. *Heart-Mind Matrix: How the Heart Can Teach the Mind New Ways to Think*. Rochester, Vt.: Park Street Press, 2012. Originally published under the title *Strange Loops and Gestures of Creation*. Great Barrington, Mass.: Golden Stone Press, 2010.

Peterson, James. *The Secret Life of Kids*. iUniverse, 2000.

Schore, Alan N. *Affect Regulation and the Origin of Self: The Neurobiology of Emotional Development*. Hillsdale, N.J.: Lawrence Erlbaum Associates, 1994.

Spitz, René. *The First Year of Life*. New York: International Universities Press, 1965.

Tillich, Paul. *Systematics of Theology*. Chicago: University of Chicago Press, 1973.

Windle, William F. "Brain Damage by Asphyxia at Birth." *Scientific American*, vol. 221, no. 4 (1969).

Index

Aborigines, 260, 262
adolescence, 48–49, 187–88. *See also* child (children)
anesthesia, self-induced, 23–24
answer, the, 10
anxiety
  breeding, 116
  childbirth and, 65
  conditioning, 90
  as contagious, 97
  free-floating, 47
  intelligence and, 71
  tool production and, 56
assimilation-accommodation, 81–84
assumptions, of underlying beliefs, 9, 11
autistic, 14–15, 22, 105
autistic thinking, 10, 11–12, 23
autonomy, 49
awareness
  bodiless, xvi
  choiceless, 109
  of force of mind, 3, 32
  personal, 49, 136
  transitional change of, 100

balance, xi
Balinese children, 76–77, 79–80, 85

Bell's theorem, 142, 143
bioculture, 199–201
biological plan, 45–49, 114–15, 247–50
Biology of Transcendence, The, 177–229, 258, 272
Blake, William, 2, 7, 12, 16, 18, 100–101, 113–14, 124, 128, 153, 174–75, 305
bodies within bodies, 215–17
Bohm, David, 91–92, 97–98, 103–6, 108–9, 110, 144–45, 235, 296
bonding
  to the culture, 70
  disruption of, 194
  domination and, 212–13
  with the earth, 74–76
  heart-mind, 156–58
  matrices and, 45–46
  to objects, 69–70
  as stage specific, 64
  that which blocks, avoiding, 89
Bond of Power, The, 91–132
brain. *See also* mind/brain
  change, 266
  dialogue between heart and, 188–90
  "evolutionary," 283
  fields, 146

habituation and, 165
heart as, 254
judgmental capacity of, 250
mind and, 107–8
new, 135, 148
self-organizing nature, 154
shutting down of, 266–68
triune, 147–50
brain-growth spurts, 104
"By their fruits you shall know them,"
   226–28

calendrical system, 138
Calvin, John, 228
caregivers prohibition, 206–8
causal body, 109
causality, reversing, 19–20
child (children). *See also* adolescence
   boundaries and, 74
   brain, "building," 184
   brain-growth spurts, 41
   creative interactions, 79
   developmental stages, 41
   dysfunctional, 246
   ESP and psychic phenomenon, 74–75
   "fortunate" and "deprived," 198
   ideation that shapes, 13
   lifeboat, 219
   mind-brain, understanding, 40
   modeling parent example, 112
   mother and, 48, 73, 221
   movement toward synergy, 86–87
   nature and, 40
   open-acceptancy, 152
   personal power in the world, 48
   play and, 161–62
   as potential genius, 43
   pressing from without, 40
   primary perceptions, 74–76
   signaling what is wrong, 44
   structuring knowledge and, 72–73

childbirth, 61, 65–66, 71, 193
church, as mediator, 226
coherence, 190–91, 264–65
compassion, power of, 217–18
complementarity, 146
conflicted behavior, xxiv
consciousness
   brain and, 108
   "broadcast" out, 155
   implicate order as, 103
   "at large," 157
   in perception, 120
   thought and insight and, 106–7
cosmic chaos and order, 265
Crack in the Cosmic Egg, The,
   backstory, 1–3
   beginning to write, 2–3
   as direct outgrowth of experiences, 2
   excerpts from, 3–35
   insight resulting in, 95–96
   reader assumptions of, viii
cracks in the cosmic egg, 27, 29, 272
creative competence, 85–87
creative logic, 82
creator and creation, 275
crying, 64
cultural conditioning, 203–4
cultural counterfeits, 282–83
cultural patterns, passing, 236–38
culture
   as artificial, 111
   biology conflict with, 245–46
   body rejection and, 258–59
   changing, 242–43
   darkness of mind and, 236
   defined, 180
   encultured mind as, 242
   as field effect, 201–2, 238, 240,
      242–43
   in ideation, 231
   reality and, 12

role of law in, 239
self-creating, 275
as set of ideas, 201
shaping by, 180
use of term, 275
war and, 239–40

Darwin, Charles, 209, 232–34, 236,
    279–80, 293–95
death
    acceptance of, xviii, xix, xxiv
    concept, as personal destiny, 84
    evolution of mind and, 293–95
    resurrection and, 213–15
Death of Religion and the Rebirth of
    Spirit, The, 230–73
DNA, 246, 248, 252, 263–64
don Juan, 25, 26–28, 30, 31, 34

ECG (heart), 219
Eckhart, Meister, xxv, 147, 152, 155,
    174–75, 187, 192, 288
EEG (brain), 219
eleven, age, 82–83, 87–88, 162, 178
Eliade, Mircea, xix, 149
enculturation, 202–3, 205, 250, 283
error-correction error, 116
error proliferation, 114–18
ESP, 74–75
eternity and time, 128–32
Eurekas!, 35, 138, 272, 298, 299, 301,
    303
evangelists, 221–22
evolution
    devolution and, 190
    intelligence and, 234
    of mind, death and, 293–95
    resumption of, 259–63
    strange loop wave, peak of, 289
    as work in progress, 306
evolutionary stages, 284–86

Evolution's End, 133–75, 176, 198
excitement, 53
experience, content of, 128–29

"fall of man," 291–92, 293
family triad of needs, 192, 193–95
fathers, 220
fear
    of abandonment, 110
    childbirth and, 65
    creating that which is feared, 32
    of death, xviii, xix, xxiv
    reliance on IT and, xxv
    survival mentality and, xx
field effect
    culture as, 201–2, 238, 240, 242–43
    defined, 297
    non-physical, 297
    that produced Jesus, 269
fields of intelligence, 138, 145–46
fields of potential, 141–42, 295,
    302–3
fixed assumptions, x
formal operations, 169–73
form and content, 112–14
fragmented thinking, 33
freedom, energy of, 123

gating level of the ancient RAS, 195–96
Geller effects, 81–82, 83, 88
genius, 101–3
Gerber, Marcelle, 58, 59, 68–69
greatness, vii, xv, 187, 301
Great Stability, 17
Guru principle, 126

Hamilton, Sir William, 298–99
heart
    as a brain, 254
    dialogue between brain and,
        188–90

inner vision from, 264
neural system, 189
relationship and, 250–51
unity and communion and,
251–52
universal, 251
HeartMath, 243–44
heart-mind connection, 156–58, 177,
180–81, 251
Heart-Mind Matrix, The, 274–306
Hilgard, Ernest, 20, 21, 22
holonomic movement, 98, 104, 110
hypnagogic state, 10, 11
hypnotism, 20–21, 154

IBM machine narrative, xx–xxii,
xxv–xxvi
idealism, xiv–xv, 121, 187
imagination
capacity as "divine genius," 16
creative, 123–25
defined, 123
inability to develop, 165–66
seeing without, 125
imbalance, xi–xii
incorporation-integration, 287–88
independence, from the matrix, 46
infant(s). See also child (children)
"in-arms" period, 115
as born prematurely, 67
childbirth and, 61
crying, 64
delivery room and, 60–63
free-floating anxiety, 47
male, circumcision, 67–68
mother and, 47–48, 54, 67, 194
newborn, 71–72
smiling, 56–58, 60, 89
television (TV) and, 267
in Uganda and Kenya, 58–59,
68–69, 70

insight
about, 94–95
as creative thought, 105
enticing, 96
playful, 98–101
thought and consciousness and,
106–7
translating, 95
wisdom, xi
integration, 287–88, 290–91
intellect, 136–37, 157, 170, 172–73,
276
intelligence
as ability to interact, 43–44
allowing full development of, 42
anxiety and, 71
biological plan for, 45–50
cells as, 43
emotional, 196
evolutionary, 181–82, 234
fields of, 138, 145–46
growth of, 44
insight, 106
as interaction, 50–52
interaction with possibility and, 113
living earth and, 88
matrix as mother and, 54
play and, 158, 162
slowness in forming, 57
stress and, 53
well-being and, 158
intelligence of the heart, 94, 177, 271
interaction
infant-child ability, 51
intelligence as, 50–52
mind-brain and source of
information, 55
with possibility, 113
reciprocal, 276
with unknown and unpredictable,
52

internal civil war, 284
intuitive perception, 243–44
IT, xv, xx–xxii

Jesus
    "cause one of the little ones to
        stumble" and, 212–13
    crack in the egg sought by, 27
    cultural power struggle and, 226
    don Juan and, 26–28, 30, 31
    field effect that produced, 269
    God within and, 121
    healing minds and hearts and, 217
    mythical story of, creating, 221–22
    new cultural synthesis, 29–30
    "ontological construct" and, 31
    reality-adjusted thinking and, 28
    Socrates and, 271–72
    upstaging, 273
    "Whatever you ask in my name"
        and, 31
    white alabaster image of, 93
Jung, Carl, xvii, 17, 64, 97, 153

keys and locks, 111–12
knowing, xi, 35, 44, 50, 69, 79, 135,
    175
knowledge, structuring, 72–74
Krishnamurti, 98, 109

Langer, Susanne, 32, 34, 201, 231, 235
Laski's formula, 299–301
learning
    bonding and, 64
    deep and abiding, 85
    importance of play in, 255–56
    joyful, of cultural conditioning,
        203–4
    stress and, 52–54
LeBoyer, Frederick, 59–60
left-handed thinking, 89–90

limbic system, 148–50, 154, 156, 159,
    161, 211–12
logical thinking, 32, 33
love, 26, 72, 101, 128, 202, 219, 280,
    283
Loye, David, 232, 294

MacLean, Paul, xix–xx, 134, 147, 165,
    182, 192, 233, 284, 297
Mae-Wan Ho, 190–91
Magical Child
    backstory, 36–38
    central issue of, 99
    critical problems we face and, 96
    excerpts from, 38–90`
    reader assumptions of, viii
    "Time-Bomb in the Delivery
        Room" and, 282
matrix, establishing, 70–72
matrix shifts, 45–50, 73, 129–30,
    304–6
meditation, 102, 125
metanoia
    conversion, 9
    defined, 6
    in education, 29
    Indians, 18–19
    restructuring, 8
    resyntheses, 7, 14
    slow, of necessary concepts, 11
    trance as, 25
mind
    as catalyst that changes the earth,
        80
    of the child, 13, 42
    darkness of, 236
    as emergent process, 295
    emerging, 13–14
    emptied, moments of, 301–2
    force of, awareness of, 32
    formal transformation of, 6

instruments of, 107–11
intuitive perception and, 243–44
matter and, 142–45
as self-awareness, 306
separation from brain processes, 49
states of, 154–55
synthesizing aspect of, 11
mind/brain, 96, 98, 102–4, 107, 112, 124, 135–36
mind fields, 296–99
mirroring
cause and effect, 235–36
DNA in, 252–53
of heart and brain, 251
of own limitations, 32
pattern formed by, 14
process, 4, 30
by reality, 7
of relationship, 255
mirror-to-mirror, 281–82
missing stage, 186–87
model imperative, 192–93, 199–200, 207
Monroe, Robert, 129, 130, 155
Montagu, Ashley, 198, 246, 280
morphic resonance, 296
mother
childbirth and, 61, 65–66
children and, 73, 221
emotional state of, 205–6
infant and, 47–48, 54, 67, 194
model imperative and, 207
shame and, 208–9
Muktananda
author and, 98, 99, 100–101
background, 91–92
fluid dynamic state and, 131–32
insight and, 127
meeting with, 93
on perfection as already achieved, 121

picture of, 99, 100
qualities of, 101
Siddha meditation, 97, 98, 102
view of creation, 131
muscular-mindedness, 52, 53, 85
mythologizing great beings, 269–71

nature
biological plan, 247–50
bonds for matrices and, 130
children and, 40
developmental rule, 141
exorcising, 54–60
laws of, x
operation by profusion and selectivity, 306
plan, ignoring, 39
scale of, 247
negation, power of, 204–5
neurons, 140–42, 236
"new difference," 197
non-conflicted behavior, xviii–xxvii
non-locality, 139, 142
non-ordinary events, 20, 83
NO! word, 204–5, 207
nurturing, 203, 280, 283, 285–86

operational thinking, 78, 169, 172–73, 261–62
operation bootstrap, 99

pain, as good for you, 209
Palos Verdes cliffs narrative, xxii–xxiv
Paraclete, dissolution of the, 224–25
passion, power of, 217–18
Paul, 223, 224–25, 271, 272–73
Penfield, Wilder, 107–8, 147
perception, 114, 120, 122, 124, 132, 169–70, 243–44
perceptual attitudes, 124
perfection, 33–34

physical body, 39, 48–49, 109, 122–23, 150, 155

Piaget, Jean, 12, 25, 41, 79, 172, 210

play
 adult management and, 168–69
 child, 161–62
 death of, 254–55
 electronic toy and, 167–68
 as foundation of creative intelligence, 158
 importance of, in relationships and learning, 255–56
 intelligence and, 162
 R-system and, 161
 television (TV) and, 163–67

pleasure, 209, 228, 250, 252, 255–56, 257, 259

political correctness, 225–26

positive coherency, 264–65

prefrontal development, 182–86

prefrontal lobes, 172, 182–86, 210–11, 280, 286, 292

Pribram, Karl, 134, 147, 284

primary perceptions, 74–76, 83

Purity of Heart Is to Will One Thing (Kierkegaard), xxvii

questions, viii, 15, 303–4

reality
 ability to relinquish, 23
 connection between thought and, 41
 creative participation in, ix
 culture and, 12
 "modulated," 249
 non-ambiguity and, 12
 as not fixed, x, 4–5
 openly shaping, 12
 redefinition of, 82
 resyntheses of, 7

revelation of, 144
 structure, as negotiable, xix
 virtual, 268, 277, 278
 as what we do know, 34–35

reason, breakdown of, 292–93

reciprocal loops, 278

relationships, play in, 255–56

religion
 birth of, 254–55
 as disaster, 229
 guilt and, 257, 258
 life as a gift and, 273
 origins of, 256–57
 science as, 263
 sexuality and, 257–59

resonance, 142, 252–53, 288, 296–97, 302

revelation, 94, 96

reversibility thinking, 79

Roberts, Bernadette, 174

R-system, 147–48, 154, 159, 161, 165–66, 183

Salunkhe, Dr. D. K., 127–28

savant, 138, 139

Schore, Allan, 205–6, 207–8, 209, 210–11, 247

science, 15, 16, 263

self-awareness, 170, 294–95, 306

self-generative thought, 105

self-realization, 102

sexuality, xvii, 158, 256, 257–59

Shakti, 102, 103, 119, 128

Shaktipat, 93, 102, 103, 107, 113–14, 127

shame, 208–10

Sheldrake, Rupert, 147, 295, 296

Siddha Yoga, 91, 102, 109, 118, 133

sight, 152–53

Skeels, Harold, 42–43

socialization, 202, 203

sock and aftershock, 241–42
sound, 153–54
spirit, rebirth of, 231, 259–63
spiritual awareness, xiii
Spitz, René, 56–57
Steiner, Rudolf, 176, 187, 254, 268, 296, 306
sterling silver sales narrative, xxv–xxvii
strange loops, 177, 232, 234, 247–49, 283, 287–90
stress, 46–47, 52–55, 65, 67, 69, 208
subtle body, 109
suggestibility, 87, 170
supercausal body, 109
Systematics of Theology (Tillich), xxvii

technology, 96–97
television (TV), 163–68, 267, 277
thinking
    autistic, 10, 11–12, 23
    imagery and, 158
    left-handed, 89–90
    logical, 32, 33
    operational, 78, 169, 172–73, 261–62
    reversibility, 79
    thinking about, 87–89
thought, 106–7, 117–18, 153

time, eternity and, 128–32
trance experience, 22, 24
trance states, 20, 23, 24
transcendence, x, 179, 227, 286–87
transcendent state, 213–15
triune brain, 147–50
tubulin, 248
Twin Towers, 240–41

unknown, ix, 9, 30, 45, 51–54, 67, 90, 117

vaccination, 119–23
vision, 34

wake and dream, 150–-52
war and culture, 239–40
Whitman, Walt, 35, 138–39, 247, 293
Whitton, Dr. Joel, 83
wholeness, living model of, 120–21
Windle, William F., 61–63
wisdom, 244–45, 250
witness state, paths to, 173–75
Wolff, Robert, 260, 261, 281
world-built world, 7
world deterioration, 199
worldview, 3, 5, 20, 22

yin and yang, 38–39

About the Authors

Photo: Rick King

JOSEPH CHILTON PEARCE
(JANUARY 14, 1926–AUGUST 23, 2016)

Joseph Chilton Pearce was an American author of a number of books on human development and child development and is best known for his books *The Crack in the Cosmic Egg* (1971), *Magical Child* (1977), *Evolution's End* (1992), and *Biology of Transcendence* (2002). Joe was born in Pineville, Kentucky. He served in the U.S. Army Air Corps during World War II. He graduated with a B.A. from the College of William and Mary in Williamsburg, Virginia, received a Master of Arts degree from Indiana University, and did post-graduate studies at Geneva Theological College in Beaver Falls, Pennsylvania. Joe taught college humanities until the mid-1960s and thereafter devoted himself to writing and lecturing. In the following decades, he wrote on themes ranging from child development, mind-heart connection, expanded human potential, and spirituality. Joe believed that active, imaginative play is the most important of all childhood activities because it cultivates mastery of one's environment, which he termed "creative competence." Children denied that form of play develop feelings of isolation and anxiety. He believed that child-parent bonding is crucial and sees modern clinical childbirth and lack of breast-feeding as obstructions to that bonding. Joe died in August 2016 at the age of ninety.

MICHAEL MENDIZZA

Photo: John-Michael Mendizza

A documentary and educational filmmaker, Michael Mendizza has researched and explored sensitive issues: domestic violence and rape, the impact of media on learning, cultural and human development, the nature of intelligence, holistic learning models, the changing family, prenatal learning, the roots of violence, creativity, and peak performance. For three decades Michael has gathered and published interviews with notable researchers, scientists, authors, and performance specialists, including David Bohm, J. Krishnamurti, Ashley Montagu, Gabor Maté, Bruce Lipton, and, of course, Joseph Chilton Pearce, along with many others.

In 1994 Michael founded Touch the Future, a nonprofit learning design center focused on optimizing human potential beginning with the parent-child relationship. It is based on the principle that feeling safe, physical affection, and play in early childhood will help prevent violence. Today, Touch the Future's top agenda is to provide a lasting foundation for Joe Pearce's legacy and to extend this model for Optimum Learning Relationships to specific populations: preschool, Head Start, child care providers, public education, and amateur athletics.

Michael and Joe's friendship and mentor relationship began in the early 1990s. In 2003 Michael and Joe Pearce coauthored *Magical Parent–Magical Child: The Art of Joyful Parenting,* applying what athletes call The Zone to parenting and education.

Michael is also the author of *Playful Wisdom, Always Awakening: Buddha's Realization Krishnamurti's Insight* with Rinpoche Samdhong, *Flowering: J. Krishnamurti* with Evelyn Blau, and most recently, *Unconditionally Free,* the most up-to-date and comprehensive overview of J. Krishnamurti's life, insights, and impact throughout the world.